WORK WITH PASSION

WORK WITH

PASSION

HOW TO DO WHAT YOU LOVE FOR A LIVING

REVISED AND UPDATED

NANCY ANDERSON

NEW WORLD LIBRARY
NOVATO, CALIFORNIA

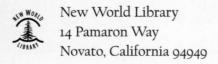

New World Library
14 Pamaron Way
Novato, California 94949

Front cover design by Cathey Flickinger
Text design and typography by Tona Pearce Myers

Library of Congress Cataloging-in-Publication Data

Anderson, Nancy, 1936–
  Work with passion : how to do what you love for a living / Nancy Anderson.— Rev. ed.
      p.   cm.
Includes bibliographical references and index.
ISBN 1-57731-444-1 (pbk. : alk. paper)
1. Job satisfaction. I. Title.
HF5549.5.J63A53 2004
650.1'01'9—dc22   2004008325

First printing, revised edition, July 2004
ISBN 1-57731-444-1
Printed in Canada on partially recycled, acid-free paper
Distributed to the trade by Publishers Group West

10   9   8   7   6   5   4   3   2

For my brothers and sisters everywhere,
that you may find your passion
and show it to a waiting world

Contents

CHAPTER 10

STARTING YOUR OWN BUSINESS

Passion Secret *10 Freedom comes from self-discipline.*

277

CHAPTER 11

CELEBRATING WHEN YOU GET THERE

Passion Secret *11 Celebrate your achievements; then continue to move on and up.*

299

APPENDIX 1

THE ELEVEN STEPS TO PASSION

335

APPENDIX 2

THE ELEVEN PASSION SECRETS

339

PREFACE TO THE
REVISED EDITION

When *Work with Passion* was published in 1984, reactions to it ran the gamut. Some critics said I was out of touch with reality. Others said the book was a practical and inspirational guide to career success. Many readers called or wrote to thank me for putting their deepest desires into words.

Today the concept of working with passion has entered the mainstream; witness the many books and magazine articles on the subject. There is even a popular Internet site that asks you to begin your job search by first selecting your passion! On television and radio talk shows, when the subject of careers comes up, the hosts invariably ask, "What is your passion?"

But how do you know what your passion is? How can you tell the difference between a personal interest or hobby and a true passion? Does your passion go out of style? What if you have several passions: Can you follow them all? Do you have to wait until you retire to do what you really want? Does the new global economy make it impossible to make enough money and still do the work you love? Shouldn't you just be glad you have a job?

In this edition of the book, I've included many more answers to the above questions. I've also added new client stories, as well as my own thoughts about the changes I've seen since I began working as a career and life consultant in 1976, such as the tremendous increase in the number of entrepreneurs, the power and influence of women in the workplace, and the impact of the Internet.

In spite of these changes, the reasons that people cannot find, much less follow, their passion remain the same: lack of focus and overextension. In fact, the distractions of modern life and the availability of the Internet make it even harder for many people to concentrate on finding work they really love.

Setting aside time to think may be the last item on your agenda. If you're just sitting and thinking you may believe you are not *doing* anything. Surely there must be a quick and easy way to find out what you want to do with your life. The truth is, discovering who you are and what you value is neither quick nor easy. But there are steps that lead to mental and emotional clarity. However this edition of *Work with Passion* helps you to discover your passion and how to express it to serve others while earning a good living, I wish you a pleasurable journey to success.

INTRODUCTION

*The world will never be happy until all men [and women]
have the souls of artists — I mean when they take pleasure in their jobs.*

— Auguste Rodin

People often tell me that they wish they could find their passion, as if passion were somewhere out there hiding behind a tree. Passion is an intense feeling that moves through your body when you encounter yourself, others, and external events. You feel passion when you care deeply about someone or something, when you want to do your best, and when you want others to do their best. Passion is how you know you are *alive*.

If you are like most people, you shut down your feelings at an early age to protect yourself from real and perceived threats in your environment. This is particularly true if your parents or other early caretakers were verbally or physically abusive or if they did not acknowledge or express their feelings. Later you may have suppressed what you felt to ward off criticism or ridicule from your peers, bosses, or mates. Today you may not know how you feel. Or if you do know, you may not trust or know how to express those feelings. The problem is, if you suppress your feelings long enough they often take revenge on you in the form of illness, mood swings, or prolonged depression.

Awakening from emotional numbness begins with a decision. You finally get tired of living to please imaginary and real critics. You want to be true to yourself, to experience *life*, with all its trials, tribulations, and joys, rather than resigning yourself to a long wait for death. But just as it took time for you to put your feelings to sleep, it will also take time to bring them back to life.

Like the prince who hacked his way through the brambles surrounding Sleeping Beauty's castle, you need to be determined if you want to find the passionate self you lost so long ago. You may want to work with a support group or a counselor to help you identify and express your feelings. You will certainly need to take more risks. You may need to leave an abusive relationship, go to school, find a new job or improve the job you have, start your own business or streamline the business you've already started, or get involved in a creative project that showcases your talent.

As you read the stories of my clients, you will see that the more in touch you are with how you feel, the more honest you can be, with yourself and others. As a result, you make better choices. You avoid people and situations that are not good for you. You eat a balanced diet, you get plenty of rest, and you laugh frequently. You pray or meditate, and exercise regularly. You like and respect the people in your life, and they like and respect you. You do the work you love, and you do it with your whole heart and soul. In time, you make all the money you need.

Begin your journey toward a more passionate life by eliminating the distractions from your life. Distractions include spending time with people who drain your energy, surfing the Internet, watching too much television, overspending, overeating, overworking, and oversocializing. Letting go of distractions can be difficult, since bad habits are like "old friends" who once served a purpose.

Most of the time distractions are avoidance techniques, effective ways to numb uncomfortable feelings or to put off until tomorrow (or forever!) what you need to do today. Eliminating these habits can also feel threatening, since change for the better opens up unstructured time. Many people are so afraid of opening up empty space in their lives that they immediately fill it back up again with other distractions!

Since courage is the chief quality of people who work and live with passion, the best antidote to fear of the unknown is facing your fear head-on (I discuss the six basic fears and how to cope with them in chapter 1). Courage is a function of our intuition, that mysterious force that leaps over the barriers of primal fear and disbelief to bring new light into our lives and the lives of others. Courage is also the product of faith; the more faith you have the more open you are to the unknown. Living by faith does not mean that you are never in doubt. On the contrary, faith and doubt accompany us throughout life. Doubt exists to keep us from being too gullible; faith exists to keep us from being too cynical. Rather than blaming God, the devil, the IRS, our mates, or the economy for our woes, when we have faith we look for the meaning in our experiences.

I wrote this book to help you embrace change for the better. While you may experience more fear when your heart is open to new experiences, you will also experience more joy and emotional fulfillment. In each of the eleven chapters you will find passion "secrets" that let you know you are heading in the right direction. When your life reflects these eleven secrets you will be reunited with your passionate self.

HOW TO USE THIS BOOK

To help you get in touch with your passionate self I "talk" to you in this book as if we were having a conversation. In each chapter, I provide exercises and stories to help you to understand what you do naturally and easily. Chapter 2 guides you through the important autobiography-writing exercise, since understanding and letting go of the past are the first steps toward working with passion. The exercises in the third chapter will help you to identify your top-five strengths and values, which define the job, business, and relationships that will work for you. Chapter 4 shows you how to write your six months' want list and to make a collage, exercises that help you to set goals you can reach.

In the remaining chapters, I discuss the three personality types and the niches in work that are appropriate for each type, how to do research, how to meet people who share your passion, when to write a résumé or proposal, how to get offers, how to start your own business or private practice, how to handle success, and how to know when you "get there." Throughout the book, my clients' stories show how adversity often serves as the spur to professional and personal growth. You will find a summary at the end of each chapter for reviewing what you've learned. There are also two appendices: a summary of the eleven steps to passion and the eleven passion secrets, as well as a list of recommended resources that I think you'll find helpful and enlightening.

You may not need to do all the exercises in the book to discover what you want to do for a living; for some people, just reading the book opens their minds to new possibilities. But for most people self-awareness is a process: the light dawns while they are writing the autobiography, when they select their top-five values, when they discuss the insights they've gained with a friend or spouse, or while talking with an expert about what they want to do.

Some people realize only after landing a new job or starting a new career that they have found their life's work. In other words, you may fall in love gradually, just as you do when you're developing any relationship that stands the test of time.

I recommend that you read all the way through the book before you begin doing the exercises. As you read, absorb and integrate the concepts. Since learning is a gradual process, don't skip any of the steps in the book; for example, don't do the exercises in later chapters without first writing your autobiography. Skipping the feeling work only keeps you in your head; and you can't find your passionate self until your heart is engaged. The exercises are designed to bring your feelings to life in stages. If you skip a stage your heart may get frightened and your emotions may shut down.

After you finish reading the book, let at least two weeks go by before your begin doing the exercises in the book. This would be a good time to purchase a blank journal or several writing tablets to use as you work through the chapters. While you work on the exercises be sure to take frequent breaks, rest when you get tired, exercise regularly, and eat a balanced diet. Avoid substances and activities that numb your feelings, such as alcohol, rich food, and excessive socializing. Remember that the treasure you are looking for is inside you, not in the "job market."

I commend you for your willingness to look within for the clues to finding your heart's desire. Self-scrutiny can be scary, but with courage as your companion the journey to passion will be a fascinating and rewarding adventure.

1 FINDING YOUR PASSION

Are you as happy on Monday morning as you are on Friday morning? Do you make the money you need? Do you admire your boss and the company's philosophy? Do you like your colleagues? When your day is over do you look forward to another day of challenge and excitement? Would you buy the product or service that you, your company, or your firm sells? If you are an artist, or you have your own business or private practice, do you enjoy working for your clients or customers? Do you have security, recognition, and advancement potential? Are you the same person at work that you are in your private life?

If you answered no to any of the above questions, then I will tell you what I tell my clients when they begin the process of finding their passion: you can love your work and make the money you need. You can have a life full of adventure and satisfaction. You have many choices and opportunities. You literally do not have enough time in this life to do all the exciting things that you could do. But first, you must know yourself.

Well, that's easy, you say, I know myself — let's move on to finding the work I like, writing a dynamite résumé, and meeting the right people.

Surprisingly, few people, even highly paid professionals, know themselves. Most people I meet are so overextended they don't know what they feel, much less what they want to accomplish with their lives.

Passion Secret *1* *Know what you feel as well as what you think.*

To find the right work you need to know what you feel as well as what you think, since your feelings tell you what you value. Feeling is not the abdication of thinking; on the contrary, people who do not feel make dreadful errors of judgment.

Taking time to integrate your thoughts and feelings is how you get to know yourself, what is unique about you, your weaknesses as well as your strengths. You discover what annoys you as well as what excites you, what you do naturally and without effort. Although you may need to go to school to acquire technical knowledge, such as computer skills, sales training, or ways to improve your craft, you do not need to change drastically, to drop out, or to get fired to create the results you want.

People come to me because they are dissatisfied with their situations. Their creativity is stifled. They do not know what kind of job or business is best for them. Perhaps they clash with their supervisors; or maybe they are disenchanted with corporate politics and structure. Or they feel a general boredom; they need a new challenge but cannot, for one reason or another, *focus* on which steps to take to solve their career problems.

Frequently, my clients think that if only they had plenty of money, then they could do the work they love. This is a common fallacy that is often demonstrated in the lives of people who win the lottery. Because money comes too quickly and without effort, they lack the skills to handle the changes wealth makes in their lives. Many of these people wind up losing the money they won. Too late they discover that happiness is the result of loving what you are doing, not of how much money you have in the bank.

Very often, your creative self thrives on a sense of urgency rather than ease and comfort. My most challenging clients are the ones with large trust funds or inheritances. Because they have so much money there is no need to act. They procrastinate, scatter their energies, and get distracted by their money. As a result, the creative self inside these clients is asleep, like a warrior with no battle to fight. Conversely, my best clients describe themselves as desperate. They tell me they will do *anything* that will help them to find satisfying work, including doing the exercises included in this book.

The Russian writer Fyodor Dostoyevsky learned firsthand the importance of being satisfied with your work. When he was put in prison for holding views that ran counter to those of the authorities, Dostoyevsky was moved by the misery of prisoners who were assigned to carry a huge pile of sand from one side of the camp to the other. Each day, every week, for months on end, they carried the same sand in wheelbarrows back and forth across the camp. Some of the prisoners were in such despair they threw themselves on the electrified barbed-wire fence and committed suicide.

In contrast, in another prison camp Dostoyevsky noticed that the prisoners sang as they went to and from work each day. These men were building a railroad, so at the end of each day they felt accomplished. This led Dostoyevsky to conclude that people can be happy — even in a prison camp — if their work has meaning.

If your work is not meaningful, you may try to make up for that lack on the weekend with hobbies, friendships, travel, love affairs, drugs, overindulgence in drink, or other escapes. By noon on Monday you are deflated, counting the days until next Friday. You wonder if that's all there is to your life.

When you begin looking for satisfying work it helps to think about nature's way. You do not find a pine tree growing in the middle of the Mojave Desert. If you like variety and have always been independent, ever since you were a tiny bud, then do not plant yourself in a big corporation. Look for a job that allows you plenty of variety and room to grow, in a small business with fewer than twenty employees, or start your own small business or private practice.

You will know you are in the right job when you sense that you are becoming a better, wiser person. You are glad to be learning the information offered to you at this job, and you like the other plants around you. The gardener (yourself, the owner, boss, or supervisor) gives you just the right challenge, does not overwater (rescue) you, does not expose you to too much sun (provide unrealistic expectations), and does not neglect you (offer no praise and plenty of criticism).

Let us assume that you need replanting — you are a seedling that is not flourishing. Know that the environment in which you can grow to your full potential is available. Remember this statement; say it every day: "I need to identify *my* part of the garden." Do you like to work alone? Then you are a shade plant (an introvert). Do you like to work with one other person or in a small group? Then you are the flower that needs a mixture of sun and shade (a partner type). Or are you happiest working on a team? Then you are a flower that thrives in full sun (the extroverted team type). I will discuss the three personality types and temperament in more detail in chapter 5.

Before you move to a new environment, look around you. Are you in the right place where you are? Have you done everything you can to improve this situation? Do you need to change your attitude about the job you have? Are you doing too much and then assuming that the job is the problem, when really it's your tendency to overwork?

Even working with passion feels wrong if you do it too much. Modify your schedule and see if that makes you feel better before you move to another job. Maybe you are not taking enough risks where you are, or you are not taking advantage of the opportunities before you. If this is the case don't move to another job; you will only repeat your dissatisfaction. Work out the problem where you are. If you do leave, do so only after you've given your all. Everyone notices excellence, so leave any situation through the top, when you are feeling confident and complete, instead of angry and resentful.

Over the years, I've seen men and women leap into the unknown in the face of tremendous fear and anxiety. But the prospect of doing what they loved was enough to help them overcome their fear of failure.

When they did the work they loved, everything else in their lives fell into place. Like these clients, when you do well in your life's work — whatever that is — you feel well. Your sense of personal worth is keen, and you are able to see others' worth.

As Dostoyevsky learned when he was in the prison camps, it is through the dignity of the work we do that we achieve self-esteem. Helping my clients to discover the work they love allows me to do what I do best: first, to heal their hearts and clear their minds; second, to design a marketing strategy; third, to stay with them as long as necessary. Since I keep my practice small and focused, many of my clients stay in touch with me throughout their careers; I know so much about them, they say, that they like to run current problems by me.

A typical conversation in my first meeting with my client is a variation on the following theme:

I ask, "What bothers you about your work?"

Response: "I feel stifled, unappreciated. My employees and customers drain my energy.... I am so busy I can't think straight. [Being too busy and feeling drained are signs of poor boundaries: my client is giving too much because of his or her need for approval.] My associates' attitudes are poor, my boss is not a leader I admire, I can't seem to get my ideas across, and top management doesn't really care about the employees. We're just faces at desks to them. [Note that all these complaints are an external rather than an internal analysis of the problem.] The job (or business) I'd like is unavailable. I have background, training, and experience, but I can't put my skills to full use. I know I have potential, but I can't seem to focus."

"What have you done about this on your own?" I ask.

Some of the responses include, "I've been thinking about doing something different for months. I've talked to my boss and my friends, but that doesn't help. I bought a really good book on how to write résumés; then I wrote my résumé and emailed it to several people who had openings. I got many responses, so the résumé worked."

When I ask what the results have been, they respond, "Nothing feels right to me. Either the jobs are not what I want, or I'm not what they want. I'm doing something wrong. The whole process has affected everything else in my life, too. I'm not much fun to be around right now, and my home life isn't the greatest. My family (wife, husband, lover) doesn't know what to do; they have their own problems to think about. I know there's something out there that I can really get my teeth into, but what and where? I don't know the market; I don't know where I fit."

Fortunately, before we meet I will have read and digested the first section of my client's autobiography, a fascinating summary of the family's beliefs about money and work (an exercise covered in chapter 2). The client's current situation reflects those beliefs, although she is not conscious of that fact. As she works through her story, she becomes aware of the hidden agenda that works against her conscious intentions.

DISCOVERING YOUR NEEDS

The right "fit" in a job comes when your work satisfies your needs. Having your needs met is similar to having the right nutrients in your diet: you feel happy and content when your body is well nourished. Your needs may or may not be conscious. If you grew up around self-centered people, for example, you may have decided that you were not supposed to have needs, and so you suppressed them. Throughout your life, you may have gravitated toward people who expected you to put their needs first because this was familiar to you. Whenever you put your needs first you felt guilty and wrong since that's how you were conditioned to feel by selfish people.

Let me assure you, when you are happy and content everyone benefits, although selfish people will get angry when you refuse to sacrifice your needs for theirs. But if you remain firm they will adapt to your new boundaries. If not, once they've left your life (and they will) you'll have the time and energy to focus on what you want to do.

Once my clients understand and accept the value of their needs, they make better choices. I can assist them in making this vital connection because they trust me enough to reveal what they truly need.

(Passion clue: If you are embarrassed about what you need you are close to your passion! This may not be obvious at first — but think about how vulnerable you feel when something or someone is very close to your heart.) The purpose of this book is to help you to acknowledge the value of your needs without feeling guilty or ashamed.

HOW YOUR FEELINGS WORK WITH YOUR MIND TO ACCOMPLISH YOUR GOALS

When you know what you want and you have the courage to go after it, your mind and feelings work as a team to help you accomplish your objective. As with any search you have to know the right key words. Your feelings provide your mind with these key words, since your feelings reflect what you really want. The mind then goes after the goal following a logical, step-by-step process.

For example, if you want more confidence, your feelings bring someone into your life to challenge your way of doing things. Let us say you doubt your ability but you are not fully aware of that fact. On the surface you look confident, but your underlying doubt communicates itself to people in your environment who sense what you really feel. These people are not taken in by surface appearances, and so they challenge you to prove that you know what you are doing. While these people can make you feel uncomfortable (we all like people who agree with us!), you are forced to stand up for what you believe or admit that what you are doing doesn't work and correct it. The encounter with this critic helps you to clarify your values or to improve your performance. As a result, you gain genuine confidence. This is how your feelings work with your mind to transform you into a more effective person.

The educational systems in most countries train the mind, not the feelings, which leaves students in a quandary when they graduate and discover they lack emotional intelligence — the ability to "read" what is really going on with you and other people. People who trust their feelings see beneath surface appearances, and they respond appropriately. In contrast, those who lack emotional insight may know a great deal of information, but they cannot identify others' underlying motives because they are disconnected from their own emotions. As a result, they feel isolated and alone, even though they may be surrounded by people.

Formal education stresses objectivity and impartiality about facts and data so that emotions do not cloud judgment. Thinking is a linear process; it is logical and analytical. In most people, thinking takes place in the left hemisphere of the cerebral cortex. The function of the left side of the brain is to put the events and feelings you experience in order. The principle of rationality produced the Enlightenment, which challenged superstition and emotional excess. Rationality brought about the scientific and industrial revolutions, as well as tremendous advances in technology and efficiency. However, the emphasis on rational abilities often came at the expense of the right side of the brain, the source of imagination, feeling, intuition, and creativity.

Yet too much emphasis on the right brain causes mental chaos and confusion, such as what you see today with members of cults and fanatic religions. The fanatic in any age is emotionally attached to an impossible ideal, so the mind rejects alternatives that don't fit the individual's utopian worldview. By contrast, a tolerant mind is open and inclusive because it wants what will work in the real world.

By definition, being balanced is having the ability to be comfortable with the functions of both sides of the brain; thinking is not more valid than feeling since both are needed to make wise decisions. When you close your mind or shut down your feelings out of fear or obstinacy you become rigid; you may even lose touch with reality. To open up the mind and heart, slow down and listen to what you may not want to hear. You may be uncomfortable with some of your thoughts and feelings, but you will feel alive again.

Like your physical body, the social and cultural body loses its balance when it rejects reality, as when people hold on to what is dead and gone out of fear of the unknown. They get angry, go on strike, sue people, or fall into despair and hopelessness. Think of the "feather-bedding" that occurred on the railroads when the need for firemen was eliminated. Instead of adapting to change and believing that people have the capacity to find other work, union leaders insisted that the railroads keep firemen on the job, even though there was nothing for them to do. This led to added expenses for railroad companies, expenses that were passed on to the consumer.

Companies need to adapt to change if they are to survive in a competitive world, just as you need to find new ways to use your skills if you are to stay employed. Particularly now, in this global market, you must not take your work or your company for granted. While this may put pressure on you, rest assured that your creative self thrives on this pressure, since it forces you to come up with solutions. Necessity is indeed the mother of invention.

Living without a safety net can be scary, but the alternative is to yearn to be taken care of from cradle to grave. While this may sound like the ideal life, too much security is death to your creative spirit. Look at the resistance to initiative and innovation in any large bureaucracy or totalitarian country, and you will see what I mean.

During times of rapid change and growth it is important to focus on what you can control. Don't watch the news every night on television — once a week is enough gloom and doom for anyone. Don't spend time with negative people; their fear will only drag you down. Don't read newspapers, books, and magazines that only talk about how bad things are. Pessimism comes and goes; only the truth lasts forever, and the truth is that change is inevitable and refreshing.

Focusing on what you can control is not the same as being in denial; rather, it is accepting what you cannot change as well as being aware of what you can change. When you are alert you catch downward trends before they catch you off guard. Then you take action rather than waiting for an outside event to force you to act.

You will not miss out on anything important when you pay attention to your inner world. In fact, when you are finished with the exercises in this book you will be head and shoulders above most people in self-awareness. My clients tell me they are astounded by the leaps in consciousness they gain as a result of doing this process. This awareness stays with them the rest of their lives, helping them to reap great benefits in their private and public lives.

Thinking Creatively

Imagination, spontaneity, intuition, and feeling: all are functions of the right side of the brain. The right brain is irrational, nonlinear, feeling, and innovative. The right side of the brain is the source of hunches, insights, irrational thoughts, and moments of inspiration that come seemingly from nowhere. That information is then processed by the left side of the brain, which is strongly developed in most of us.

The exchange between the left and right brain occurs rapidly, in milliseconds. For example, if the thinking side of your brain rejects your feelings and intuitions about some goal you've always wanted to achieve, you stop dreaming. The result is that instincts and feelings (need I say passion?) become repressed and stifled.

Your mind and feelings work best together when you focus on what interests you. And what could be more interesting than *you*? Are you aware of the power of your mind, that your thoughts create your experience of daily life? When were you taught about the magic keys to powerful living: spontaneity, flexibility, and following your heart's desire? If you are like most people, you have a sense of limitation, which you developed early in life. This occurred the first time you doubted yourself. You thought you were too young or too uneducated (or too *something!*) to know what you knew. Because you doubted yourself you cut off your awareness. In the process, you capped your passion.

That strong desire still lives within you; it didn't go anywhere. You frustrated the urge to create out of fear, but you and I will bring your passion out of hiding so that you can express it in your work, revealing the creative spirit within you. If you believe that attaining passion in your work will not happen overnight, you are right. However, what *can* change overnight and literally transform your life is your attitude, your way of framing the problem. This change of perspective can come to you in a dream, a conversation, or from someone whose insight shocks you into awareness and gets you to "see the light."

Change begins with a strong desire to change. Then your attitude makes a shift, although it may take some time to bring the new goal — a new job or your own business, for example — into being. In time, you will see the outward manifestation of your new way of thinking.

THE POWER OF LOVE

Since the subtitle of this book is "how to do what you love for a living," I want to talk about the word *love*. I'm not referring to the romantic version of love, that giddy, swept-away feeling you have when you and your date gaze into each other's eyes over a candlelight dinner. Love is much more down-to-earth and hardworking. True love is like your best friend; it stays with you long after the candle flame dies.

Look up the word *love* in your dictionary and thesaurus. Write down the definitions (of the "unromantic" version of love) on a piece of paper. Carry them with you for three weeks. Notice how many times you observe the working form of love, and how many times you give that kind of love. For example, when someone in a grocery store pays attention to your needs, is it because he loves his work? Is he expressing love *through* the work he does? Then notice the times when you express love in your work. Can you see that the right work is a conduit through which you give love to others and get paid for it at the same time?

Loving your work assumes that you know how to love. You care so much you give your all, whether you are remodeling a house or editing someone's book. As the years go by you grow into a better, finer expression of yourself, which is not always a comfortable experience. Don't expect always to love your work. Sometimes you want to leave it, because love demands so much of you; just like with married love and the love you feel for your children, there are times when you're ready to throw in the towel, but you don't because love for them overrides your desire to leave. (This does not mean that you stay with abusive people; your love for yourself insists that you leave them.)

Love's power not only remodels your values, it also alters the values of those who receive your love. In spite of what you experienced in the past you can decide to give love freely right now, even if you are not yet in the perfect job. Loving without expecting a return will speed up the process of finding the work you want to do. You don't have to do anything you hate — you can choose to do the work you love to do. That is power.

Keep in mind power's spiritual meaning, an internal force that is not affected by external reality. You may think that presidents, kings, movie stars, corporate executives, and wealthy people have power. They may, and they may not. The power I am describing is like a compass with a true north, which is how one of my clients expressed the feeling of inner satisfaction. Your worth does not fluctuate depending on who loves you, or on what is going on outside of you.

When you love it changes your experience of yourself, your world, and life in general. You no longer feel trapped like you did as a child when you felt restricted by authority figures. Love sets you free to be you. You are open to others' advice and instruction, but you look within when you need to make a decision. Love controls your impulses, risking the rebellion of the hostile forces within you. By hostile forces I mean the impatient part of your human personality that wants the easy way out of life's challenges. The loving part of you knows that quick and easy solutions are easy in the short run but terribly hard in the long run. This is why love makes you wait until you get it right, whatever "it" is. Love wants you to think about consequences before you act. Love is patient because it knows that time reveals the truth.

Many people believe they can think rather than feel their way to passion. They search job sites on the Internet, read books on writing résumés and holding interviews, attend meetings and seminars, explore the "hottest" careers, or scour every list imaginable for information and contacts. They do, in fact, get jobs using these techniques, but six months later they are dissatisfied because the jobs do not match their values (remember that only your feelings can tell you what you value).

Thinking your way to your passion is like trying to find a marriage partner when you don't know how to love or when you've never felt loved. You are at a loss as to what a loving person acts like, so you pick the first person who shows interest in you; or you pick someone based on superficial values, such as money, looks, and status. Then you discover that he or she expects you to do all the loving! This is what many people do when they look for a job or a business; they hope to be chosen before they've decided what to choose and why to choose it.

Power Is in the Present Moment

In the introduction I talked about how wounded many of us are as we're growing up, so I'd like to say a few kind words to parents, teachers, and other authority figures who may feel offended by my references to typical child-rearing practices. Sadly, abuse of children is all too common, and we all need to be aware of that fact. While you had authority and an awesome responsibility you did the best you could or, in some cases, you may have done less than your best. If this book stirs up feelings of remorse, make amends to the people you injured, including your children.

Abuse is defined as mistreatment, cruelty, neglect, and any action that damages the body, mind, and spirit, such as physical violence, insults, disparagement, the "silent treatment," and ridicule. If reading the book reveals that your parents or other caretakers abused you, acknowledge that the abuse took place. Then have compassion for the child you were; genuine sympathy will heal your wounded heart. Perhaps you can talk with a friend or therapist about what was done to you so that you can work through your emotional pain. If your parents or other family members are still abusive to you, stay away from them.

Conversely, if you realize that your parents' actions were kinder and wiser than you knew at the time, thank them for their dedication to you. If you realize that your actions were kinder and wiser than you knew, commend yourself. My point in this section is that the past is not the focus of power; rather, the present moment is the point of power.[1] By changing the way you look at the past, you change its effect on you. In that sense, your life is renewable from moment to moment.

Maturity is the willingness to accept responsibility for your actions, and to cooperate with others to achieve mutually desirable goals. Action, putting your passion to work, requires help from other people. The first step is to know yourself — to have mental clarity. The bad news is that this internal awareness is often hidden beneath layers of fear.

Fear keeps you from experiencing your true self. That is why you need to identify and confront your fears head-on to find this passionate person who lives inside you. Fears are like the demons in fairy tales the prince must conquer before he wins the princess's hand in marriage. These tales are parables that describe the psychological process of becoming a whole and complete individual. As you meet and face your fears you'll find that most of them are imaginary ogres left over from the long-ago past.

THE SIX TYPES OF FEAR

The six basic fears, according to Napoleon Hill, author of the classic book *Think and Grow Rich*,[2] are the fear of poverty, the fear of criticism, the fear of illness, the fear of losing love, the fear of old age, and the fear of death. Hill calls these fears "ghosts," since they are more imaginary than real. Different fears often work as a team, especially when you take risks, such as leaving a job, opening your heart, or saying what you think in public. Then fear rises up to terrorize you. These six fears fight for existence, but they crumble before calm, detached scrutiny. Examine the following six basic fears. Which of them affects you the most?

Fear of Poverty

Fear of poverty is often the most powerful fear of all because your survival depends on having enough money. The fear of poverty has many symptoms: indifference, constant worry about money, indecision, excessive caution, and procrastination. This fear is not limited to poor people — it can also haunt people with a great deal of money.

One of my young clients, John, had more than $50,000 in the bank and a steady stream of income from an inheritance and investments. Yet he feared losing it. He was immobilized, and his career choices seemed limited. He worried, procrastinated, and refused to take risks.

"John," I asked, "what do you want to do with your time each day?" (This is a question that gets fear off balance, since it engages the logical mind.)

John responded, "Everything I think of loses interest for me after an initial investigation, Nancy. When I get bored I hang out with my friends or my family, or go for long drives by the ocean. [Here you have an example of why it is hard to take action when you have a great deal of money: there is no sense of urgency.] Being someone's employee doesn't appeal to me — I know how independent I am. The other alternative is to invest in a business, as a partner. The question is, what business? I don't want to use my money to buy a job."

"Why do you have to use your money? What do you want to do? Figure that out first — not the money question. Once you've done some research and you've identified what excites you, money will assume its proper place in your thoughts. It won't be such an obsession."

It turned out that John was fascinated with racing cars. He had raced Formula V Fords as a hobby, and the thrill of the track showed in his eyes as he talked about it. He still worked with Formula team members on occasion, but as a volunteer. I suggested that he talk to racing professionals and learn about the income possibilities. His investigation took weeks, but John found his heart's desire — and was he excited when he came in to see me.

"Nancy, this is it! I finally know what I want to do!" John said. "After I talked to a number of people in racing I realized that I know how to organize and run a successful racing team. Organizing the team comes first. Preparing a cost-benefit presentation is next. Finally, I need to approach businesses whose sales would increase as a result of sponsoring our cars. Their name and logo would be on the cars for prospective clients to see at the track. They get to watch an exciting race and identify with the company in an atmosphere that brings them to their feet. This helps the companies to sell their product or service to special customers — those who love speed and drama."

John's story shows how important it is to find people who share your passion. You don't have to sell them on your ideas; they already agree with you! A year later, I went to John's first regional race and met his teammates. They had three beautiful royal blue cars, several spon-sors, and lots of enthusiasm. The race was an exciting triumph. John did not finish first, but he was on his way. We shook hands and planned the next race date.

"The best part about this year is that I discovered a way to keep my savings and investments and earn the income I need in another way. As I talked to people, I discovered they had needs I could meet. For example, some wanted leasing arrangements — they were new drivers who wanted to lease a racing car to learn to drive. Others needed a good mechanic. I know how to repair those cars, and I can earn good money doing it. I see now that a year ago I was concentrating on loss. As soon as I concentrated on gain, my income increased," John said. He added that the Indianapolis 500 was his ultimate goal.

John solved specific problems — repair and leasing. He lost his fear of poverty because he had confidence in his ability to repair and lease racing cars, his passion. It had never occurred to John that he could make money at what he loved, for he thought — like many others — that he could not combine fun and profit.

For many of us, the beliefs that money is bad and that work is drudgery are based on an overliteral interpretation of the Garden of Eden story in Genesis. When Adam and Eve were expelled from the garden for disobeying God, Adam was doomed to work by the sweat of his brow and Eve to suffer alongside him. Yet I read this story as an allegory of human maturation, not of condemnation for disobedience. The underlying message is that we cannot remain children in a parental cocoon forever; we have to grow up, go out into the world, and make choices if we are to become independent adults. It is painful to give up the illusion that someone has all the answers. Some people never leave the safety of the family, preferring to remain in a dependent state.

No truly spiritual book says that work and money are bad. What they all say is that you will be happy when you love the work you do, and when you do not let greed's tentacles get too firm a grasp on your mind. As the apostle Paul said, it is the love of (or lust for) money that is the root of evil, not money itself, since money is a neutral commodity.

The misinterpretation of the Puritan work ethic is another source of the belief that work is drudgery and money is bad. The Puritans were so named because they sought to purify the excesses of the Anglican Church, which at that time was led by power-driven priests. Plain clothing and a democratic way of worshiping God, as well as thriftiness, hard work, and adherence to basic principles were the original Puritan objectives. For the Puritan, the word *pleasure* meant vice and debauchery, not enjoyment.

Most likely the Puritans who decided to make worldly success evil did so because they envied others' success. Making success wrong is also a way to rationalize failure. "Pleasure," in the modern sense of the word, is not seductive, sinful, irresponsible, or the devil's lure. Pleasure is satisfaction. Remember Rodin's quotation at the beginning of the introduction, that when you take pleasure in your work you will be happy? When people say that work is not supposed to be pleasurable, is it because they don't believe they can find the work they love? Could they be envious of people whose work is satisfying?

The economy goes up and down, and technology brings constant change, but passion is always current since it is an expression of your soul. When you love your work and you do it well, people will seek you out, whether they are employers, clients, or customers. You make it through good and bad economic times because you are doing the work you were destined to do.

Fear of Criticism

Fear of criticism brings with it self-consciousness, lack of initiative, lack of ambition, and an inferiority complex. This is the most damaging and prevalent fear in our culture. Well-meaning (and some not so well-meaning!) parents, friends, teachers, and peers instilled in you the fear of what others thought; often this was a projection of their fear of what others thought of them. If only you had known!

Picture a pretty, intelligent young woman with talent in the graphic arts. Sharon had run her own freelance business ever since she was a teenager, yet she was gripped by the fear of criticism. She had finally overcome the fear of rejection in her work because she knew she needed only a few clients to make a profit. Yet certain nagging self-doubts remained.

"You handle your business problems so well, Sharon. Where is this fear coming from?" I asked.

"No matter what I do, my father and stepmother still think I'm flaky. They always ask, 'Why don't you settle down and get a real job?' [You see why people who do not take the risks you take cannot understand you?] And my best friend seems to think I'm battling hopeless odds. She says that because there is so much competition, I shouldn't expect to be successful."

How many times have you been discouraged by friends and family members who threw boulders of criticism in your path? Sadly, you are often most stymied by those closest to you. Unless you realize that your bravery stirs up the fear of failure in them you will take what they say personally. In other words, it's not you who bothers them but what you symbolize: change! In Sharon's case, once she took action her confidence increased, as did her understanding of people who criticized her. She set up interviews with potential clients to discover their design needs. As she listened to what they wanted to accomplish, Sharon's mind was flooded with ideas that she turned into workable solutions to their marketing problems.

Once Sharon realized that it was her own fear of criticism that held her back, she felt compassion for others' fears instead of anger with them. Since she was less self-critical, she did not get discouraged when she was around critical family members. But she did seek out people with whom she could talk about the challenges of self-employment, men and women she met at entrepreneurial gatherings.

Most fears are based on faulty beliefs, not reality. Healthy fear protects you from danger. Unhealthy fear keeps you from doing what you love.

Fear of Illness

Fear of illness causes hypochondria, avoidance of exercise (you believe you may overtax yourself), susceptibility to germs (you think you may catch something, and you do), self-coddling, and intemperance.

Prevention is the best defense against the fear of illness. Take good care of you; don't overextend your physical resources. Identify and express your emotions as they occur so that they do not have to express themselves as illness.

Keeping your body active is a surefire way to keep your mind alert. Especially during a career change, a self-initiated training program will release tension, improve your overall self-confidence, and increase your energy. I always insist that my clients exercise regularly. Once my clients are in shape, they are amazed by the body's natural hunger for movement. Excellent physical health also helps them to cope well with stress and to bounce back from setbacks and delays.

Fear of Losing Love

The fear of losing love — the most tragic fear — creates jealousy, faultfinding, possessiveness, clinging, and even gambling (to buy the love you want so badly). This fear comes from the erroneous belief that love is something you can actually "lose." Yet love is a force that lives inside of you; it is not affected by who loves you. When you love you get to keep that experience forever. Although you grieve when a loved one dies or leaves you, when you are a loving person you do not fall apart, contrary to what the lyrics of popular love songs say. You are happy with people, and you are happy when you are not with them.

Loving means caring about and supporting a person without expecting a payoff, which is no easy feat, especially if you did not experience love in childhood. You will need to love yourself before you can truly love others. This means that you are true to yourself in your relationships; you don't betray your values to keep others close to you, or to gain their approval. Loving yourself means that you take responsibility for your actions, but you do not berate yourself for mistakes. You correct them and move on.

19

Whatever your situation is today, resolve to be a loving friend to yourself, no matter the cost. When you stand on that firm foundation, relationships will assume their proper place in your life.

Fear of Old Age

Fear of old age involves denial of or apologies for your age, and thinking of yourself as slipping or declining in some way. This fear kills off initiative, imagination, and self-reliance. It just is not true that getting older has to be a diminishing experience.

For a woman, fear of old age is often connected to strong traditional security needs. Movies, magazines, television shows, and music videos bombard a woman with the message that she needs to be physically alluring to attract the man she needs for economic support. As she grows older, if she starts looking "old," she fears her man will discard her for a younger woman and she will lose her security.

Geneticists say that admiration for beauty is programmed into the human brain in order to propagate the species. The problem is that few women (or men!) are or will remain the perfect "10." However, both men and women can be attractive regardless of their age when they take good care of their bodies, minds, and spirits. Eat and drink moderately, don't smoke, exercise, wear clothing and colors that are right for you, keep an open mind, and have a cheerful heart. Then you will be irresistible, regardless of your age.

Fear of old age often teams up with the fear of criticism and the fear of losing love. "What will people think of me if I'm alone? Being alone means no one wants me." You can see how these three fears work together to promote an acute sense of inadequacy — but only when personal worth is based on having a partner.

Getting older adds depth to life, and it leads to greater understanding. If there is a man in her life, a woman is grateful for his presence. If she is alone, she treasures the life she has. For a man, the fear of old age is connected to the fear that he will lose his economic independence and sexual power. This fear causes him to be competitive with other men, including his sons, whom he fears will best him, take away what he has or, worse, show him up in front of his peers, wife, or partner.

A man's fear of old age is connected to his sexuality, as is a woman's, but sometimes with a more competitive edge. The man who is moving into his mature years would do well to read biographies of famous men. He may be startled to discover how many of them came into their greatest productivity late in their lives (and to learn how many were influenced by the kind of woman described above!).

Healthy men and women radiate strength, humor, and vitality. They are curious, perceptive, knowledgeable, affectionate, and warm. Believing in themselves, they believe in others. They do not take life or themselves too seriously. These men and women savor life; they linger over it, as they would a good meal. They recognize the value of quiet reflection, alone and away from others to balance and weigh their thoughts and feelings. As a result, they are the source of balance and encouragement for others.

Fear of illness and old age vanishes when you prepare for getting older. Make health your priority when you are younger; manage your money; nourish your mind and spirit and, most important, do the work you love. Then you won't have to wait for retirement to enjoy life.

Each stage of life is as necessary and beautiful as the seasons of the earth. The spring and summer of life are for charging full speed ahead, taking risks to gain life experience. As you reach your autumn years it is time to turn to the inner life, to reflect and consolidate learning. The winter of your life is an opportunity to develop a spiritual connection in preparation for the new birth to come, the transformation that nature always promises.

Fear of Death

Fear of death causes preoccupation with the idea of death, fostering lack of purpose and concentration on what you cannot control. People who fear death often numb their feelings as a way to avoid awareness of their impending deaths. Without the feelings, they live in the illusion that time is not passing by. Concentrating on the future is also an effective way to avoid the present. For example, one of my clients worried about old age and death even though she was in her early fifties. Sarah's preoccupation with her demise was reinforced by all the other fears: the fear of poverty, losing love, criticism, and illness. Underneath all her fears was an unconscious belief that life was meaningless.

Sarah's thinking had been influenced by older European parents who survived the horrors of World War II. As a child, she listened to their conversations with their friends as they talked about the war and its aftermath. Even though the parents immigrated with their daughter to the United States and went on to have good lives, they remained pessimistic in their thinking, especially Sarah's father.

Sarah had identified with her father, not her more adaptable mother, and this was the source of Sarah's fear. Like him, she lived in fear of an uncertain future, which was why she was so anxious. Rather than talk with her about death and old age, since that would be colluding with her fears, I asked Sarah to set small goals each day. She was recovering from the end of a marriage in which there had been a great deal of co-dependence. Additionally, a downturn in the economy had affected Sarah's business, so she had many challenges to face and work through.

To help her concentrate on the present, and to keep her fears under control, I asked Sarah to write a summary of her accomplishments at the end of each day. I also suggested that she get a part-time job to keep cash coming in while the business got back on its feet, since I knew she had a tendency to isolate herself, which only exacerbated her fears.

As the months went by, Sarah learned to train her mind to concentrate on what she could control. As she worked on her autobiography, she also broke the sympathetic attachment to her father, replacing it with a more objective, grown-up relationship. This was not easy for Sarah, since giving up the bond to her father forced her to look at fearful behavior she had formerly projected onto him.

A few years later, Sarah said she knew old age would be no problem for her because she would only get better at her work as she got older. She also said that when death came she would deal with it. This is an example of the power of the mind, how it reproduces what we program it to think. Today, Sarah has occasional lapses into negative thinking but, on the whole, she is stable and optimistic. Her business is growing, and she has new friends and colleagues. The divorce and the downturn in the economy were difficult challenges, but these events forced her to grow beyond her limitations. As is so often the case, Sarah found a jewel of great price buried in the midst of her adversity: faith in herself and the process of life.

In the next chapter I will show you how to write the kind of auto-biography I have my clients write. Summarizing your life can be a daunting task, but it will also be an exciting journey of self-discovery, as you can see from the above stories. Taking time to write about the people and events that influenced you is hard work. But once you understand and let go of the past, you'll move forward into a happier, more productive future.

SUMMARY

Passion Secret / *Know what you feel as well as what you think.*

1. Write about a time when although your feelings told you what to do, you ignored them. What happened? Next write about a time when you listened to your feelings. What was the result of this decision?

2. Which of the six basic fears affect you the most?

3. Now that you've identified your worst fear, what would help you to banish this specter? Who or what can help you do this?

4. Describe a time when you overcame your worst fear. If you took the same action today, what would be the result?

2 WRITING YOUR LIFE STORY

Each client reacts differently to the exercise we will cover in this chapter — writing your autobiography. "I'm not a writer!" some say. "What has that got to do with a job?" say others. "How will I have time to do that with all the other demands in my life? Why can't we just start the process of interviewing?" Some clients get so upset about the exercise that they stop in the middle of the process. It is amazing how people will walk away from personal power.

If you are like most of my clients (and me!), you'd rather get better without feeling the pain your past choices have caused you. However, feeling the pain serves a purpose; it reminds us of what will happen if we make those choices again. In that sense, pain can be an effective teacher. As Sarah in the last chapter learned, adversity brings many rewards in growth and understanding.

Passion Secret 2 *Understand the past; then let it go.*

Why is writing an autobiography so important? Notice I said "writing." Unlike talking, writing uses all your senses. This is why I recommend that you not create your autobiography by speaking into a tape recorder. Writing down on paper what you have thought, felt, and experienced makes those thoughts, feelings, and experiences more real. Then you can examine your reactions objectively, from today's perspective. In addition, you see the uniqueness of your personal history when you put it in writing. Taking the time and energy to complete such a project gives you a new understanding of the thread that runs through all your experiences.

We all have an incomplete picture of the past. Although memories sometimes float up into our consciousness, we have little sense of how a memory and the event that triggered it tie into our life as a whole. Seeing our lives as a unified whole is difficult. Each day there are so many demands and distractions: family, job, bills, and the world's unending problems — all are so immediate, so troubling. We feel guilty about concentrating on ourselves.

Philosophers from Plato to Descartes to Sartre were concerned with how to live a good life. In the late nineteenth century the American philosopher William James took a pragmatic view. James said that you could change your life by changing your experience. For example, you do not sing because you are happy; you are happy because you sing. Thus, if you act cheerfully, you will be cheerful. You do not have faith because your life is going well; your life is going well because you have faith.

When you act as if something will come about, it *will* come about, James said, since experience is based on how you think. While acting "as if" can be a way to avoid reality (what elephant in the living room?), this technique prepares your mind for success, since what you think about becomes your experience. The following client story shows this cause-and-effect concept.

Mark's Story

One of my younger clients, whom I will call Mark, was concerned because he had no professional work experience, and yet he wanted to

WRITING YOUR LIFE STORY

start out on a job as a manager. He came to my office with a three-page résumé in his hands, nervous and unsure of his future. Mark had just finished college with a bachelor's degree in business administration. He had mailed dozens of résumés, but he had problems getting interviews. And when he got an interview he heard the same line: "You don't have any experience." Mark was discouraged. How could he get experience if no one would hire him?

I asked him to write about his abilities and achievements, what he did naturally and easily. Mark had worked his way through college by helping to manage a delicatessen. "Did you do anything to increase efficiency and profits in the deli?" I asked. After puzzling for a few minutes, he said, "Well, I moved the mayonnaise closer to the mustard!"

Then he remembered an even better idea — he had created a sandwich that became the most popular one in the deli. He wrote about his willingness to stay late when business was good, which showed his initiative. Very quickly, we cataloged these examples into marketable strengths and abilities. Becoming aware of his strengths, Mark saw himself as an experienced manager. From then on, he presented himself as a confident, aware self-starter, and soon he got exactly the job he wanted. Not surprisingly, the man who hired him said his decision was based on Mark's self-assured presentation.

Since Mark's passion was automobiles, through our marketing survey we found a tire company that had the training program and the potential for growth that he needed. The manager who interviewed Mark liked his thoughtful approach letter (a technique I discuss in chapter 8) and his thorough research on the company. He was flattered and considered himself fortunate to have a person with Mark's initiative. Mark performed beautifully in his new job — in one year, he rose to a managerial position.

We develop a commitment to whatever we spend time on: the more time we spend, the stronger the commitment we make. If we worry about failure, failure is what we manifest in our lives. When Mark changed the way he thought about himself, his experience changed. His first step was to become aware of his thinking. Then he saw and heard what he was doing wrong. You too can become aware if you use the techniques discussed in this book.

In addition to learning how and when to use these tools, you will learn how to recognize and tap the valuable resources of your childhood — *spontaneity* and *flexibility*. These two words define personal power. When your mind is open and free of judgment, you have the best tool for solving problems at your disposal — awareness. To look at people and events from a detached point of view opens the door to innovation, to change, and to alternative modes of thought and action.

Think of two-time Grammy-winning opera singer Renée Fleming, professional tennis whiz Venus Williams, astute mystery writer Elizabeth George, and creative men like Thomas Edison, Albert Einstein, Steven Spielberg, and George Lucas, to name only a few people who unlocked their power by remaining open to possibilities and opportunities. Be flexible and spontaneous like these brave people — do what you are not supposed to do. Don't bind yourself to the conventional, safe way of thinking and doing. Instead of fearing an event in your life (especially failure), try viewing your experience with detachment, as if you had no stake in the outcome. Then the meaning of that experience will become clear to you.

A SAMPLE WARM-UP WRITING EXERCISE

Doing these warm-up writing exercises will prepare your writing muscles for creating your autobiography. To help prepare you to do this exercise, I asked my client Jonathan to let me use his work. (I changed his name, like that of all my other clients, to protect his privacy.) I include my comments to show what his self-assessment reveals about him.

Jonathan's "How I See Myself" Exercise

"Basically, I find this is a difficult thing to do," Jonathan wrote. [An honest beginning!] "So I'd say it is one of my personal traits that I don't do well focusing on the present moment. [This was evident in our first meeting. I had a hard time getting Jonathan to stay on point. His mind works very fast, too fast, which is his problem; he is all over the place. Jonathan helps information technology companies to maximize the effectiveness of their sales organizations, but he is not sure this is what he wants to do. He's very intuitive and focuses on possibilities, not on the here and now. He is an introvert who tries to be more extroverted than he is — thus the conflict.]

"I am forty-five years old and still trying to figure out my place, where I fit in, what my contribution [life's work] is," Jonathan wrote. "I am adventurous and willing to take the initiative, to try new things; I'm learning to cross tightropes without a net. I am a successful consultant, able to listen to and sort out complex issues and problems. I am a struggling entrepreneur, learning how to live with the uncertainty of not knowing where my next client is coming from. Funny, I started with career, when my most important work is my relationship with my wife [is this true?], followed by parenting my young daughter and teenaged son, who lives with his mother. Maybe that is another paragraph. [You see how easily Jonathan gets off the subject? This section is about *his* self-image. Jonathan starts with himself, but then he writes about his wife and children. Perhaps he's afraid to focus on himself for fear of being thought selfish].

"For now I will say that I am committed to creating a relationship with my wife that is fun, mutually rewarding, enhances our creativity both separately and together, and that runs on positive energy rather than drama and criticism," Jonathan wrote. "We both take 100 percent responsibility for our relationship and commit to telling the truth, feeling our feelings, and keeping our agreements." [Wait a minute, what is going on here? Jonathan defines the problem in a way that guarantees failure; he needs to describe what he alone is responsible for, to say that he will tell the truth. It's hard to know who uses drama and criticism in the marriage, his wife, Jonathan, or both of them? Is Jonathan trying too hard to please his wife because he wants her approval?]

Jonathan's "How Others See Me" Exercise

"My wife sees me as smart and insecure, with a nice, easygoing social manner, good at making other people feel comfortable [too much so, I'd say!]," Jonathan wrote. "She says I'm self-protective, basically a very kind person, with self-absorbed edges, creative, interested in personal growth. She likes it when I am lighter, enthusiastic about nature, photography, and when I am very deeply and sweetly romantic, but sometimes I am a jerk. She says I'm very prickly about people asking questions, like I think that a question is a maneuver for control; in some of the heart ways I am very steady and dependable; in other ways I am erratic."

"Erratic" is a good description of how an introvert feels when he is torn between spending time with people and time with himself. Jonathan desperately needs more time alone, but he feels guilty for needing to be alone, which is why he fights with his wife. When he's angry with her, he has an excuse to be alone. Jonathan needs to write about what he knows in order to gain confidence, but writing is a lonely process, and it runs counter to what he thinks he's supposed to do — be an available husband and father.

"My daughter thinks I'm a great dad who spends too much time on the mobile phone doing work. [Another criticism of Jonathan.] She thinks I'm an excellent storyteller [so do I; he should use this skill to make a living!]. She thinks I'm fun to snuggle with early Saturday mornings when we read books and make up stories together. My son sees me as making an effort to spend time with him but has difficulty with my interactions with his mother."

Jonathan's former wife remains bitter about his exit from their marriage; sadly, she uses their son to get back at Jonathan for leaving her, even though she has another man in her life. Jonathan gave in to her during the marriage to keep the peace, so now he is afraid to allow his son to choose when he wants to be with him, since that means his former wife wins in the struggle for power. I suggested that Jonathan wait until his son is older, say, sixteen to eighteen, then see what he chooses to do on his own. Jonathan's son has the same problem as his father: he's afraid of women's emotional power.

"My clients say I'm an expert at partner strategy," Jonathan wrote. "They tell me that I have a combination of strong people and analytic skills and am focused on results. I go the extra mile to deliver, I'm a professional who cares about my client's success. My boss and co-workers say I have a strong ability to gain the trust of the client, as well as surface issues that need to be addressed for the project to succeed. I possess strong analytic skills; I am a good thinker/problem solver; I'm able to leap small buildings with help from others."

Jonathan's sense of humor saves him from being too pessimistic. Notice how clear he is when he talks about himself at work. There's no guilt, no confusion, just the facts. I see the same clarity when my women clients talk about themselves at work, but in relationships it's another matter. Since they fear disapproval, they sacrifice themselves to please the men in their lives. Like Jonathan, they can't focus on themselves without feeling wrong and guilty. This dynamic goes back to what they experienced in their relationship with the parent of the opposite gender.

Jonathan's mother was an alcoholic whose husband traveled to get away from her. Like most children of alcoholics, Jonathan has a hard time holding on to his identity when in relationship with a woman who reminds him of his mother. Until he knows he will not betray himself for her approval he'll be vulnerable to her control.

Jonathan's "Balanced Self" Exercise

"I am an ambitious learner, willing to take risks, trusting that my path will unfold (eventually)," Jonathan wrote. "I'm challenged rather than defeated by impatience; my mind is focused on the present moment; I feel secure and confident, not scattered and unsure of myself. I have all the time I need to be alone, to think, and to write. I allow myself to go as far as my talent will take me. I have good boundaries with my wife, children, and clients because I respect and trust myself. I exercise every day. Keeping my body fit helps me to stay in balance."

Note that Jonathan's description of his balanced self begins and ends with what he can control: his attitude and his actions. There is no mention of what his wife and the children think of him, only how he relates to himself and to them. This makes Jonathan's goals attainable because they are measurable. Additionally, by getting in good shape he has grounded his intuitive insights in physical reality. Do you see how effective these self-description exercises can be? In three paragraphs Jonathan has defined the problem and the solution.

When Your Descriptions Don't Match Up

Another client, Joe, found so much difference between his description of how he perceived himself and the description of his balanced self that it disturbed him. Balance was unattainable, he said. When I asked why, Joe said, "Well, look at the words: 'I am calm, financially secure' — that's the opposite of what I am!" he said. His self-image was pretty bad. "Joe," I said, "do you fear being calm and financially secure? Would that change your life script?" He hesitated. "You've answered my question," I said.

You may find you do not really want to be happy and secure, in your most private thoughts. We all develop an attachment to misery; it feels so noble to suffer. After all, no one will envy us if we are miserable. Besides, what right do we have to feel happy and secure when there are so many suffering people in the world? Shouldn't we fail in order to pay for being better off than they are?

As I said earlier in the last chapter, misguided interpretation of religious texts and collectivist ideologies cause many people to cast a wary eye toward success. Too much creature comfort might be bad for us. This is the long-suffering view of life, the fear that without struggle life would be meaningless. (By struggle, I mean a sense of futility, not the effort that any achievement requires.) In Joe's case, his self-image gradually began to conform to a more balanced image. First, he had to see that his beliefs interfered with any possibility of changing his picture of himself.

If something in your past troubles you, guilt may be interfering with your ability to cultivate a positive self-image. Perhaps you hurt someone or did something that makes you feel uneasy. Or perhaps you have not admitted to yourself how much someone hurt you. These old, unfinished situations can keep you from experiencing happiness in the present.

Awareness of what you think and feel comes in several stages: denial (this is not happening), which can be intentional or unintentional; shock, when someone or something breaks through your denial; anger or remorse, depending on whether you were the transgressor or the one who was transgressed against; action, internal and external change in attitude and behavior; forgiveness, letting go of anger and resentment; and detachment, or psychological freedom.

With emotional freedom as your reward you can see why it is worth the effort it takes to understand the past. When you write about actions of yours that injured others, stop and make amends. You can do this in person, in a letter, by email, or with a telephone call. If you were the injured party, and it is appropriate to do so, approach the other person and express your concern. When you talk about your hurt, you give the other person an opportunity to apologize to you, which will heal both of you and strengthen the relationship.

If talking to the person who injured you is not possible, write your thoughts in a letter. Imagine that the other person reads the letter and apologizes to you. Then, throw away the letter. Forgiveness does not mean that you let this person back into your life; that depends on how he or she treats you in the future. Forgiveness is a process, so don't rush to forgive before you have experienced the pain someone caused you. In the end, you are the greatest beneficiary when you forgive others, since forgiveness sets you free to move forward into the future. (Passion clue: The truly passionate person feels sorrow and remorse for his or her transgressions and is not afraid to confront those who have hurt him or her. Remember, passion is intense feeling.)

Emotional pain does not end with one, two, or even a dozen attempts — consciousness takes work. But one day, you will feel all you need to feel about the past. Then you will no longer need to discuss or repeat it.

YOUR WARM-UP WRITING EXERCISES

Take a pen and writing tablet or sit down at your computer and write your answers to the following questions. You can also use a cassette tape recorder for these preliminary attempts at recall. Your own voice is a good teacher and clarifier. (Do not, however, as I stated above, tape your autobiography.) Add any ideas of your own that come up while you're writing. Do not take these exercises too seriously — it's okay to have fun with them! You are not writing a term paper.

Your "How I See Myself" Exercise

Turn back a few pages and read Jonathan's self-description before you write about how you see yourself. Then answer the following questions. Do you see yourself as unique or special? How do you feel about your personality? Do you like what you see in the mirror today? Do you like your hair, your eyes, and your walk — your body design? Do you like your thoughts, hopes, goals, and aspirations? Do you appreciate all the good things you say and do each day? What about your work? Do you think you do it well, whatever it is? What makes you angry? What makes you happy? What makes you feel sad? What makes you feel powerless? If you were a character in a novel, who would you be, and what would the theme of the story be?

Your "How Others See Me" Exercise

What picture do others have of you? Be specific; identify these others as you write. Are they your parents, wife, husband, or lover? Are they your children, co-workers, boss, customers, or clients? Do your answers reflect what they have told you, or is this what you *think* they think of you? When in doubt, ask others how they see you, as Jonathan did. Do they see you as you see yourself? The answer to this question is important, so think about it. What do others think about your physical self, your personality?

Who likes to be around you? Who avoids you? (If you are an honest person some people will not be comfortable around you.) Do the people in your life see you as an optimistic, depressed, cautious, adventurous, funny, competent, or incompetent person? Are you a capable, caring father, mother, sister, brother, wife, or lover? Are you self-absorbed? Do you say what you think in spite of the fear of retaliation or rejection? Do others show how much they appreciate you? Do you give people mixed messages? Are they uncertain or confused about what and who you are? Do you say one thing and do another? Do people trust you? Do they think you are sincere? Do they tell you what they think and feel about you?

Your "Balanced Self" Exercise

You are balanced when all the parts of your personality form a unified whole. In other words, you are the same person wherever you are. Using psychological terminology, you are "congruent." Honesty takes daily effort, but telling yourself and others the truth will accelerate the process of finding your passion.

Picture your balanced self. Are you different from how you see yourself and how others see you? How so? What would you change so that you are consistent in words, deeds, and actions? By whose standards do you measure yourself: yours, your peers', your spouse's, your boss's, or your parents'? Is your balanced body different from the body you have? What about your attitude, your friends, your work, your income, and your spiritual life?

What similarities are there between the balanced you and the person you are now? Who can verify these similarities for you? What action do you need to take to bring balance to your life? What is your biggest challenge? Is it being honest? Is it the need to control your temper? Developing patience? Trusting in the process? As you may have surmised by now, the need for balance is the same at work and home.

CAPTURING YOUR EARLIEST MEMORIES

After you have done these preliminary writing exercises, you will be ready to begin writing your autobiography. Past feelings recalled in the present will give you great insight into your values, needs, goals, and behavior.

Much of your behavior was shaped by early childhood experiences. Your views of success and failure were solidified as you moved through the educational process — a process that included experiences with family, friends, and outside activities, as well as school. Let the memories come, whatever they are. There is no such thing as a "good" or "bad" autobiography. It is your experience, so naturally it is good. What you are after is a picture of how you responded to your past and the people in it. Writing your autobiography will show you these responses.

Your autobiography will consist of four or five parts: part one will include your grandparents and your parents, part two will describe your life from birth to junior high school, part three will cover high school through college and up to your thirties, and parts four and five, depending on your age, will complete the autobiography. Describe in detail the experiences you feel are important. Include significant people who assisted in your growth as well as the people who caused you pain. Keep a novelist's perspective: all the characters in a story, including the "bad guys," are important.

Before you write, read through all of the questions in this chapter. That will help you to think of the events of your life in chronological order. Slow down the pace of your life so that you can do a good job on the autobiography. When in doubt, turn down invitations, especially to large-group gatherings, since this will be too stimulating. When you are writing, your unconscious mind opens wide, so if you are not careful you will take in everyone's undigested emotional "stuff." Then you'll have to take several days just to digest it!

As you write, avoid substances that block feeling: alcohol, cigarettes, excessive food, or any activity that distracts you from the task at hand. Your goal is to know what you feel so that you can make wise choices. Exercise, eat well, and rest when you get tired.

Part One: Your Grandparents and Parents

On a blank page in your journal, describe what each grandparent believes (or believed) about money, work, sex, gender, religion, and love. Would you describe them as optimists or pessimists? If you do not know the answers, ask your parents or a relative; or extrapolate from your parents' beliefs. Pay particular attention to the beliefs of the grandparent who is the same gender as you, since he or she most likely passed down those beliefs to your parent of the same gender.

Many of my clients are surprised to discover that they do not know much about their grandparents. It's as if life began with their births! Grandparents are important because of the impact they had on your parents. When you understand your grandparents you'll understand your parents, and consequently, yourself.

Next describe how your grandparents brought up your parents. For example, did they grow up in the city or the country? Were there many children, or just a few? Were your grandparents strict, harsh, permissive, or caring? What was positive about their marriage? What did not work?

Once you introduce your grandparents and parents into your story, call them by their first names all the way through the story. This technique gives you emotional objectivity, since it creates a new category for them in your mind. I ask my clients to call their parents by their first names in our sessions, too; this is a startling concept at first, even sacrilegious to some. If they persist, however, they change the way they think about their parents; parents become people instead of authority figures they worship, hate, or rebel against. This has a direct, positive impact on how they relate to authority figures at work who may be standing in for the parents.

Additionally, if there is emotional entanglement between and among family members, I ask my clients to limit contact while they are working on the autobiography. If the dependence on the family is severe, then I request a three- to six-month moratorium on contact: no phone calls, no letters, no social interaction. Time apart gives my client a chance to break old habits and to clarify values. So much creative energy is wasted in emotional entanglement, which is not the same as genuine relating.

According to Robert Firestone, author of *The Fantasy Bond*, grown-up children's entanglement with parents and siblings, and parents' entanglement with these children, is rooted in the fear of death. Unlike "the genuine companionship and closeness that occurs in families that do not have dishonest or neurotic dependency ties, real togetherness is replaced by special attention, intrusiveness, and possessiveness on the part of parents and their children. Children and their parents come to expect this kind of counterfeit 'love.'"

Firestone believes that the reluctance on the part of therapists and others to disturb these bonds is due to "the fear of breaking into one of the strongest and most effective defenses against death anxiety." Fear of death is inherent in being alive, "it is mankind's 'incurable' neurosis," he says. To remove this fear, we fixate on fantasy love and "withhold our feelings for the things that remind us of our mortality."[1]

Working with passion will stir up fear of death, since when we care deeply about our work, we simultaneously know that it is finite, like our lives. The alternative is to live in bondage to parents and children, or their substitutes, to maintain a sense of security. But it is false security, since time moves forward, whether or not we believe it does. Without deep feeling, we come to the end of our lives never having lived, never having risked the unknown.

In his essay on the difference between him and Freud, Carl Jung said the only way out of the biological bondage to our parents and our offspring is through taking a spiritual leap, the intuited recognition that we are souls on a journey through life, unattached and free: "There is nothing that can free us from the familial bond except that opposite urge of life, the spirit. It is not the children of the flesh, but the 'children of God,' who know freedom. We moderns are faced with the necessity of rediscovering the life of the spirit; we must experience it anew for ourselves."[2]

Jung was talking about the natural progression toward the spiritual life that occurs as you pass through the stages of your life. As you grow in spiritual strength, entanglement with your family and other people ends. People who hold on to the past, however, remain stuck at an earlier stage of life, causing them to reject new ways of thinking and behaving. Jung noticed this pattern in patients whose parents were long-lived. As soon as the parents died, however, his patients took a giant leap forward in consciousness and maturity.

This is not to say that children do not need the base camp a good family provides. But you are not a child — you are an adult who is trying to find the work you love. Rest assured, the family members who share your values will remain an integral part of your life. If, on the other hand, they do not share your values, trying to force closeness will only lead to endless conflict. As thoughtfully as possible, go your separate ways. A relationship in which everyone lives and lets live is the most loving relationship of all.

The next step in your autobiography is to describe how your parents met. That meeting is important because it sets the stage for what happened next in their partnership. Were they equally matched? Did your father do what he wanted to do? Did your mother? What was going on in their marriage before you were born? Were there other siblings before you? How did they react to your birth?

It is important to know the answers to the above questions because as a baby you absorbed the emotional content of your environment, particularly what was not expressed openly. Your mind had yet to develop the ability to filter or analyze this information, but you felt it and reacted accordingly. You can see this when babies fret for no apparent reason around certain people and situations. When they feel safe and secure they quiet down.

What was going on with your early caretakers affected you for good and ill. You took in their fears, hopes, and dreams with your oatmeal. Just knowing this can explain why certain situations and people still have a powerful impact on you. Your body and mind store everything that happened to you. As you write about the past these memories will make themselves known to you. You can use this information creatively, turning trauma into productive activity, as artists do when they use past events in their creations, or when people create a product or service based on a need that was not fulfilled when they were young.

Next we turn to you as you walk into a personal and collective story.

Part Two: Birth through Junior High School

Pre-School Years

Where were you born, and under what circumstances? Was it in a hospital or at home? Was the birth easy or difficult? Where were you in the birth order? Infancy is extremely important. Find out what kind of baby you were from your family. Go through old photographs and select a picture of yourself. Keep it near you from now on. This person is still you, the little child who is part of your personality. Looking at this child every day will be a reminder of your innocence, curiosity, and belief in the future. The picture of you from long ago will encourage the grown-up you of today.

What was going on in your parents' marriage when you were born? Most important, why were these two people together? Did you have both of them throughout your life? Was your early life comfortable and predictable? Was it full of change, moving, and upsets? Were your parents happy with each other and their life? Or did they fight and argue most of the time? Did they love you and tell you so? How? How did your family express their feelings? Was there laughter in your home? Did you tell your family you loved them? How important was love in your life? Where did it come from?

How did you know you were special or not so special? What were your brothers and sisters like? Did you like them? Did they like you? How about other relatives? Did you identify with your father or with your mother? Did you have an adult outside the family who took an interest in you? How did she or he influence you? Was either of your parents an alcoholic or addicted to other substances or activities, such as food or work? How did their addiction affect you at that young age?

Did you have friends when you were young? What special things did you like to do? What made you feel lonely or unappreciated? How did you know when you had succeeded or failed? How were you praised or reprimanded? What was considered "good" or "bad"? Did you have pets? If so, what kind?

These are all pre-school influences. Can you see how important they are to the development of the character in your story? Any good story depends on the consistent behavior of the main character in the plot. The best books hold our interest because of the characters — their unique and consistent reactions to events. Be generous with details; little things that come to mind can be quite enlightening. We are looking at your story to discover what you have experienced so far. Now let us go on to your school years.

Early Socialization

Where and when did you go to school? Were you glad to go or sad? Were you afraid? Did you feel encouragement from home? Did your parents like school? What did they tell you about it? Did you go first, or did your siblings? How did you get to school — by bus, bicycle, car, or walking? Who went with you? What was your first reaction to your teacher? How did you interact with your classmates? Did you learn easily? What subjects gave you trouble? When did you do well, and why? Did you make new friends quickly, or were you cautious about making friends? Did you ever bring them home? What did your parents think of your friends? Did you ever run away from home?

If there was alcoholism in your family, how did it affect you during those years? Include a discussion of how the drinking in the family affected you later on. Do not underestimate the impact of alcohol on your life. Unless you have extensive education about this problem, the emotional legacy left to you by family members and friends who drank excessively can be devastating to your self-esteem.

According to Freud, addicts regress to an earlier stage of life to avoid the stage of life they do not want to go through. Thus, people who numb their feelings with alcohol, drugs, or other substances do not develop the emotional muscle they need to cope with the demands of that stage of life. Those who remain stuck in that stage wreak havoc on their children, who are not aware the parents are back in time. If you had any problems with alcohol and drugs in your teens, what stage of life you were avoiding with this choice? What feelings were you numbing out? Girls often use food as a way to suppress the fear of sexuality and anger, either by starving their bodies or by overeating. With boys, taking drugs and drinking can mask a lack of confidence.

What teachers influenced you the most? Was their influence good or bad? Did they encourage or discourage you? Ridicule is the number-one enemy of passion, so if teachers ridiculed your efforts, go back in time and tell the young person you were to ignore what these people did to you. Sadly, there are those who should not be in the teaching profession because teaching is not their true passion.

Did you work hard in school, or did you do what you needed to get by? What kind of grades did you get? What did your parents and teachers think about your work? What did you think about yourself in relation to other students? Did you feel inferior, superior, or about average? Were you the creative or the practical type of person who was not interested in academics? Did anyone ever tell you that you could succeed in life even if you did not get high grades? Did anyone recognize and encourage your creativity and practicality? For example, did anyone suggest that you start your own business or go into one of the trades?

What sports or extracurricular activities did you participate in? Why? Did you feel prepared to go on to each grade? How did you feel when you left grade school? What did you look like? Were you tall for your age, of medium height, or short? What effect did that have on your peers? Were you admired or ignored? How did you get the attention you wanted at school? Did you have crushes on people? Did you notice the opposite sex, or were you attracted to people of the same sex? Did the people you were interested in notice you? Did you win awards for any effort? Were you a quiet or outgoing person?

Your character is pretty well jelled by now. The socialization process has had an effect. You are about twelve years old now and coming into puberty. Surges of hormones are changing your whole world. This is a very impressionable time for you. The junior high school years will accelerate your feelings, sometimes to the breaking point.

Junior High School

During junior high school you either open up or close off your feelings. Now is when you make decisions about yourself that will direct the course of your life. Peer pressure is enormous. Your conformity, or lack of it, to the behavior of your peers is extremely important. Who were your peers? How did you conform? When did you rebel? Did you ever rebel against your parents? If so, how did you rebel; what was the outcome? Was it constructive or destructive?

Describe how you felt about junior high school — excited, scared, bored? Where did you go to school? Did you stay in the same town? Did your family move in those years? Did you adapt to the work that was required of you in school? What were the teachers like? Did you take the classes you wanted? Who counseled you about school? Were you thinking about college?

Did you have a close friend with whom you could talk things over? Did you have a girlfriend or boyfriend? Several? What was your earliest sexual experience? How did you feel about your sexuality? What about others' sexuality? Were you ever caught masturbating? What was said? Did you have an adult to talk to about sex? List any early sexual activity and describe how you felt about it (whether homosexual, heterosexual, or incestuous). When you come to your teenage and adult years, make a similar list. Who made you feel good about being sexual and passionate? Who teased or ridiculed you? Who said it was bad? What did you like about your culture, such as clothing, music, pop music, television, and movies?

Did you have trouble getting up in the morning? What time of day did you feel most alert? Was it always the same time of day? Is this still when you do your best work? Or do you force yourself to work against your natural clock? Did you go to school events, like football or basketball games? Did you have school heroes?

Were you a reader? If so, what books did you read for fun? What movies and videos did you like, what celebrities impressed you? Did you have any heroes or heroines? Are you still attracted to the same kind of person? Did you spend time alone with your thoughts? Were you busy, always into some activity? Were you taught anything about how the mind works, what creativity is? Did you feel in or out of control of your life? Who inspired you? What was happening in the country and the world that held your interest? Did you feel optimistic or pessimistic about going to high school? How did you prepare for the change?

Part Three: Senior High School, College, Life in Your Twenties

Were your parents active in your high school life? How active were you at high school? Were you in student government? How much did you participate in school clubs, drama, or singing groups? Did you ever work with your hands — pottery, art, or woodwork? Did you excel at this? Did you work at part-time jobs during school and in the summer? When did you first earn money? Was your work behavior similar to either parent? Did you receive any memorable advice, correction, or support from bosses or other mentors? At this point in the story, take two weeks off from writing to think about what you have written. You've covered a great deal of your history, so take time to integrate what you are learning about yourself.

Your senior high school years most likely solidified many of your attitudes and interests. You tried and rejected many self-pictures. Remember how you copied the latest fads after studying them with magnifying intensity: clothes, walks, jokes, mannerisms, dances, cars, dates. Your focus was external, you were watching to see what was acceptable, what "they" thought. "They" usually meant four or five of your friends and their friends. This was a small but influential group that had an impact on the formation of your character. Remember that your character is formed by the decisions you make, for good or for ill.

By now you may have begun to limit your possibilities. You have heard many stories about "what life is" and accepted some of them as true. You have narrowed your paths and perhaps begun to stop dreaming and envisioning. The confusion about your identity increased if you were pressured by your parents or other caretakers to make decisions that you were not ready to make, such as when to leave home, what to do for a living, what major to select in college, or whether to have sex with or get married to your romantic partner. How did you cope with the pressure? If you made choices you were not ready to make, what was the outcome? If you did not give in to pressure, from where did you get your strength? Or did you always have a strong sense of self?

Study your character now; you are about eighteen years old. How has the socialization process affected your self-image? You are looking for consistency of character, choices you make that are by now predictable. Do you choose what will make you independent? Do you go your own way, or do you follow others' leads? What choices did you make about friends, family, loves, work, and/or future college plans? Would you make the same choices today? If you answer yes, why would you make those choices; if no, why not?

How much direction did you have during your senior year in high school? Did you know what you wanted to study in college? Is that what you ended up studying? If so, how did you know this course of action was right for you? What did your close friends do? Did you move away from home? Did you stay home while you worked or went to school? How did you feel at your graduation and other senior-class activities? Did you take an active role in the events? What did you enjoy most about your senior week?

Did you finish high school? If you quit school, what happened next? What did others think about your leaving? Did you ever complete your high school education? If so, when and why?

What did you do the summer after high school — work, play, or prepare for college? Where were you? Who did you spend time with? If you had no plans for college, what did you plan — and why? Who did you want to be like? Who did you not want to be like? Did anyone advise you on a career that would be right for you? Who told you what you did well? What did you settle for? Did you pick the college you went to? Why? Did you have help with finances? What did your parents think about higher education? Were you encouraged by them to go as far as you wanted? If not, who gave you the encouragement to go to college?

In your jobs — whatever they have been up to this point — what did you do? How were your relationships with your bosses? How did you get along with co-workers, with customers? In your school and work life, how did you relate to authority figures — teachers, principals, counselors, bosses, government employees, business owners? How did they relate to you? Did they trust and admire you, or did you feel rejected or judged by those who were "above" you?

How did you spend your money? Did you save any? Who taught you how to manage money? Did you buy your own clothes or car? Did you travel? If so, where did you go?

The Time of Choice

At college, did you choose your major, or did someone else design your course of study? Did you have financial aid or scholarships? How and why did you pick your courses? What classes did you like and not like? How did you feel about your college life? Did you feel like a part of the campus? What was your greatest success? What was your greatest failure? Who were the significant people in college? Have they stayed in your life? What professors made the greatest impression on you? Why? How did they reward your efforts? Did you take part in campus life — sports, clubs, or class activities? Did you have an active social life? What made you laugh? Were you serious or detached about being in school? What were your grades like? Did they move up, down, or stay the same?

Did you notice any big emotional shifts in your attitude toward life in general? Did you ever have a friend betray you, lie to you? How did that affect you? Did you question what you were being taught? Did you take part in any campus rebellion? What were the issues? What happened?

Who were the student leaders you admired? Were you one of them? Did you ever feel like quitting? Did you? What happened then? Did you go back and finish? How old were you when you were in college? When you graduated? In your senior year did you begin a job search? Who and what did you consider? Were you recruited? Who recruited you? Did you feel happy to leave college? How would you summarize your college years — as fulfilling, empty, or exciting?

Did you marry or get engaged? Did you pick a person who turned out to be a replica of either parent? Did this choice force your growth, or encourage old patterns of behavior? Take another break from writing at this point. By now you will be amazed by the discoveries you are making about yourself and the characters in your story. You are no doubt surprised by the amount of energy it takes to write an autobiography. Processing the past is hard work, so take frequent breaks. Go for long walks, rest, and eat nourishing food. When you are ready, begin writing about young adulthood.

Young Adulthood

Now you are about twenty-two years old. Look at your character. How are you different now from how you were in earlier years? How are you the same? How have your experiences changed your values, what you think is important, good, and true? As you observe the unfolding story, can you see any repetition of patterns — behavior that coincides with your early years? Were your beliefs in flux? Were you confused about your future? Did you have a sense of direction? Did you feel prepared for the stage of life that was ahead of you?

When did you fall in love? How many relationships did you have before you married? When did you marry (if you did)? How did that event change your goals? Many of us find that when we look back over our early decisions, we realize we felt that we were caught up in circumstances beyond our understanding and control. Did you feel like that? Or were you aware of what you were doing?

You are moving into adulthood now. What are you like? Are you self-confident or insecure, on a firm path, or are you following someone else's lead? Did you change towns, jobs, and relationships? Where were you living, and with whom? Who were the most significant people in your life at that time? If you were in a new job, how did that come about? Did you like it? Were you making enough money? Were you and your spouse or lover sharing expenses? Were you working? Where?

What kinds of friends did you have? Were they supportive? Did you stay in contact with your parents and other relatives? Were they involved in your life? Did they help you financially? Did you buy a home, or rent one? Did you have children? What effect did they have on your life? How did becoming a parent affect your self-image? Did you take parenting seriously? You may have had several children. If so, did you have a favorite? If you had a boy and a girl, which one was easier to know and enjoy? How would you describe your family life — as smooth, difficult, or a mixture of the two?

Part Four: Life as an Adult

Experts in the banking industry say that by the time we are twenty-eight years old, most of our financial habits are set for life. This is also true about your other habits, the way you interact with others, how you work and live, and what you believe; all these are solidified and highly resistant to change. How would you describe yourself when you were twenty-eight? What choices did you make that turned out to be wise? What choices did you make that did not work? What did you learn from these choices? Did you get professional help when you were stuck, from a therapist, coach, or mentor? Or did you learn from experience?

Write a paragraph that describes your personal relationships during the decades from thirty years of age to the present day. What patterns do you see? For example, are you the dominant or submissive friend and partner? Or are your relationships based on equality? Do you leave people, or do they leave you? Who stayed with you throughout the years? Why have these people remained in your life? What do you have in common?

Next describe your work relationships. How do you relate to co-workers and other people in your field? Then describe how you relate to authority figures, such as bosses, your parents, or other people in positions of power. Do you feel secure or intimidated around these people? Are you yourself, or do you lose your identity? Are you afraid of anyone in authority? To express your resentment do you try to undermine this person's authority? What would you do if you were not afraid of this person? By someone in authority, I mean a person who knows what he or she is doing, not someone who is in a position of power. As I'm sure you know, people can be incompetent and in power. What is important is how you relate to both kinds of people. Are you direct or indirect? Do you try to change or topple incompetent people from power? Do you comply, or walk away?

Continue writing your story in ten-year intervals: from age twenty-eight to thirty-eight, from thirty-eight to forty-eight, and so on, until you are in present time. Note the people who influence your thinking, your view of life. Summarize the choices that work, as well as the choices you no longer make. What you are looking for is the theme that runs through your life. Are you the victim or the victor? Is your goal growth and self-awareness, or looking good to others? Notice when you passed through the stages of life, as well as the times when you were afraid to leave the past behind.

What external events influenced you during your adult years? What trends and developments had a particular impact on you? What people in the public eye did you admire and respect? Who disappointed you?

My Life Today

End your story with a summary of yourself today, personally as well as professionally. Where are you now? Why? What work are you doing? Is it satisfying? Is your social life pleasing?

Summarize your sexual experiences from high school until now. Do you have friends you like and admire and who like and admire you? Do you have honest relationships with your family members? Do you force yourself to be with them out of fear of criticism?

What makes you laugh? Do you laugh frequently? What makes you sad? What makes you feel powerful? What fascinates you? (Passion clue!) What do you do when no one tells you what to do? What books do you read; what music thrills you; what would you do today if you knew you could not fail?

How would you describe your current job? Is your boss anything like your parent of your boss's gender? Are you in business for yourself? Do you want to be? (If so, then chapter 10 will be of particular interest to you.) If you have children, do you like being a parent? Do you do it well? Did your life turn out the way you thought it would? How does your life differ from your expectations of it? Is life better than you planned, or worse? Does your story resemble your favorite fairy tale from your childhood?

Do you handle money well? Are you in debt? If so, how long would it take you to get out of debt? If you are burdened by possessions you do not need, are you willing to sell or give them away? Can you scale down your life so that you can focus on what is important to you? Can you record every penny you spend, and save what you can every month? When you have six months' living expenses saved, can you invest in a conservative plan? Until then, can you make do with what you have? Most people believe if they had all the money they needed, they would do what they love. Actually, the opposite is true for the clients of mine who succeed, as you will learn in chapter 4.

Once you start writing your autobiography, the memories will come flooding into your mind. When the dam of fear is eliminated, your conditioning, your loves, your hates, your indifference, your irresponsibility, your sexuality, and your humor will come washing through. I wish I could tell you about all the wonderful autobiographies I have read. I have laughed, cried, felt dismay, admiration, and sheer joy at the capacity we all have to experience life's ups and downs and survive them. The human spirit is remarkable in its ability to survive even the most brutal circumstances.

Your story, told with complete openness, is a valuable document — something for you and those who love you to treasure. While you are writing your story I urge you not to show it to the people who are close to you, unless they are going through a similar process. When you know that people are going to read what you write you edit your thoughts and feelings, which sabotages the process. When you are done you can show your story to the people who are worthy of your trust.

You will experience uncomfortable feelings as you write about the past. For example, if you did not acknowledge your anger in the past it will come up now as you write. Getting a massage, practicing deep breathing, and finding a sympathetic ear will help you to uncover and process buried anger. When you know what made you angry you will see that behind your anger lurks fear. Look back at the six basic fears. Which fear made you bury your anger? What matters is that you cared (passion clue!) as much as you did. You are capable of intense feelings.

You will also see the positive aspects of the past, such as the talents, traits, and other personal characteristics of your grandparents and parents that serve you well. For example, a sense of humor is often passed down through the generations in families, as are other wonderful gifts. There is no right length to your story, but most people will have between forty and fifty pages when they are finished, more if they are inclined to write.

When you are done, read your story slowly. Try to imagine the outcome as if it had happened to someone else — this will give you more insight, understanding, and compassion. Looking at your story as if it were another's will give you the chance to act as an editor, not a writer. These are two different skills. It is a rare writer who can edit his or her own work. You are too close to it, too emotionally involved. Many writers say they need at least four years' distance from any event to write about it objectively, so don't be surprised if it takes a while for you to detach from your story.

Ask yourself these questions: Did this character accept the misinformation he or she received? What beliefs are outmoded? How much of what happened in the past still decides the present? See if you can identify any patterns and reactions that are learned behavior. The following story shows how one client's old behavior pattern interfered with his career.

Frank's Story

At age forty Frank, a printing executive, was stuck in a repetitive pattern. He performed well in whatever job he got — up to a certain point. Then conflicts would arise. The problem always revolved around an intensely personal clash with his superior, after which he would quit or get fired. Add to the turmoil a well-developed case of hypertension: Frank was angry most of the time! "When I'm not kicking dogs, I'm

thinking about it," he laughed. His sense of humor had kept him func-
tional, but that was about it.

Going over his autobiography, I discovered a significant series of
events. Frank was the second son, following a brother who excelled in
everything: school, sports, and social life. The father was a perfectionist — exacting and successful. He often made comparisons between
Frank and his older brother. Frank remembered one in particular:
"Why can't you be like your brother? He does everything so easily; you
always do it the hard way." Whatever Frank did, it was never quite
good enough; he always missed the mark.

Frank spent a great deal of time trying to live up to his father's
unreasonable standards. Seldom did he hear praise (believe me, one can
never get enough praise). His accomplishments came as a result of fear,
fear of reprisal. Frank also became conditioned to be the person
doomed to fail — fulfilling his father's unfortunate prophecies. His self-
esteem dwindled.

I asked Frank if he saw any similarities between the relationship
with his father and his relationship with the bosses he had chosen. The
pattern began with his expectations of failure, not success. Or, if success came, it had unpleasant strings attached. He felt that even when
you win — at building a business for example — you lose personally in
some way.

Frank was startled to see that his bosses were, on the whole, unpredictable, judging, and hard to please, just like his father.

"Could you possibly be choosing to work for your father?" I asked.
"If so, you'll never make it."

"You're right," he said. "I can see that I believe I'm really not that
great!"

Not all of Frank's problems were solved with this information
about his early experiences, but a light of recognition did go on for him.
From that base, we worked together until he began to think of himself
as an independent adult, rather than a boy who wanted his father's
approval. Updating the "software" in his brain helped Frank to let go of
the self-destructive decision ("I'm not as good as my brother") that

compelled him to work for men who reminded him of his father. For Frank, the fear of criticism brought him exactly what he thought he deserved: punishment and contempt. The happy ending to Frank's story is that he now enjoys a prestigious position, and he loves the independence that goes with his new maturity. In a recent conversation, Frank was buoyant and optimistic.

"I'm having a great time over here," he said. Then he lowered his voice, conspiratorially. "It's a piece of cake," he admitted. We both laughed, remembering the times when Frank saw life as one long battle he could never win.

Find Time to Be Alone

I hope that after you write your autobiography you will continue to set aside some time each day — even just a few minutes — to be alone with your thoughts and feelings. As I said in my earlier garden analogy, weeds of doubt and fear take root in your mind unless they are pulled on a regular basis.

When you begin to write your autobiography, you will notice a reluctance even to sit down alone. You might find diversions, relish interruptions, run errands, do chores. You might even read something and then move about — restless, maybe even annoyed. Good. That means that you have been inoculated with new information and it has gotten under your skin. Almost all my clients experience restlessness when they begin contemplating the changes they are about to set in motion.

Remember that the Western world is a highly extroverted culture that rewards external activity. If you are an introvert, as about 25 percent of us are (according to David Kiersey and Marilyn Bates, authors of *Please Understand Me*[3]), you need time alone to recharge your batteries. If you are an extrovert, as about 75 percent of us are supposed to be (although I believe much of this is conditioned), you recharge when you're around people.

Just make sure you do not use talking to people as a substitute for the hard work of writing and processing what you write. Unlike talk, which can be forgotten over time, our words in print are a permanent record of what we thought at the time. Writing an autobiography is the ultimate act of courage, said one of my clients. She was a court reporter, someone who knew the power of testimony in print.

Just before the moment of clarity — the "aha!" — you will feel the greatest confusion. So if you feel stirred up or puzzled about how this introspection will produce results in the outside world, congratulate yourself. You are beginning to know yourself.

SUMMARY

Passion Secret *2* *Understand the past; then let it go.*

1. Write about a time when you were successful (or when you were a failure, if you wish).

2. Write a few paragraphs of self-description. How do you see yourself? Describe your personal qualities, your physical, mental, and emotional self.

3. Describe how others see you. What image do you think others have of you?

4. Finally, describe your balanced self. What aspects do you want to enhance to achieve this balance?

5. Writing your autobiography is an extremely valuable exercise. It helps you to achieve clarity.

6. As you write a summary of your life to this point, notice your earliest memories. Who was there, and what happened? Take your character through your life. Part one covers your family background and relationships — particularly a solid word sketch of both grandparents and parents.

7. The remainder of your autobiography takes you through the rest of your life. Pay close attention to the significant people who aided or assisted in your growth, and to those who injured you as well, since they were also part of your growth. Recalling these people and events is not always pleasant. If you feel residual anger, acknowledge and express the anger by writing about it. Understand the past; then let it go.

3 IDENTIFYING YOUR STRENGTHS AND VALUES

The third step to finding your passion is identifying your strengths and values. In step two — writing your autobiography — you took inventory of your past in chronological order. Through writing your autobiography you got in touch with your family's belief system about money, work, sex, gender, religion, and love in various stages of entrenchment. In some cases, you may have needed a crowbar to dislodge the misinformation.

When I first started working as a career consultant I was not aware of the family's impact on an individual's career. In those days, my intention was to help my client find a job, not to remodel his or her view of the past. After doing an initial personality assessment, I focused on conventional job-search techniques: researching the job market, making contacts, preparing for and holding interviews, writing résumés and thank-you letters, and negotiating job offers. This process did help my clients get jobs, but a few months later they would call back with the same old problems.

What am I doing wrong? I asked myself. Why aren't my clients happy? Since I had been trained as a writer I decided to ask my clients to write their stories to see if that would help me get to the root of the career problem. After I read a few autobiographies it became clear to me that there is no separation between personal and public life. Behavior learned in the family was made manifest in the career, as we saw with Frank in chapter 2.

Making the connection between my clients' reaction to their upbringing and their career distress made my job much more complex and therefore much more interesting. After all, I had been trying to figure out why people do what they do my entire life. It was no accident that I took all three quarters of Shakespeare in college, along with conducting an in-depth study of political science!

Once I focused on the politics of the family my work became a daily adventure, like solving a mystery. Could I find the answer? Would my clients be true to themselves, whoever those selves turned out to be? Would they be able to overcome family and cultural conditioning to do what they wanted? Without knowing it, I'd found my passion. My clients were equally fascinated when they heard my interpretation of their stories. As they worked through their autobiographies and the other assignments that later became part of this book, they encouraged me to share my ideas with a larger audience — which is why you are now holding this book in your hands.

In this chapter, I offer you more examples of how childhood deprivation sets up one's driving need in life. When this need is met in your work you feel complete, a creative way to use past injuries or neglect. For example, let us say you were not recognized when you were growing up (whether you were recognized or not is not the point). The need for recognition motivates you to do what it takes to get that need met. If you try to meet this need constructively, you work long and hard to become good at what you do. In the process you gain recognition, you make money, and you serve a function in society. Since you've recognized yourself through your work you no longer need outside recognition. You have experienced the inevitable growth that comes from working with passion; you do what you want to do, and that turns you into a better person.

I know that some people remain hung up on childhood deprivation; for them there is never enough to fill the hole in their hearts, never enough money, love, material possessions, or power. But for my clients who persevere in their efforts to find the work they love, that love repairs the damage they experienced in childhood. Why is this so? Because giving love to others heals their hearts and spirits. The strengths and values exercises in this chapter will help you to discover what you need to feel complete. When you know your top-five strengths and values you have a template by which to measure choices in your career and private life. Successful jobs and relationships use all your strengths and fulfill all your values. When your job and relationships do not match these values you fail, regardless of how much money you make.

GETTING EMPOWERED

In the last chapter, I said that power was the ability to take action. It is the energy (passion) that motivates, guides, and directs people who have the life they were born to live. Working with passion is simple, but it is not easy. On the contrary, a passionate life is an ongoing process of challenge and growth. Each new goal you set has its stages of drudgery and triumph: a beginning, a struggle, and a victory.

You may deny your passion because you are embarrassed about it, or because you are afraid of what others will think if you express yourself in your work, or because you think you cannot get what you want. But you cannot "lose" passion. It only goes underground, where it waits until you are ready to take the action that will release its power. How do you become aware of your power? First, notice when you feel powerless, when your actions do not match your thoughts and feelings. Then notice when your actions are aligned with what you think and feel. Think of how powerful you feel when you are honest and direct.

Honesty and directness are the hallmarks of self-acceptance. Honesty eliminates the kind of communication that undermines your personal power, just as directness puts an end to subversive tactics. For example, one of my clients, Jan, was afraid to express her anger to the men in her life. So instead she expressed it in passive-aggressive ways. When she was angry she seethed in silence or withdrew to lick her wounds. After we had been working together for a few years (yes, change takes time!) a man Jan had been dating called to say hello. Jan was involved in a project, so she asked if she could call him back in about thirty minutes. He said okay. When Jan called back there was no answer; her friend had turned off his cell phone.

In the past, Jan would not have told the man what angered her; rather, she would have expressed her anger in sarcasm, crankiness, or moods that hovered in the room like black clouds. But the next time they talked Jan asked her friend why he was not there when she called back (she had learned to be honest and direct). At first Jan's friend was evasive, but when she pressed for an answer he said that another woman had joined him for the evening, but she was only a friend, he assured Jan. When Jan asked how the other woman would have felt had he taken Jan's call, he was quiet; then he said he didn't know. Jan said, "You've answered my question, and you've explained why you turned off your phone."

It would have been better for the man to have called Jan as soon as possible to tell her what happened and to apologize and ask what he could do to make amends. It was early in their dating relationship, so Jan did not expect him to be focused on her. Regardless of Jan's reaction, he would have kept his self-respect, and he would have regained Jan's trust. But because he waited for her to take action he lost both his self-respect and Jan's trust. Since he had not taken responsibility several times before, Jan knew that he would repeat this behavior, so she told him she did not want to continue dating. At the end of their conversation, he asked if an apology would help. Again, he wanted Jan to take the initiative.

The next day, Jan received an email from the man saying how shocked he was and how sad he felt (note that his main concern was for himself, not for what he had done to Jan). In her reply Jan said she understood how he felt but that "loss is the consequence when you treat someone the way you treated me." She went on to say that she hoped he'd learn from the experience and take what she said next as a gift.

"One way of not hurting others is to do what you say you're going to do when you say you're going to do it," Jan wrote in her email. "Another is to try to be as honest as possible with everyone involved, including the woman who came to have dinner with you the night you called me. And last, always try to do the right thing, even when it's hard — you earn a lot of respect that way, even though it might make some people mad."

Jan's directness had an immediate positive impact on her business as a piano teacher. She eliminated difficult students, and soon better students came to her. As a result of her courage, she enjoyed her teaching business again.

"I had been thinking I was in the wrong business," Jan said to me. "But the problem was that I was not being honest about how I felt. I was afraid if I were honest and direct my students would get mad at me and leave. But those are the very students I don't want to work with; they took forever to pay their bills, and they did not practice!"

Jan had learned from experience that it is best to get feelings out in the open rather than holding them back, "even though it might make some people mad." Her greatest fear had been that people would get mad at her or reject her when she expressed her feelings, as they had done in the past. But in spite of her fear of being alone and losing certain customers, she took the risk she needed to take.

Perhaps Jan's friend will learn to be more direct because of his experience with Jan, and perhaps not; taking the easy way out is a tough habit to break since evasiveness sometimes works. Evasiveness begins in childhood as a way to undermine authority and to avoid responsibility for our actions. Boys copy their evasive fathers and girls copy their evasive mothers. Parents who try to please everyone teach their children to be dishonest and indirect, behavior that winds up making honest people angry, as was the case with Jan. Chameleon-like behavior may work in the short term, but sooner or later the truth comes out.

We are all passive-aggressive to some extent, but when we are direct we stop confusing people. It is true that we are vulnerable to rejection and criticism when we are honest, but Jan would have forgiven her friend had he been genuinely contrite instead of concerned about losing the relationship with her. In other words, his concern was not about being honest, it was about keeping Jan in his life. Examining her hidden motives had taught Jan to trust her instincts, so she knew when to say when.

My clients expect me to be honest and direct with them, so I can't hold back because I'm afraid they won't like what I have to say. Sometimes they are not aware of what they are doing until I call it to their attention. Other times they know but feel compelled to continue self-destructive behavior. After they get over their initial shock they thank me for caring enough about them to tell them the truth. They also know that I expect them to tell me when I'm off track so that I can serve them better. If we are fortunate, we have a few people in our lives that care enough about us to point out our inconsistencies. We need to be grateful for honest people; they are our best friends and most effective coaches.

Another way to become aware of your power is to watch the signals from your unconscious mind. These flashes of insight can come in dreams, in slips of the tongue, and in the behavior of people you attract. For example, say you attract pessimistic people who drag you down. Once you admit that you are being too pessimistic yourself, these people don't bother you anymore. Acknowledging your pessimism releases your power, since you have accepted a part of yourself you formerly rejected.

You can consciously enter the rich storehouse of hidden thoughts and feelings through your imagination. The imagination serves as a bridge that takes you from one place to another, from one self-image to another.[1] If you can imagine being an honest person, for example, that image will "build the bridge" to a more honest you. This is how Jan became an honest person; she rehearsed the part and then practiced it in her relationships. This took a great deal of trial and error, but in her interaction with the man she was dating she finally got it right. She acknowledged her anger and then did something about it in a thoughtful, constructive way. Then she felt powerful rather than powerless. Today, Jan is enjoying a mutually respectful relationship with a man who is honest and direct.

Conversely, the imagination can also work to bring negative outcomes into your life. Frank (from chapter 2) used his imagination to keep a self-destructive scenario alive. He imagined himself as the victim of his father's perfectionism, a role he played in battles with his overly demanding bosses. Frank was stuck in this role because he did not want to see his father as he was; that would have been too painful. Frank chose to picture himself as not being good enough, so he concentrated on his flaws rather than on his father's emotional inadequacy. So who was really the perfectionist?

It's hard for some people to accept that parents are human beings before they are parents. Our tendency is to idealize our parents and the family out of our natural need for security. But if they are not happy with themselves and their own lives, some parents will project their flaws onto their children, particularly on the children who are the most sensitive, as was the case with Frank. His father said he was not good enough when, in fact, it was the father who was not good enough, in the sense of not being a fair and balanced parent.

Letting go of a child's illusions about his father was not easy for Frank, since he had spent his life thinking his father was a competent, powerful man. Imagining his father as a flawed human being set Frank free from his false picture of himself. Then he was able to relate to his father as an adult. As a result of his detachment, and his honesty about his life, Frank's work (and life) became a "piece of cake."

We all play the roles we assign ourselves early in life. Some of these decisions we made are healthy, such as "I want to be a professional dancer when I grow up." And so the child does whatever it takes to make that goal a reality. Some decisions are not so healthy, as when children decide they don't want to work "that hard." So they play the role of victims when life gets difficult, behavior that attracts people who decided it was their job to rescue others. When rescuers get tired and complain or leave, the victim gets angry, and the rescuers feel guilty and go back to rescuing the victims. Strange as it may seem, getting angry and feeling guilty are the payoffs for victims and rescuers. Changing this self-destructive behavior is a complex enterprise, as the next two stories demonstrate.

PLAYING AT KNIGHTS AND MAIDENS

One of my clients, whom I'll call Lance (short for Lancelot, of course), had always wanted to be the hero, the savior, the knight in shining armor who swoops in with teeth flashing and with sword cutting through the brambles to victory. The result: the maiden swoons with delirious relief, the dragon tiptoes off to the cave, and the other knights gnash their collective teeth in envious admiration.

Lance took on the role of the hero when his father left his mother for another woman when Lance was a boy. Devastated by her loss, Lance's mother turned to her oldest son for advice and comfort, saying that now Lance had to be the "man of the family." The mother did not realize what she was doing; she was too frightened and lonely to think clearly. But as a result of her dependence on Lance he grew up assuming that carrying more than his share of the load in a relationship was normal. With this picture of relationships in place he went through life attracting people, especially women, who expected him to take care of them.

Lance believed that people could not handle pain and rejection because that was his experience in childhood. Thus he did not attract competent people into his life since they did not fit the pictures in his mind. Over and over his imagination replayed the same scenes from his childhood, with the same negative results. Because he gave so much of his time and energy Lance was too tired to work with passion.

As he wrote his autobiography, Lance realized that he could not make people happy. While it was true that his mother suffered because of his father's irresponsibility, Lance saw that it was wrong of her to have put him in a position of power that he was not ready to handle. At first he was very angry with his mother for doing this to him (feeling anger about what was done to us is the necessary first step in coming out of denial). But when he accepted that she had not known what else to do, he forgave her. Then Lance had to forgive himself for giving too much of his time and energy to others.

Breaking the pattern of putting others' needs first took time, since Lance got approval when he rescued people. At least at first they approved of him. But then they got mad because he couldn't fix them. Not surprisingly, Lance was married to an alcoholic, so time and again he relapsed into his old rescuing ways until he went to Al-Anon and got help.

Following the Al-Anon program helped Lance to see that it was his wife's decision to drink, and that only she could decide to stop. So he stopped nagging, blaming, and trying to change her. Instead he told her that although he loved her, he would leave if she did not stop drinking and get help. It took all Lance had to not back down since he was afraid to be alone, but he stood his ground. His wife stopped drinking and went to Alcoholics Anonymous meetings. Today, she is sober and sane, and Lance has the time and energy to work with passion.

Another of my clients was taught by her mother from an early age that she was being loving when she took care of her younger siblings and selfish if she did what she wanted instead. Can you guess who gave more in Ann's relationships?

Through the work she did on her autobiography, with her therapist, and with a support group, Ann learned that there is a difference between caring and rescuing. She saw that caring is motivated by love and genuine concern, whereas rescuing is motivated by guilt and the fear of being thought selfish. Ann's siblings, on the other hand, learned early to use guilt to manipulate generous people like Ann. As she became more objective about this family dynamic she saw how easily her siblings had manipulated their mother and why her mother had pressured Ann to follow her example: she was afraid to stand up to her children for fear of losing them.

Ann ended the family guilt game when she told her mother that her siblings could and would work through their problems when they had no other choice. She said that as long as the mother rescued them, they would have no motivation to change. To her surprise, Ann's mother agreed with her, but she lacked the courage to follow Ann's example, since she was afraid her children would reject her and then she would be alone. Unlike her mother, Ann learned to cope with the anxiety that accompanies emotional risks. Even when she relapsed into her old rescuing ways, she picked herself up and tried again. Each time, she strengthened her emotional muscles. Today, Ann feels free to concentrate on what she wants to do.

As Lance and Ann's stories show, the blocks to passion are often rooted in your reactions to the authority figures in your childhood. These reactions may have worked for you back then, but now they undermine you in every area of your life. Lance could not do the work he loved because he felt guilty when his wife was unhappy (his mother's legacy). Until he realized that he was not a bad person because he wanted his wife to take responsibility for her own happiness, he was destined to take on more than he could handle. Similarly, before she could succeed Ann had to let go of her fear that she was a bad daughter and sister when she focused on her needs (her mother's legacy).

When we are children we make decisions about ourselves based on our experience with our parents or other early caretakers. Since these adults were in control of us at the time, we had no choice but to comply with their wishes if we wanted to survive. As adults, however, we can change those decisions. We can decide to see parents as human beings just like us, not as authority figures we put on pedestals. The desire to be free from the parental matrix is a sign of emotional maturity. The mature individual rejects the notion that an outside authority has the right or the ability to direct his or her life. We could say that the purpose of authority is to outgrow the need for it.

The problem with the above-mentioned white-knight-on-a-white-horse syndrome is that it destroys the confidence of the person receiving the help. As time goes by, the person being rescued believes that he or she can't solve problems, as was the case with Lance's wife and Ann's siblings. Resentment builds, and initiative is weakened. "Well, why don't you do it? You always know how to do everything," says the one being helped. Being the great provider, though well intended, leads to emotional slavery and dependence on the part of the one being helped. In addition, the knight (who is only human, after all, as Lance and Ann discovered) gets tired of carrying the whole load. At the heart of this dynamic are the desire to control and be controlled and the fear of criticism. Self-acceptance means that you can live without approval. You care what others think, but you look to yourself for approval of your thoughts and feelings, not to others. The self-accepting woman knows what she wants, and she does what it takes to achieve her goals. She does not try to get what she wants through her relationship with the man in her life.

Similarly, the self-accepting man expresses his emotions without embarrassment: he grieves, he gets excited, and he admits when he is lonely and confused. Rather than projecting his uncomfortable emotions onto women or demanding that they feel these feelings for him, he does the emotional work for himself. As a result, he connects to himself and others. Men who reject emotions, on the other hand, have trouble with women because they reject the feeling part of their personalities, as was the case for Jonathan in the first chapter. On the surface he feared women's power, but what he really feared was the power of his own emotions. As he became more accepting of his feelings he stood his emotional ground around women, including his mother.

Alcoholic, controlling, or indulgent mothers wreak havoc in their sons' psyches, causing some of them to reject and fear women. Because they reject their own sensitivity they are compelled to go after others' sensitivity, making fun of others' feelings through sarcasm and ridicule. Domineering, abusive, and controlling fathers cause their daughters to reject and fear men, including the aggressive male that lives inside them. Because they are afraid of their masculine power these women pick men through whom they hope to accomplish their objectives. Then when the men fail, they get angry.

The work of adult life is to right the imbalance of a disturbed child-hood. We have to learn on our own and with the help of others what our parents did not or could not teach us by example: how to be healthy, whole human beings. A clear mind and a loving heart are life's most worthwhile achievements. Once Lance accepted the value of his feelings he related well to himself and to his wife. When Ann listened to her feelings, in spite of internal and external pressure, she brought balance to her life.

Limited Choices, Plentiful Choices

In his book *The Third Wave*[2] Alvin Toffler provides an accurate descrip-tion of the development of Western society, including the roles that men and women play. He describes this development as a series of "waves." The first wave, agrarian society, was composed of small units — the villages. The power structure, which was local, was defined by land and position of birth. Thus, the structure of this society was hier-archical and authoritarian.

The second wave of civilization, according to Toffler, brought an end to the former localized power structure. The Industrial Revolution and resulting technological growth changed civilization and gave a factory-like definition to life: schools, families, and work meshed like the gears of production. Standardization, specialization, synchroniza-tion, and maximization of resources — all these led men into second wave "centralized" thinking, while the women stayed behind in the first wave. The wife "produced" for her family, not for the larger market. Toffler explains his theory further:

> As the husband, by and large, marched off to do the direct eco-nomic work, the wife generally stayed behind to do the indirect economic work. The man took responsibility for the histori-cally more advanced form of work; the woman was left behind to take care of the older, more backward form of work. He moved, as it were, into the future; she remained in the past.

Men, prepared from boyhood for their role in the shop, where they would move in a world of interdependencies, were encouraged to become "objective." Women, prepared from birth for the tasks of reproduction, child-rearing, and household drudgery, performed to a considerable degree in social isolation, were taught to be "subjective" — and were frequently regarded as incapable of the kind of rational, analytic thought that supposedly went with objectivity.

According to Toffler, sexual differences and sex role stereotypes were sharpened by the misleading identification of men with production and women with consumption, even though men also consumed and women also produced. In short, while women were oppressed long before the second wave began to roll across the earth, the modern "battle of the sexes" can be traced in large measure to the conflict between work styles, and beyond that to the divorce of production from consumption. The split economy deepened the sexual split as well.3 Toffler believes that social turmoil is reduced when people shift from second-wave thinking to third-wave thinking, echoing my belief that self-acceptance and flexibility speed growth and understanding. When we hold on to the past because we think that is the only way to live, we miss golden opportunities for growth.

The Lancelot of the twenty-first century is a fuller person than the Camelot character of the past. He laughs, cries, and feels more. Sometimes he notices that he does not really want to slay the dragon anymore. (He has slain enough already.) As for maidens and kings and jealous knights, my client Lance changed their roles, too. He sees his wife as a woman who is capable of change and growth, rather than a helpless victim. He no longer tries to please his boss; instead, Lance tries to please himself. Similarly, the Guinevere of the twenty-first century does not define success by how well she motivates the man in her life. Success is being true to herself wherever she is.

UPDATING YOUR STORY

To update your story to match the times in which you live, think about a time in the past when you achieved a particular goal. You may have to practice remembering success. Keep in mind that most people equate success with money, fame, and power and have a hard time recalling an *emotional* success. If you don't believe it, ask a friend or co-worker how he or she would define emotional success. Then ask when they last achieved that objective.

This commitment to defining success in material terms is the main reason that people can't accept themselves as they are. Until they achieve a certain level of monetary success they feel inadequate. They compare their lives unfavorably to those of rich people who are in the spotlight, without knowing what is really going on with those people. I have worked with people who, by any definition, would be considered successful. But they had the same inner pain as those in less fortunate financial circumstances.

Glorifying material success is reinforced everywhere in our culture: on television and in movies, newspapers, and magazines. The focus is on celebrity, fame, and riches. This says a great deal about the shallowness of our values, how easily we can be fooled into believing that money and things bring happiness. But that's the challenge of life on earth: to enjoy it without being enslaved by material possessions.

You will notice that I use stories of ordinary people in this book, not those of the rich and famous. Once my clients did what they wanted to do, however, their lives became extraordinary. I hope their stories will inspire and encourage you to follow your heart, rather than your wallet. Ironically, once you do what you love, and you do it well, you will have all the money you need (*need*, not want).

Stop reading now and write a happy ending to your story. First define what you mean by happiness; make sure this definition includes spiritual and emotional rewards as well as material success. Then make a list of the people you know who are happy. Can you see a common thread in these people's lives? Do they do what they love for a living?

Are they intensely excited about what they do? Do they accept themselves as they are, rather than comparing themselves to others?

Remember that the definition of power is the ability to take action. Consider the actions happy people take — with themselves and others. Study your list. If you list only two or three people, then you need to alter your definition of happiness.

Passion Secret *3* *Know your strengths and values.*

Self-acceptance begins with an accurate understanding of what it takes to make *you* feel good about you. As you do the exercises in this chapter, do not compare yourself to an ideal. Comparison sabotages your path to personal power, since your power lies in your uniqueness. Powerful people do not reject any part of their experience. I cannot overemphasize the necessity of self-acceptance: you must have a genuine appreciation of your individuality to be successful. Whenever you compare yourself to another person ask yourself how such a comparison can serve you, given that it cannot reflect all of your strengths or the uniqueness of your personality.

Comparing yourself to another is as effective as political tyranny in its ability to limit your choices and development. If you believe that you are a "nobody" — that it is only rich people, corporation presidents, movie and media stars, and political figures who have power and the ability to take action — you are tyrannizing yourself. You are the dictator you dislike, the one who tells you every waking hour what to do, what to think, and what to say. Look at your life, discover the action you need to take, and then take it. Then you will truly feel powerful.

Tom's Story

Here is a story of how being competitive can backfire. One of my clients, whom I'll call Tom, was so intent on proving he was "right" and that his ex-wife was "wrong" he sent her child support checks late and wrote her name in the tiniest of letters.

"You're trying to eliminate her, Tom," I said.

"You're right; as far as I'm concerned, she doesn't exist," he said bitterly. We had been wrestling with Tom's resistance to change, and the anger that resistance masked, for weeks. Both these traits were showing up when Tom went on interviews. One prospective employer called me, since Tom had given him my name as a reference. He said he thought Tom had a bad attitude and that though he thought Tom was technically qualified, he hesitated to hire him.

"How do you know he has a bad attitude?" I had asked.

"Well, he was stiff with his answers about his past job. He's defensive about that period of his work life. It made me wonder what happened. I just got the impression he was mad, and tense, and he would have trouble with his co-workers." He explained that Tom needed more maturity before he could be a good manager.

When I told Tom what the employer said, he was surprised.

"I had no problem with my last job. It was my divorce that made me angry," he said.

"I think your pride got hurt when she left you." I said. "When are you going to accept responsibility for your part of the reason the marriage failed, Tom? Didn't you tell me recently that your wife says you're a poor communicator? Do you want to repeat the past? Don't you want to learn from your mistakes?"

"Of course I want to learn," Tom said.

"It's been five years since the divorce. When you write her name so that the bank teller can't even read it, you think you are controlling her still, getting back at her, and making her nonexistent. Actually, she's controlling you so much now that you can't get hired."

Tom was quiet and looked uncomfortable. "How do I stop feeling angry?" he asked.

"First, admit that you like playing the role of the wronged victim. That way, you get everyone's sympathy. But sympathy is the last thing you need. Ask yourself why you want everyone to feel sorry for you and mad at her." I knew Tom had lived as a victim for so long it was going to be hard for him to admit that he was being competitive with his former wife. "I felt so angry when she left," Tom said. "I still feel powerless every month when I write that check to her. I am still mad that I have to give her money. She left me for someone else, and I got hurt.

I know that I'm living in the past, dragging around a dead carcass, thinking each month about the whole marriage and the divorce," Tom added. "But what do I do about the anger? Aren't I justified in feeling angry?"

"Not if you see that your former wife left you because she got tired of the way you treated her. It's normal to think only of yourself when you're a child, Tom, but not when you're an adult. You deliberately withheld affection from your former wife as a way to control her."

Tom's autobiography had revealed the origin of his cruel streak. When Tom was a boy his father left his mother for another woman. His mother could not afford to take care of the children, so she sent Tom to live with his aunt; his siblings were placed in foster homes until their mother got on her feet. Tom decided that since no one cared about him he was never going to care about anyone. This was not reality, but it was Tom's conclusion, based on what he knew at the time.

"That's a completely different way for me to look at my story," Tom said. "I had no idea the problem was my anger about being left with my aunt."

"What's important is the decision you made back then, that you were never going to care again because no one cared about you. You've got to challenge that decision. Your mother cared about you so much she put you where you'd be safe. You're here now, and everything turned out all right. So why not forgive and forget? Until you do, you won't get hired. What employer would want to put a time bomb on the work site?"

"I see what you mean. I wouldn't hire me either," Tom said. "Not the way I am now."

Changing the way he thought about the past changed Tom's view of himself. When he talked with his wife about our discussion that night she agreed with everything I had said. The next time I saw Tom he seemed like a different person. He was more relaxed, more humble, and less defensive. In a few weeks, he got a job offer from a well-respected computer firm. When he called to tell me the good news, Tom told me, laughing, "My boss said he hired me because of my good attitude."

Tom's story is an example of mastering passion secret 2: understand the past; then let it go. Being blocked in his career was the consequence of his refusal to let go of his anger with his former wife. Once he realized that he was still competing with her, Tom saw how outmoded that behavior was, and he corrected it. Then he moved forward in his career and in his marriage.

The next exercises will show you what you do when you are having the most pleasure. Keep in mind that passion is an intensely pleasurable experience.

WHAT'S YOUR PLEASURE?

I designed the following exercises to help you discover what gives you the most pleasure. Take a few minutes and think about what you do when left to your own devices. Do you gravitate to certain activities, such as reading books, working in the garden, going for walks, talking to certain people, traveling, or taking time to contemplate? The first exercise will help you to identify what you do when you are "working" at what you like. (You will need several sheets of paper or several pages of your journal to complete this exercise and the ones that follow.)

Focus on pleasure in this exercise — the times in your life when you were enjoying yourself. Look up the definition of the word *pleasure* in your dictionary and thesaurus. What thoughts do these definitions of pleasure bring to your mind? Most of us think that work and pleasure are antonyms, not synonyms. You will find that this exercise gives you a fresh way of looking at work.

You probably do not stop to analyze happy times; you just have them. Spontaneous, joyful times hold the keys to your natural strengths. By analyzing pleasurable moments, you will discover those strengths, the qualities that allow you to perform effortlessly and naturally. Use big, positive, cheerful words to describe your pleasures. Also ask yourself why you remember these particular events. The answer to this question will give you insight into your values, the motivation behind the choices you make when you feel free. The lists below will help get you started.

1. *Pleasures in school.* When did you feel the sense of accomplishment that came from doing well at what you liked? How about extracurricular activities? What did you like? What fascinated you?

2. *Pleasures in hobbies or special interests.* What hobbies did you enjoy? What activities were you motivated to engage in on your own?

3. *Pleasures you felt when you received test results.* Discuss when you did well on educational, psychological, or other kinds of tests.

Work-Related Pleasure

Now answer these questions about pleasure you have felt at work.

1. Have your pleasurable accomplishments ever reduced costs and increased income? For example, did your ability to laugh increase rapport with a customer so much that they bought more? Was your curiosity responsible for discovering a costly error? Did your computer skills make a job go faster and be more understandable? These are strengths — marketable qualities that make businesses work better.

2. Have you solved problems and had fun doing it? (Problems can involve people, data, or objects.)

3. Have you improved efficiency because you were relaxed and enjoying yourself? This could be something quite simple — perhaps you learned a new software program, saw a better

way to file or translate documents, or recognized an easier way to get a job done. Perhaps your teaching skills helped a co-worker improve performance. Your decision made your work and others' work easier and more enjoyable.

Comment on the pleasure you felt in developing new ways to market the products or services your company sold. Your ideas need not have been put into effect; list any times when you came up with improvements that you knew would work.

THE EDUCATIONAL SKILL GRID

Looking at the work pleasures you wrote about, select the words that best describe your natural strengths. Strengths are not always the same as skills; they can be intangible traits you use when you have to solve a problem, such as finding your way in a new town or circumstance. Are your strengths optimism, warmth, honesty, good humor, imagination, communication (writing, reading, speaking, talking), intuition, flexibility, and perseverance? These words describe what you do when you are being yourself. These are the strengths you use when you do the work you love, when you get paid to be yourself.

You will probably find that ten to twenty words keep cropping up as you write about pleasurable times in your life. These key words are your strengths. List these words across the top of your educational skill grid, as in the sample that follows. Next, look at your classes in high school or college that you enjoyed the most. You may want to list your classes in chronological order, checking where you were using your strengths. Write down the reasons why you liked these classes so much.

List any course or subject you were taught outside school as well — in seminars, training programs, or home study courses. Look at your key words, and ask yourself if others would agree with you about these strengths. For example, did you hear from teachers or classmates that you were analytical, original, hardworking, creative? (Again, choose the words that reflect your individual abilities.)

One of my clients summarized her favorite classes and her corresponding strengths as follows. To save space she included her considerable listening and speaking skills in the one category she called "communication." Below I will show you the skill grid in table format, which my client used, as well as in the paragraph form, which you might find easier to use.

Sample Educational Skill Grid: Table Format

	Analysis	Problem Solving	Communication	Organization
1. Intro Chemistry	X	X	X	X
2. Human Sexuality	X		X	
3. Fundamentals of Music	X		X	X
4. Concert Choir	X		X	
5. English Composition			X	X
6. Elementary German	X	X	X	
7. Conversational German	X	X	X	
8. General Psychology	X	X	X	X
9. Language Lab (German)	X		X	X
10. Elementary Speech	X		X	X
11. Intermediate Algebra	X	X		X
12. Physical Education				
13. Work Experience I	X	X	X	X
14. Work Experience II	X	X	X	X
15. Elementary Algebra	X	X		X
16. Continue as above				
Total	13	8	12	10

Sample Educational Skill Grid: Paragraph Format

Strengths I See	Verification
	Who agreed with you about these strengths? Write a short paragraph about that.
1. Analysis (Example)	1. Professors gave me high grades and lots of praise. Other students complimented me on my papers. I received the most praise for my accurate analysis.
2. Communication (Example)	2. I contributed in class and answered questions. I spoke when called on without fear. My papers were well researched and written; my teacher read part of my paper to the class. In all my classes I got praised for listening.
3. Continue as above	3.

WORK SKILL GRID

My client Emily was not aware of what a good listener she was until she completed the educational skill exercise; she didn't think of listening as a strength. As a musician and language teacher she took her sensitive ear for granted. When she got a job interviewing people on her own radio show, Emily felt right at home since she was using her top strengths, what came naturally and easily to her.

As in the education-oriented exercise above, focus on strengths that give you pleasure. These are far more important than your job title or function! Make a list of your jobs and businesses, beginning with your most recent position. Choose the technique you want to use, using either the table or the paragraph form. Since most jobs today require computer literacy, make a separate grid for your computer skills. Write a list of the programs you are familiar with, and the strengths you use when you work on your computer, laptop, palm pilot, and other technological tools. Are any of these tools pleasurable for you to use? Observe the patterns.

As before, record who would agree with what you recorded as strengths (your key words), who noticed that you were enjoying yourself.

Sample Work Skill Grid

Strengths	Analysis	Communication	Organization
1. Job A	x		x
2. Job B	x	x	
3. Job C	x		x
4. Continue as above			
Total	3	1	2

DEFINING YOUR STRENGTHS AND ASSETS

Now rank your strengths in order of ability and frequency of use. You will list your top-five strengths at the end of the chapter.

Strengths I See	Verification
1. Analysis (Example)	1. Salesmen relied on me for data and told me I was good at my job.
2. Communication (Example)	2. My ability to communicate with all kinds of people was noticed by customers and salespeople.
3. Organization	3. My boss said I was very efficient.
4. Continue as above	4.

Your assets are your natural resources — gifts granted you at birth — your height, smile, posture, bone structure, and temperament. If you are an introvert, for example, your strength is your ability to live deeply, not widely, to work alone or in a small group of people. Your strength is independence, the ability to work well without much supervision. If you are an extrovert, your strength is teamwork, the ability to work with others, to relate to large groups of people. Unlike introverts, you do not get worn out in meetings or when you travel.

Don't forget about the assets of your race and nationality, your ethnic roots, and your heritage. For example, your family may come from a long line of storytellers, as is often true of those with Celtic roots, or your forebears may have been great cooks, or perhaps they valued artistic expression, or maybe you've inherited the tactile skills of craftspeople or the business sense of entrepreneurs. Think carefully and prepare an extensive list of your personal assets, in your journal, on a pad of paper, or on your computer. Do not confuse your strengths (you've already listed those!) with your assets. Your strengths are the result of individual effort and interest; your assets are your natural abilities and gifts.

Next, have someone who knows you well prepare a similar list. Ask this person, From your perspective, what assets do I possess? Better yet, ask several friends to respond. They will enjoy doing it, and you might gain some insights! Ask your friend to think carefully about your characteristics. Have them list your assets in one column and your strengths in another.

DEFINING YOUR VALUES

Values change over time; what was once important to you may not be of interest to you now. However, some values remain constant throughout your life. These values reflect what you think is good, true, and worthwhile. Of all human activities, your work has the greatest potential to fulfill your values. In fact, your values should define your career choice. When you know yourself and what you value you are more likely to choose a position that allows you to get paid to be yourself.

Observe what you do, not what you say, consistently. This will tell you what you think is important. Some values are conscious and easy to identify; others require more work to bring to the surface. Study the following fifteen values; they apply to your personal life as well as to your career.4 Write about each value in as much detail as possible. Focus on those that are the most important to you now, on what you need to feel happy and content.

1. *Security.* Freedom from worry; safety, certainty, and a similarity between prediction and event. Security is not money; it is the need to know what is going to happen.

2. *Status.* The state or condition of a person in the eyes of others. When you value status you are concerned with

what people think of you; your job title, position, and col-leagues are important to you.

3. *Compensation.* Pay or remuneration for services rendered. Everyone wants to earn a good living; if compensation is one of your top-five values, then how much you are paid is important to you.

4. *Achievement.* Accomplishment of a desired objective; a thing done successfully. Mastery of a task, project, or goal. If you like overcoming obstacles, then this value is important to you.

5. *Advancement.* To improve, to progress. Advancement can be growing in expertise, knowledge, and tolerance.

6. *Affiliation.* The desire to associate with like-minded people or a team with whom you identify. This is an important value if you are extroverted and you need interaction with a group of people to accomplish your objectives.

7. *Recognition.* Special notice or attention for individual or team effort. People who value recognition will work long and hard to have this value met.

8. *Authority.* The power or right to command, direct, and manage. This value is typical in people who enjoy leading others.

9. *Independence.* Freedom from the control of another. People who value creativity often choose independence as one of their top values because they need freedom in order to create.

10. *Altruism.* Concern for the welfare of others. This value is important to people who want their work to help others.

11. *Creativity.* Finding new, improved ways to do anything; the urge to innovate and make new combinations. People who value creativity get impatient with too much supervision and structure. They need air!

12. *Ethical harmony.* Importance of having moral values, environmental concerns, and so on reinforced in work setting. Honesty, fair dealing, and walking the talk are vital to people who pick this value.

13. *Intellectual stimulation.* Mental electricity, the need to be around people who like to think. You need to be in an environment that encourages, supports, and promotes thinking, such as an academic, creative, or research position.

14. *Variety.* Diversity of activity, tasks, and people. People who value variety get bored when their work is repetitive; they like something new coming in all the time.

15. *Aesthetics.* Desire for beauty in the work setting and surroundings. Aesthetics is more than the love of beauty and fine-ness; it is a desire for connection with the Divine.

Select your top-five values and list them in your journal or on your computer. Choose the ones that are the most important to you now, what you think is good, true, and worthwhile. Now list your top-five strengths. When you know your top-five strengths and your top-five values, you narrow your focus to work settings that reward these strengths and values. That is what you take to the marketplace — your strengths, not a job title.

Now you have the template to assess any business, job, or creative activity. Look at your five strengths. These are what your employer, clients, and customers need from you. Your five values are what you share with them. In other words, the people who hire or work with you will have the same values. Their products and services will reinforce these values. For example, if you value creativity, your employer or boss values creativity too; most likely, their products or services are sold to creative people. It is only logical that the business, job, or creative activity that makes use of your top-five strengths and that fulfills your top-five values will be your passion.

SUMMARY

Passion Secret *3* *Know your strengths and values.*

1. Self-acceptance means that you accept your human nature:
    your honesty and dishonesty, kindness and cruelty, stub-
    bornness and open-mindedness. Self-acceptance takes
    great courage, since some traits can be ugly, such as greed,
    lust, and jealousy. But if you look without judgment at
    these traits they lose their unconscious hold on you. Accept
    the lighter side of your human personality too: your
    courage, kindness, and generosity. Being balanced means
    being comfortable with your flaws and your assets.

2. Get in tune with your times. Update your computer skills
    and your attitudes; small changes set the stage for greater
    changes. Imagine the end of your life story just as you want
    it to be.

3. Your imagination is the bridge that connects you to the
    treasures in your unconscious mind. Visualize what you
    want. Then do what it takes to make these images a reality.

4. To move into the next phase of your life, reject hierarchical
    and authoritarian thinking. Accept people as your fellow
    human beings.

5. If you are the rescuer, like Lance, try to let people do their
    own thinking. Be grateful for your sensitivity and compas-
    sion, but don't let compassion be used against you by
    people who take advantage of your kind heart.

6. If you play the role of the helpless "maiden" (regardless of
    your gender!), grow up and take responsibility for your life.
    Focus on what you need to do for yourself rather than on
    what you can get others to do for you.

7. Male-female stereotypes (aggressive knights and passive maidens) are obsolete. Instead develop both your intuitive right-brain thinking and your logical left-brain thinking.

8. Make a list of happy people. Who are they? What do they do? Are they passionate?

9. Acknowledge any anger and resentment that keeps you from living in the present. Make amends to people you injured. Let go of the past; then you'll move forward into a better future.

10. Focus on the times when you were enjoying yourself, when you felt confident and glad to be you. What is the pattern in these times?

11. Recall your most pleasurable times in a work setting. What personal strengths were you using?

12. What courses did you like the best in school? What strengths did you use in these courses?

13. List your most pleasurable experiences in a nonacademic setting. Choose either the table or the paragraph technique to help you discover what you do when you are enjoying yourself.

14. List your top-five strengths. List instructors or others who agreed with you about those strengths.

15. List your top-five strengths in your most recent jobs. Who agreed with you about your strengths?

16. Define your assets, those natural resources given to you at birth.

17. Ask a friend to make a list of your assets and your strengths.

18. The values exercise will show you what you need to be happy now in your work. When your work matches these values, you will succeed.

19. List your top-five values and your top-five strengths. Your five strengths are what you have to offer employers, customers, and clients; your five values are what you share with them. Keep this list handy; you will need to refer to it in succeeding chapters.

4 SETTING GOALS YOU CAN REACH

The fourth step to working with passion is setting goals you can reach. When you concentrate on short-term objectives you develop the discipline you need to reach long-term goals, such as physical fitness and financial prosperity. Set goals for a six-month period or less. You get more excited about an event that is closer in time. (Passion clue!)

People who set goals they can reach are realistic; they do not overextend. They focus on the task at hand, not on the end result. Like a river, they reverse course, ebb toward shore, tumble over rocks, form swirling rapids, glide into still lagoons, and fall hundreds of feet to join with other waters. Ever onward they move, seeking newness, pushing forward to their eventual destiny — a bigger body of water (and a smoother ride).

Passion Secret *Remember that getting there is all the fun.*

Have you noticed that once you achieve a goal and you think about what it took to get you there, you realize that getting there was all the fun? This chapter will help you to become even more conscious of the importance of the journey, and that enjoying the process is the key to a contented life.

Like the force behind a river, your imagination carves out your life's journey based on your beliefs. As you change your beliefs your life alters course. Your imagination may have brought you a daily existence that is no fun at all. Do you suffer from a chronic shortage of money? Do you experience little or no satisfaction in your work? Do you have conflicts you believe you cannot resolve? Few friends? No love in your life? If it is any consolation, most people use their imagination to structure negative outcomes: no fun, no money, no love, and no joy. Yuck! Life becomes a drag — and you become apathetic.

FOCUSING ON THE JOURNEY, NOT THE GOAL

To see your life as a process — a journey — means that you are constantly integrating past experiences with today's experience, all the while remaining open to what life brings you. When your mind is jammed full of bits and pieces of undigested information, however, it is hard to make sense of your life, much less to take advantage of opportunities as they arise. Always be very patient with yourself when you are learning. You have already heard some of the ideas presented in this book. In fact, I say little that you do not intuitively know already. What I hope you learn in this book is how to use this knowledge.

Most people set economic independence as their ultimate goal. Money, they assume, will give them the freedom to do what they want to do, to go where they want, and to answer to no one. But few accomplish this objective because they are focused on making money rather than on doing what they want. The truth is that you don't need a great deal of money to do what you love. What you do need is self-discipline.

For example, if you want to write a book, get up an hour earlier every morning and write. If you do this for three months, you're a writer; if you can't sustain this daily regimen, then give up writing as a goal; it's not what you want to do. Perhaps you want to be involved in some other aspect of publishing, such as sales or production, or maybe you want to work for or with writers.

The point to remember is that making the attempt to write will let you know if writing is what you enjoy doing; in other words, getting published is not the goal, although that's exciting; the writing itself is. Whatever comes of your effort you will learn what you need to know, even if it's that you're not a writer. Good! Now you can eliminate that goal from your list and focus on what will hold your interest over a long period of time.

Let me reiterate: it is the journey that matters, not the goal. It is not the trophy, but how you run the race; not the quarry, but the chase. If you are not learning as you go, curious about the next step, understanding the process, and patient enough to let time be your ally, you have yet to discover the secret of a satisfied life: focusing on the task in front of you.

Economic independence is a laudable goal, the result of hard work and patience. But the first "law" of money is to do what you love, then the money will come. *How* the money comes cannot be predicted, but it will come, often in surprising ways, as my client Joanna discovered.

Joanna's Story

Joanna had two advanced degrees in public health administration. Her father was a physician, her mother a nurse. Both encouraged Joanna to pursue a career in health, and they paid for her education.

By all external standards, Joanna was successful. She held a succession of responsible positions in public health administration. Yet she was dissatisfied. She experienced ongoing conflicts on the job, largely because of the bureaucratic management in her nonprofit organizations. Decisions were made slowly, and her programs were so watered down by the time they were implemented that she felt discouraged most of the time. Joanna came to me wanting a new job, and she expressed a strong desire to get out of the medical field. She had no feeling of accomplishment, since she had been following someone else's passion — her parents'!

"I'm so frustrated that I can't do the kind of supervision I'm capable of," she said. "The agency where I work is a nest of conflict. I'm sick of the petty gossip and people not focusing on results. I can't stand the delays and the endless meetings. In fact, I never could, but now I have reached my limit. The problem is that I can't imagine what else I can do. I want to change, but how? I want to go somewhere else, but where?"

Making a transition from a solid career to something unknown at age forty scared Joanna. I assured her that she could make such a change, even though it might take time. But first she would have to stay where she was and change her attitude about present circumstances.

"First things first," I said. "Rather than jumping into another job, do a few preliminary assignments. First, write your autobiography. That will show both of us any unconscious beliefs that may be holding you back. I want to know how you got so far off track, what made you act against your best interests. Your story will help me to know who you are apart from your parents and the kind of decisions you make easily, as well as the relationships you need in work. Then we'll have specifics to talk about."

The completed exercises revealed much about Joanna. She was an adopted child. Her mother was a quiet and passive woman, and her father the authority in the family. Joanna identified with her father and, at the same time, she resented his control. This ambivalent attitude toward male authority, what some psychologists call a "father complex," was at the root of Joanna's career (and life) dilemma: she wanted to be in control, and yet she lacked the self-confidence that leadership requires.

Most career dissatisfaction stems from lack of self-confidence. My clients gain confidence as they go through the steps that lead to competence. If they skip a step because they are in a hurry, they will have conflicts with authority figures who act as gatekeepers blocking the path to success. Frustration forces my clients to go back and get it right, whatever "it" is. When they have gained greater confidence they move forward in their careers (and lives).

When Joanna was younger and life got difficult she turned to alcohol and drugs to help her cope with her frustration. One day, as she wrote in her story, she admitted that she was an alcoholic and started going to Alcoholics Anonymous meetings.

"Then I had to tackle all my other issues," Joanna wrote, "such as getting involved in relationships in which I took care of the other person."

Taking care of other people can be a subtle way of avoiding taking responsibility for our own lives. The other person is usually a reflection of what we need to change about ourselves, and that is precisely what binds us to them. Additionally, Joanna was an extrovert, so she had a hard time sticking to a demanding project, such as writing her autobiography. She was easily distracted, worrying about having a relationship or enough money. But eventually she completed it.

"What a struggle my life has been," Joanna said, as we discussed her story.

"Yes, you've been doing everything you can to sabotage yourself," I said, smiling. "But now I think you're ready to get out of your own way."

Most of my clients are not aware of the internal conflict that blocks them from success. They project that conflict into their environments, usually onto people with whom they have problems, such as bosses. Joanna believed she would always struggle but never get to where she wanted to go, like an airplane that warms up on the tarmac but never takes off.

Becoming conscious of inner conflicts is hard work. It is much easier to blame others or to fall into despair when we fail. But since failure is the objective of an "I'm never going to make it" script, you can see why people like Joanna sabotage themselves. Unconsciously, they make choices that guarantee failure, since doing so verifies their opinion of themselves and of life in general. For Joanna to feel confident, she had to question her father's authority. In other words, she needed to admit that her father was not the all-knowing expert she thought he was when she was a girl. At first, Joanna could not see the connection between her father and her failures.

"You're blaming him for your choices," I said. "The problem is not him; it's your unconscious rebellion against his power that keeps you in thrall to him. So he looms large in your mind, like the villain in a melodrama. You make most of your choices in reaction to this movie running in your mind. Talk to the girl you used to be. You need to show her how to see him as a person, not as a scary ogre. For example, say to her, 'if he were not your father, how would you describe him?'"

"I know exactly what she would say," Joanna said. "She'd say, 'he's smart, he has a bad temper, and people have to walk on eggshells around him.'"

"Okay, now ask her if competent people are hard to get along with."

"No, they are usually fair and easygoing."

"So what does that say about your father?"

"That he's not confident," Joanna said, looking shocked. "That's the last thing I'd think about my father."

"But if you call him John instead of Father, it's obvious, isn't it?" I said.

(Note that the word *John* does not have the emotional power of the word *father*; John is just a man's name, which was why Joanna felt confident when she talked about him. Try this yourself. Say your father's name. Then say, "my father." See the difference?)

"Yes, it is. I think John's lack of confidence goes back to his relationship with his father. From what I've heard he was a mean guy, brutal with his male children, and controlling with the girls."

"So perhaps John has copied his father's behavior. If you think of John apart from you, that will help you to separate from your old view of him. Then you can assess choices based on a realistic picture," I said.

"I see what you mean. It's like moving my point of reference."

"Correct. Your values will be your reference point, not John."

Separating from our family is one of life's more difficult tasks, since when we give up the child's egocentric (and often idealized) view of the family we feel a sense of loss and sadness, as if we were all alone in the world. But what we gain is the ability to relate to family members as adults. This shift in perspective has an immediate positive effect on our relationships with authority figures: we see them as people, not as ogres who control or frighten us.

As Joanna thought about our discussion she realized that she would never be happy until she moved into the authority role, but she could not do that until she looked to herself for approval, not to her father. Many women are ambivalent about the responsibility that goes with power; it is more comfortable to be a step away from power and mad about it. Joanna needed to own a business in which she had daily responsibility for decision making. Obviously, her current career position did not fit her personality. But first she had to take a preliminary step into the business world.

"Like your father, you are the entrepreneurial type, Joanna; you need very little structure in a work setting. You enjoy risk taking and being in charge, which is best applied in work, not in relationships with people who expect you to take care of them. The entrepreneur type always has trouble being told what to do," I added.

"I thought something was wrong with me all these years. Others seem to be able to play the political game. I'm always speaking out and getting in trouble for it. What you're saying gives me a sense of relief. I need to be in the private sector, don't I?" Joanna asked.

"Yes, a small business will give you the rewards you're looking for. The private sector is best for those who enjoy making their own decisions. It's the personality fit that counts. You are interested in giving service, but in a different way," I said.

I suggested that Joanna find a transition job in a semipublic setting. She was not prepared for the demands of the free market; she needed more business training, which could only come when she made decisions and learned from the consequences of those decisions. (Remember passion secret 3: getting there is all the fun.) If my clients take too big a leap from where they are in their career development they risk failure, regardless of how smart they are. There is just no substitute for experience.

Through her market research efforts (I'll cover this step in the next chapter), Joanna found an agency that used both private and government funds as income, providing home health and nursing care to low-income families. After interviewing with the director, she was hired to administrate the program and to raise funds. As a fund-raiser, she met and talked to many businesspeople over the next year, selling a service she was familiar with. Again, this small step led to bigger change.

Moving from a staff position to the line gave Joanna the confidence that she could sell. The more comfortable she was with sales, the more comfortable she was with the other aspects of business, such as marketing. Now that Joanna brought in the money she felt powerful — a new feeling for her.

"I do fund-raising so easily, but that's because I believe in the program; it benefits so many people. It's easy to promote. This past year has confirmed all that you said to me, Nancy, that I have the ability but what I needed was experience. I like the variety and challenge of meeting so many different people: Why did I ever think I wanted to be in an office? However, I still have problems with my superior. It's a constant struggle to put my ideas into action. She is very moody, and the staff is kept in constant turmoil. I just want to do my work, but she takes all the fun out of it," Joanna said.

As we talked, I could see that Joanna was ready for the next step, so I asked her what she did when she was not working. "What fascinates you, Joanna, what do you do in your spare time?" (Passion clue!)

"Oh, that's easy. On weekends I get up at 4:30 in the morning and chop wood. Then I organize my house, the garage, and my yard. I'm so good at this I even do it for my friends. They're always asking me to help them get their homes in order," she replied, becoming very excited.

"Can you see yourself doing that for a living?" I asked.

"What?" she asked, with a shocked look on her face. "You mean housekeeping?"

"Not houses. How about businesses, shops, banks, parking lots, all are places that have to be kept clean." I said.

Joanna was silent. Her mental wheels were spinning. "You're talking about my own janitorial business. I never thought about it, but it seems logical. In all my jobs I've been told I'm an expert when it comes to time management. I just seem to know the most efficient way to do things. But cleaning? My father, I mean John, would have a fit!" she exclaimed.

"I'm sure he would, but remember, you are not to refer your decisions to John," I said, chuckling. "Don't say anything to him until you are done with this process. It's too easy to slip back into the role of being John's daughter. For now, just explore the idea."

I ask my clients to hold off discussing the process with people who do not understand what they are going through. Most people cannot tolerate uncertainty, particularly parents like John, whose mind was made up. It may not be conscious on their part, but many parents undermine their children's confidence with questions like, "So, do you know what you want to do yet?" Or, "How are you going to make any money at that?" My clients have a hard enough time dealing with their fear of failure; they don't need others' fears to add to their discomfort.

"Pick out some companies to talk to," I said to Joanna. "Then you can meet some people and see what they say about the cleaning business."

Joanna selected ten janitorial companies of various sizes. Some were large corporations whose accounts were high-rise office buildings. Others were medium-sized companies, with both small and large accounts. She also selected local entrepreneurs in her town; one was an older man whose janitorial business had an excellent reputation. After only three meetings, Joanna came in to my office full of excitement and information.

"The cleaning business is booming, Nancy!" She said. "All the people I talked to were so enthusiastic about the need for quality service. I was even offered a job with the biggest company in the city. They said they would train me for management!" I encouraged Joanna to talk to local people before she made a decision. "Often the diamonds are right in your own backyard. Let's see what the old pro in your neighborhood has to say," I said.

The entrepreneurial type can work in large companies if they are at the bottom of a learning curve. But when they are done learning they get restless and bored. Few big companies know how to satisfy those with the "growth" personality, since starting up new ventures internally is expensive; stockholders want profit maximization, not funding startups, since that eats up money they may not get back. Most of the time growth types jump ship so that they can start over at the bottom of another learning curve, in a smaller company or in their own businesses. The entrepreneurial type is fascinated (passion clue!) by newness, not by the tried and true. Conversely, the tried-and-true fascinates (passion clue!) the maintainer type. These are the people who keep any company or organization running smoothly, such as managers, controllers, accountants, human resources, warehouse, and other maintenance-type positions.

The meeting with the old pro in the cleaning business changed Joanna's life. It put her on the road to an exciting and prosperous business. John, the owner, was very impressed with Joanna's background and passion for the cleaning business. He told her he had been looking for an assistant but had not been able to find anyone who was willing to work hard and persevere through difficult times. He said that he would like to retire soon, or only work part-time. His cleaning methods were so effective that he had more customers than he could handle. John wanted to meet with Joanna again. To prepare her for that meeting, he recommended some articles for her to read.

"John said that if I want to start my own janitorial business, I must have training," Joanna said to me. "He told me that the most crucial part of the business is in how efficiently you use your time. If you don't know the fastest way to clean, you'll go broke. My plan is to reduce my present position at the agency to half-time and spend the other half working with John. The janitorial work is at night, so I'll go in to my other job midday. I can raise money in the afternoon and clean out the banks at night!" she laughed.

And that is just what Joanna did. One year later, she quit her agency job and bought the business from John. (Interesting that his name was the same as her father's; but this John was a completely different person, very supportive of Joanna's talent and independence.) He stayed on as a consultant until the transition was complete. In six months she bought two more businesses, and in her second year she personally netted nearly twice the income she had been making at her old job! More important than the money was the control Joanna had over her life; she was happy because she made all the decisions.

As the months went by, Joanna learned how to cope with the ups and downs of owning a business, experiencing the normal anxiety and fear that are part of risk taking. Joanna had days of discouragement, feeling so tired that she ached all over. She would call me and let out all the frustration. I would always ask, "Well, do you want to quit and return to your old job?"

"No way! I'm just blowing off steam. Be patient with me," she would say.

And her father had a fit! "We didn't raise you and educate you to do cleaning work! How can you turn your back on your training? All those years were a waste of our money," John said. (Note the guilt trip and the disapproval — sadly, all too common from relatives.)

"Joanna, just send John photocopies of your bank deposit slips. He'll come around when he sees how much money you make," I said. And Joanna's father did come around. Now he brags about Joanna to his friends in his retirement community: "my daughter, the successful businesswoman" is how he describes her.

A few years later, Joanna called to bring me up to date on her business and her life. "My company's name is now synonymous with quality, Nancy, just like John's was. He trained me well. I'll always be grateful. I want to pass on my knowledge and use my business to train young people in a valuable profession. There's money and satisfaction in dirt, floods, and debris!" she chuckled.

Joanna had found her passion. And in the process, she added a great deal of value to her world. She used her natural interest and ability — what she did easily and well — to become economically and emotionally independent. But first she had to grow up and leave home. The cleaning business was a good fit for Joanna because it used all her strengths and fulfilled all her values. Like all my clients who succeed, Joanna enjoyed the journey, learned as she went, remained curious about the next step, understood the process, and was patient enough to let time be her ally.

HOW TO GET RICH: DO WHAT YOU LOVE

Joanna exemplifies the secret of becoming rich: do what you love. She followed the proven two-stage process for attaining wealth. Stage one is investing in yourself: do what you love, no matter what it takes. Joanna was willing to cut back to a part-time job so that she could learn a new business. Stage two: she did what she loved until she was competent. Then she invested her extra money.

This two-stage formula for making money will not work unless you have the passion and the talent that success in any field takes. For example, you may have a passion for music, but unless you are talented you can't expect people to pay you. Music will be your hobby. When my clients express interest in an artistic career I advise them to ask professional artists to critique their work. These professionals can tell right away if my clients have the talent. They can also tell where they are in their development and what they need to do to be a professional.

The arts are highly subjective and competitive fields that require a unique combination of fortitude and natural gifts, which usually show up early in life. This is not to say that the two-stage formula does not apply to creative careers; in fact, it is even more applicable to creative people, since they will sacrifice everything for the freedom to create. When they reach a certain point in their careers, usually after ten years of training, experience, and effort, the money comes.

Gaylon Greer, in his column on personal financial planning, "How Did the Rich Get That Way?" discusses the formula that leads to wealth. Greer paraphrases the conclusions from Srully Blotnick's book *Getting Rich Your Own Way*,[1] which chronicles a twenty-year research study of a large cross-section of middle-class workers:

In the first stage, those who eventually became millionaires were not investors in the conventional sense of the term. During this stage their major investments were in themselves. Those who eventually became rich were so *profoundly absorbed* [my emphasis] in their work that they persisted and eventually excelled at it. They accumulated a vast reservoir of knowledge and experience that would eventually bear extravagant dividends....

A characteristic goal of those who failed in their quest for riches (ninety-two percent of the participants) was to someday make enough money so that they could quit their job and do "what I really want to do." Their attempts to accomplish this goal involved seeking "get rich quick" formulas that would rescue them from what they viewed as occupational drudgery. In effect, they tried to achieve the second stage success as investors first, in order to finance their quest for activities they would find deeply absorbing, which is Stage One.[2]

Greer and Blotnick agree about the first law of money: do what you love; the money will come if you follow your heart. I would add that you must do this work long enough to reap financial rewards, as Joanna did.

SETTING AND DEFINING YOUR GOALS

Now let us talk about the stages you need to go through to set goals you can reach — goals that use your top-five strengths and that match your top-five values. Before you do this exercise think of your life as if it were already completed. Write your epitaph. How do you want to be remembered? By whom do you want to be remembered? Some examples of epitaphs are: "Jack truly did live by his rule of life: 'Go as far as you can; get everything you want. Never step on anyone to get there.' With this as a guide, he lived a fulfilling, exciting, and rewarding life." "Mary was a loving wife, good parent, wise, successful, and kind." "Tom was the best kind of friend, one you could always count on." "Susan gave and received in equal measure."

Here's a particularly creative example of an epitaph: "Don't forget how I stumbled and danced; how I struggled and succeeded; how I loved and shared; how I ranted, raved, and sang. I leave you my smile, my energy, my photographs, and my caring." An epitaph written with a three-year time projection gives you the chance to imagine the legacy you want to leave behind. Write your epitaph as though you are to die three years from now.

Writing Your Epitaph

Take a few minutes right now. In your journal, quickly write four or five sentences that summarize your life.

Given what you wrote in your epitaph, what do you need to do today to make this description of your life a reality? Are you taking the risks you need to take? Are you asking for the help you need? Are you open to correction from those who have achieved your goal? If you are not (1) where you want to be in life, (2) doing what you want to do, and (3) realizing your true potential, you probably need to take a look at the way you have set your goals, both personally and professionally. You may be requesting what is not in your best interests. Shakespeare said it best:

> We, ignorant of ourselves,
> Beg often our own harms, which the wise powers
> Deny us for our own good; so find we profit
> By losing of our prayers.
>
> — *Antony and Cleopatra*, act 2, scene 1

Paul's Story

Defining your goals clearly is the first step to reaching them. A client of mine desperately wanted a new job but did not know how to describe or define what he wanted. Paul worked for a large computer company in the cash management division. As we began working together, all he could tell me was what he was dissatisfied with.

"I struggle to go to work every day. I don't like what I'm doing; it's so boring," Paul said.

After reading Paul's autobiography, I learned that he loved performing on stage. He felt right at home in front of a group of people. This natural poise in front of an audience was not being used in his current job. Most of the time he sat in front of a computer!

"Paul, no wonder you're so miserable; you're more of an extrovert than an introvert; you like to be around people, and yet your job has you isolated from people most of the time. If you do what you do naturally, that will bring you the greatest financial reward. Why not make working in front of an audience a basic feature of your new job? Can you imagine a job that uses your gift with people, and that pays you all the money you want?" I asked.

"I've always known I was a good communicator, Nancy, but my college degrees and work experience are financial. I'm not an actor; I could have done that, but I'm more practical, I know that about myself. I like numbers and business. I guess I discounted my stage presence because I couldn't imagine anyone paying me to use that skill in the business world," he said.

Like many of my clients, Paul did not connect creativity with the business world; he thought only artists were creative, until I suggested that he could combine finance and speaking as a career.

"For example, you could use that skill in presentation of financial packages, such as selling," I said.

"Sales, oh no, that's not for me," Paul said shaking his head. "I don't want to twist anyone's arm."

"What makes you think selling is twisting someone's arm?" I asked.

"Well, that's my opinion of salespeople."

"Some salespeople may be arm twisters, but not the professional ones. They are educators, which is why I think you could sell. Why don't I ask a couple of my clients who are in sales to meet with you? Then I'll ask them what they think about you, and you can tell me what you thought of them."

My clients were very excited when they called me after they met with Paul.

"He's so personable, Nancy," one client said. "What a great guy. We had a lot of fun talking about working with you and going through this process. Thanks for sending him to me. I told him to keep in touch. We're going to have lunch next week."

"He's a natural," said my other client. "Maybe it's because Paul deals with numbers, and since numbers don't lie he's honest and straight-forward. Any company would be glad to hire him. I recommended a few books on sales for him to read, and I asked him to check back with me. I also invited him to go with me to my sales professionals' organization to see how he feels about sales as a career."

My clients' reaction is a good example of how productive inter-views can be (a step I cover in chapter 9).

Paul said he was very impressed with my clients.

"You work with some nice people, Nancy," he said. "Meeting with them certainly changed the way I think about salespeople. They're both very down-to-earth and direct, and they echoed what you said about sales being educational. They also said you have to sell what you love; otherwise the job and the pressure to produce the numbers will cor-rupt you. Maybe that's what's wrong with most salespeople; they're not selling what they love."

Meeting with people who shared his values (passion clue!) gave Paul a new way to look at his career and himself. When he did his research he looked for companies whose service he could sell rather than companies that matched his experience. When he wrote his six months' want list, he followed the three necessary criteria for success: the goal must be measurable, it must be internally motivated, and he alone must be responsible for its achievement.

Paul's discussion of his career goal read as follows: "I, Paul, deserve to be independently wealthy. I have a new and exciting sales job in which I use my written, verbal, and financial skills. I work in the city of my choice [Paul wanted to move to the South], and I make over $100,000 a year. In return, I provide a service that improves my clients' financial position. I organize and conduct financial planning seminars once a month. These seminars provide useful information and also act as advertising for my company's services. I have able partners who work well with me. My business is a success because it provides a genuine service, and it is in harmony with my needs and values. Selling what I value is my passion!"

A statement such as Paul's is called an affirmation because it is written in the present tense. A good resource on how to use the affirmation technique is Shakti Gawain's best-selling book *Creative Visualization*.3 Gawain says that writing your goals in affirmation form is a powerful technique that works when your goals are authentic, meaning when they are based on what you value. Remember to select goals that you know you can achieve within six to eight months. This keeps your mind focused and your spirits high. Goals set too far in the future may not be what you really want, anyway.

Six months later, after many meetings with men and women in the financial planning field, Paul had accepted a position. His new sales job provides a training base for his ultimate venture, having his own financial planning business. Meanwhile, he is learning the business and, in return, his communication skills meet the needs of his new company.

"They told me it was my ability to make presentations that convinced them to hire me. Of course, my financial skills were important to them, but they wanted someone who could organize and set up seminars. That's a cinch for me!" Paul laughed.

Here you have the happy ending that comes when your job uses your strengths and matches your values. Goals are easy to reach because they are authentic, rather than simply a reflection of what you think you want. If you can't reach your goals you probably do not know what you really want. Self-knowledge is a process, so don't get discouraged when you fail. Instead, rewrite your goals following the three criteria for success: measurement, motivation, and responsibility.

MEASURING YOUR GOALS

The most successful companies know how to set realistic and measurable goals. They know where they want to go and why. At the same time they are flexible and responsive to changing conditions. Their products are known, their markets are defined, and a staff is selected to carry out marketing strategy and follow-up. Few businesspeople would try to sell a product without first measuring the market, the competition, and the sales team. Personal success can be the result of similar accurate measurement. You need to set goals that are measurable.

Let us say that one of your goals is to earn more money. How do you measure "more money"? How much is it, exactly? When do you want it? Are you in a position to accomplish your goal? What service are you prepared to provide in return? You are going to have to increase your productivity. How do you plan to do that? For whom do you want to work, and under what circumstances? Will your money goal allow you to "do what you really want to do"? If so, remember the formula for making money: do what you love. As with Paul, this job may be a step toward the passion, an interim opportunity that allows you to improve certain skills and gain experience. Passion is a process; each step you take prepares you to become the master at what you do for a living.

With realistic expectations, you can project likely outcomes. Write a realistic goal using the affirmation technique. For example: "I make $_____ as my total annual compensation, which includes salary, bonuses, and perks. In exchange, I perform the following services." Then write about the time, effort, and service you will exchange for the money you seek. Measure your goal; define it. Describe it in the greatest possible detail so that you can smell it, see it, and taste it. Your imagination is a wonderful mental gift given freely to you. If you use it to improve your value, the money or reward you seek will follow.

STAYING MOTIVATED

Managing yourself is very much like managing a business. There are fundamentals to observe. Once you've defined and measured your objectives or goals, you must decide if your goals are internally motivated. Just as Joanna was unable to find satisfaction at her old job, you cannot persuade yourself to work for rewards that are not genuine.

Enough has been discovered about human motivation to show that attainment of inner satisfaction depends on authenticity. The coach of a top-functioning basketball team assumes that each player is on the court because he or she wants to be there. Good competitors and coaches understand internal motivations and, as a result, they correct players' mistakes and encourage them to practice self-correction.

Internal motivation is based on how strongly you want to achieve an objective. Make your objective realistic. Practice achieving small goals; this prepares you for the consequences of achieving your ultimate goal. For example, if taking a trip to Greece is a long-term goal, go to Greek restaurants, learn the language, locate some Greek immigrants; take a course in mythology or Greek architecture. You may "accidentally" find your passion!

Finding out what motivates you is related to discovering your natural interests — your passions. Left alone, you gravitate toward what interests you because it is connected with your desires. What do you desire more than anything else? Do you desire contentment, position, prestige, achievement, wealth, power, or recognition? Do you want to make the world a better place? Needs and values are the motivators you can capitalize on to achieve your objectives. Referring back to the values exercise you completed in chapter 3, take a look at your top-five values. These values show you what you care about. When your desires match these values your work will be as natural as your play.

If you find that you are trying to suit an external source — family, friends, or other authority figures — you very likely will not be satisfied even when you accomplish goals because they are not *your* goals. Only you know what you need. Identify your needs, not with what you think you need to be happy. Then you will set goals you can reach.

TAKING RESPONSIBILITY

Once you've set specific goals that are measurable and authentically motivated, you are ready to check off the final criterion, responsibility. Only you are responsible for completing your goal. If reaching your goal depends on the actions of others, then your chances of success are minimized. Since you cannot control the behavior of others you need to write your goals so that it is your efforts that bring about the desired end.

"I want a promotion in six months" is too vague. You are relying on the behavior of a whole chain of individuals whose approval you must gain. If six months go by and you do not get the promotion, you become reluctant to set any further goals. You feel discouraged. The same goal (expressed in the present tense) might read, "I am making the necessary improvements in my performance that could lead to promotion. At the same time, I am examining alternatives in the job market and investigating other firms that will reward the increased value of my performance." In this way you achieve your goal whether or not you receive the promotion, and you do not miss out on the satisfaction and encouragement gained by reaching it. Achieving our goals initially gives us the encouragement to set even greater ones.

Your goals, and your definitions of them, must be clear, or else your mind will not know how to focus, how to eliminate the unnecessary information that can prevent you from hitting your target. The mind reproduces what you plant in it. Given good growing weather, a farmer knows to expect corn if that is what he plants. Your mind will reproduce whatever you think about in great detail. What a valuable resource!

Think for a moment. You are unique. Unlike a business that must specialize, you have a wealth and diversity of products in your skills and abilities — all of which are highly marketable. Your strengths do not depend on supply shortages, inflation, or markets drying up — you are the dream of every enterprise! The strengths you possess will allow you to achieve your goals if you know how to market them effectively. I will show you how to do this in the succeeding chapters.

The next step for setting goals is to write them out as if you were writing a business plan. The following exercise will help you to do this.

MAKING A BUSINESS PLAN

You must have a business plan before you begin any enterprise, including setting goals. Otherwise, your business — you — will have a haphazard marketing strategy. Allow your interests totally free play. If you had all the money you needed, what would you do? With whom would you spend your time? Where would you live?

Separate all your wants into categories — financial, personal, professional, and family. Focus on the next six to eight months. Analyze carefully how you word your goals. Many of my clients start out by misstating most of their wants. For example, a goal stating a request for a new job might read: "I want to make more money, have a new job, and achieve greater recognition in my field." However, a more accurately stated goal would read: "I deserve to be as successful as I desire. I make $_____ a year with $_____ medical coverage, $_____ insurance, $_____ bonus, and vacation time of _____. In return, I provide my services of _____, _____, and _____, for which I am paid. I solve problems for people. First, I increase my sense of self-worth with an accurate analysis of what I do best, easily, and naturally. I read, go to seminars, and increase my circle of contacts. I look within my company to see if internal problems interest me. I also talk to other companies whose products or service interests me. I achieve recognition because I first recognize myself as worthwhile and capable. I assume all the responsibility for marketing my special talents."

Note: All is written in the present tense; this is the affirmation technique illustrated earlier. If you want to start your own home-based business, or you are an artist or you want to work part-time, the technique is the same; begin with your values and strengths. Then, write a six-month "want" list. Imagine all the things you would like to have by the end of the next six months.

Writing a Six-Month Want List

Sit down at your computer, open your laptop, or pick up your journal or a writing pad. Write down everything you want, from a new toothbrush to a new job to peace of mind. Write quickly and freely. Step away from the computer or put your tablet down and walk around. Have lunch, let your mind wander, let go of your limitations. Think about the six months ahead of you.

Now come back to your master list and add all the other things you want. Most people have about ten to fifteen wants. There is no limit, however!

Making Your "Ten Most Wanted" List

Next break down your master list to your top-ten wants. Try not to lump them together. If a new car is one of your wants and a trip across the United States is another, do not combine them. A car and a trip are two different things. Put your number-one want at the top of the list, then the second, and so on. Note that I use the word *wants* in this section deliberately, because your imagination feels free when you say *want* rather than *goal*. However, your top-ten wants are really your goals.

Read over your top-ten wants carefully and make any necessary adjustments. Now write a paragraph describing each desire as if it has already been met. For example, a desire that specifies a new wardrobe will reflect your lifestyle. If you work in a downtown high-rise office building you will probably dress more formally than if you work in a small office in the suburbs. If you work out of your home, wardrobe is probably not your chief concern.

But let's assume that you want new clothes anyway. Here's how you would write that affirmation: "I [your name] have a new wardrobe that matches my lifestyle. I appreciate my appearance, I like my body, and I always look exactly the way I want to look. I have suits — gray, blue, and casual — and matching shirts and ties [for men] blouses and tops [for women], and three pairs of dress shoes. For casual wear, I have two pairs of jeans, three shirts, two sweaters, and three pairs of shoes. I have a beige raincoat and a down parka for hikes and skiing. I look well groomed always."

If a relationship is one of your top wants say, "I am ready for a committed relationship." Using the word "ready" addresses emotional inadequacies and fears that may be blocking you from having a relationship. The technique of writing as if you already have what you want works because writing in the present tense activates the "law of interest." Once you begin formulating goals you set this law in motion. This law draws information to you seemingly from nowhere. Why is this so? When your mind is focused it is like a search engine; it looks for what you want, information that you would have formerly rejected or not noticed. You pick up clues in the environment that were always there; you simply were not aware of them before. Suddenly, you see articles and books that relate to your goals, and you hear relevant conversations. For example, have you ever noticed that once you learn a new word it seems to pop up everywhere? Once you focus on any area, you are more receptive.

Do not use *should, ought, will,* or *perhaps* in your sentences. Using those words may signal that you are not sure you deserve to have what you want. And guess what? If that's how you feel, you will not get it! Remember, your mind is like the earth: it reproduces what you plant.

After you write a paragraph about each want, describing it in as much detail as possible, read each paragraph out loud to yourself. How does it sound? Is it authentic; do you really want what you hear? Your tone of voice as you read will give you the answer. If your voice is unsure or it wavers, think again about your want. You will have to suspend disbelief while you are doing the exercise. Do you feel excited while you're writing or reading? (Passion clue!) Next read your want list to a trusted, supportive friend. Although his or her reaction is important, it is not as important as your own reaction to what you are reading. Are you nervous, unsure, embarrassed? Or perhaps your excitement surprises you. Great! You are halfway there. Now, if you like, you can tape-record your list of wants. Or, if you are like some of my clients, you may want to create a document that you can read every time you start up your computer.

If you decide to tape-record your affirmations, play the tape every morning and night for twenty-one days, since it takes about three weeks for the subconscious mind to "lock in" new beliefs. Do not worry about how these things will come to you. Some will happen right away! Soon you will attract information, events, and people to help you bring all the things you desire into existence.

Do not be afraid to rewrite and reset your priorities. You can change your list until it is exact. You will notice yourself becoming more focused as you fine-tune your wants. Next tell your rewritten goals to someone you can trust. This person needs to be an impartial, objective listener.

Here is a list of a client's top-ten wants before she wrote the descriptive paragraphs.

1. To maintain and keep myself healthy. [Marilyn had just recovered from breast cancer.]

2. To continue to be happy in my relationship. [This goal depended on her ability to communicate, which Marilyn covers in another affirmation.]

3. To keep life interesting.

4. To not sweat the small stuff.

5. To enjoy my work.

6. To travel.

7. To continue to improve on communications.

8. To work on a relationship with my younger sister.

9. To buy the townhouse I'm living in.

10. To take classes I'm interested in, French and English.

As you can see, Marilyn knows what she wants. Now all she has to do is write the paragraphs in present tense, such as "I maintain my health" and "I communicate honestly with my partner." These sentences give her full responsibility for the achievement of her goals.

MAKING A COLLAGE

Now that you've consciously written your six months' want list, the next step is to go to an art supply store and buy a poster board in your favorite color and a glue stick. Then cut out pictures from magazines that you like. For example, you may like beautiful scenery, stylish clothing, children playing, food, travel scenes — whatever appeals to you. Arrange your final selection of pictures on the poster board. Leave it overnight. The next day, see if you still like the arrangement — if not, change it. Some pictures you will reject after further deliberation. Then, with the glue stick, coat the backs of the pictures that remain and press them into place.

All my clients look forward to this assignment. They call this chapter the "dessert chapter" because it is a pleasure after all the thinking work required in previous chapters. Making a collage is a fun, enlightening, and creative way to get to know yourself and your passion.

Your collage will reflect your passion, but it will be in symbolic form, since the collage is like a dream, a message from the unconscious mind. It may take time for you to understand the meaning of the images on the collage, since you did not pick them with your conscious mind. Your unconscious mind is more reliable since it knows what you want with all your heart and soul. If there is a conflict between the written want list and your collage, write a want list that matches your collage. After six months, look at your collage again. You will be amazed by how far ahead of you your unconscious mind was.

A Sample Collage

My client Michele was not sure she wanted to continue working in the ministry. Michele was an introvert in an extroverted job, feeling out of control because she spent most of her time with others. Like many introverts who live and work in an extroverted society, Michele was conditioned to believe she was antisocial if she wanted to be alone. Exhausted from being overstimulated, she longed for rest, beauty, solitude, and affection, as the images on her collage showed. Tears came to her eyes when I told her there was nothing wrong with her except for when she betrayed her need for solitude in order to please others.

Michele's father (see how frequently the father's attitudes affect my clients' careers?) had been a workaholic minister who used to say, "God never takes a vacation." Identifying with this rigid, perfectionist view of

life (and with that view of God!) drove Michele to take on more than she could handle. Like Joanna in chapter 3 and, indeed, like all my clients, before Michele could succeed she had to see her father as he was, not as she wanted him to be. As stated earlier in this book, career conflicts are rooted in the fear of authority, the belief (or hope!) that some human father figure knows more than we do about how to lead our lives.

Those who like to do their own thinking do not expect their fathers to be anything other than human. When Michele realized that her father overworked because he thought that's what his congregation expected of him, she learned to take care of her physical and emotional needs without feeling guilty. Michele did not need to leave her job; what she needed to leave behind was her belief in martyrdom. Her collage indicated that she was ready to take on that challenge, as many of the images suggest, particularly her image of the woman striding forward into her future with confidence.

Not surprisingly, Michele's top-five values were achievement, altruism, creativity, intellectual stimulation, and aesthetics. She had achieved everything she wanted in her church, which was why she felt bored and restless. Her top-five strengths were intuition, introversion (how wonderful that she can now list this as a strength!), teaching/ preaching, and communication/relationships. These were the strengths she would use to create a new life.

Today Michele is a much-beloved pastor in a church in a southwestern city (foreshadowed by the desert images on her collage). She does her best to be a model of the "power that doesn't corrupt" (the words on the upper right-hand side of her collage). The welcoming home in the middle of her collage reflects Michele's comfort with where she is in her life: she spends quality time with her family; she takes time to write and think (like the contemplative woman sitting next to her laptop in the upper left-hand corner); and she is compiling her favorite sermons into a book on how to stay grounded in an overly busy world — a concept shown by the picture of the man who sits contentedly beside a pile of balanced rocks and by the woman who relaxes in the modern chair.

The flowers and the stacked baskets on the lower right-hand side of Michele's collage — as well as the orderly placement of all of her pictures — indicate that she is hopeful about her future because she sets good boundaries. The image of the enchanting little girl at the top of the collage is Michele's ultimate accomplishment: she is free to be herself because she knows that's all that God wants her to be.

PERSEVERANCE: THE KEY TO SUCCESS

Now that you've set your goals and made your collage, it is not time to stash them in a drawer to look at "later." The iron is hot; it's time to strike! Your success depends on your willingness to persist in your efforts. Sadly enough, fear of the unknown (and inertia) keeps many people trapped right where they are. Most of us prefer what is familiar, even if a situation is extremely stressful — rather a known devil than an unknown one.

Change, even for the better, can be upsetting, but it can also be liberating. When we let go of obsolete ways of thinking we make room for new ways to solve our problems. In fact, the problem was the way we were thinking about the problem! In addition, changing your mind can be threatening to people who know you as you used to be. Yet the new you can also serve as an inspiration to them. Because change is stressful, as I've said before, I recommend that you exercise every day. Keeping fit will help you to persevere when discouragement threatens to thwart your efforts.

Getting your heart's desire begins with the willingness to do what it takes to accomplish your goal and to persevere through the middle and often not very exciting stage of change. During the middle stage of change it feels as if nothing is happening. You wonder about your decision to change; you worry about how long it's going to take to get where you want to go, or if you're going to get there at all. The tendency is to give up at this point and go back to what you know. Watch out! Old habits die hard.

When asked about the process of writing a book, Edith Wharton gave an accurate description of the three stages of change. She said the first stage of writing was like walking through the woods on a beautiful spring day. The middle stage was like crossing the Gobi Desert. The final stage of writing was like driving a convertible down a boulevard in Paris.

Change that lasts is of necessity a slow and gradual process, since the mind can only incorporate so much change without losing its balance. Focus your thoughts on what you can do today, and don't get distracted by what is going on in the outside world. Measure your goals; make them your goals and no one else's; and consider it your responsibility to attain your objectives. Then you will achieve the most tangible reward of all: inner satisfaction — a reward measured not only in terms of dollars but also in creativity, productivity, and healthy relationships.

SUMMARY

Passion Secret *4* *Remember that getting there is all the fun.*

1. Learn as you go.

2. Be curious about the next step.

3. Be understanding of the process.

4. Be patient enough to let time be your ally, not your enemy.

5. Write your epitaph in an affectionate manner. What did you do while you were here on earth?

6. Write a six-month want list.

7. Write your "ten most wanted" list. Write a paragraph (using the affirmation technique) about each want. Tape up this list somewhere.

8. Check your want list against the three goal-setting criteria: measurement, motivation, and responsibility.

9. Rewrite and re-record your list if necessary.

10. Spend five to ten minutes a day (for twenty-one days) listening to, reading, and thinking about your wants. Allow no distractions during this time. If you have taped your want list, make sure your voice on the tape is full of emotion, excitement, and enthusiasm. Let your mind envision the want as you listen to the tape. You will love the sound of your own voice!

11. Be sure you stay in shape physically. Vigorous exercise helps you develop the perseverance necessary for your inevitable success.

12. Make a collage. See what part of your life — your mind, body, heart, or intuition — is emphasized by the images you choose. Sometimes we are starved for one or more of the above; for example, if you need rest, as Michele did, then the collage reflects quiet images, sometimes with lots of space between the pictures. If stimulation is your need, then hot colors and motion might attract you. If affection is the theme, you might choose pictures of puppy dogs and babies — soft, cuddly images to express your need for giving and receiving love. If you long for a spiritual connection, you may be drawn to images of beauty, the sky, angels, or great religious art, all of which point to a desire for peace of mind.

13. Don't give up during the middle stage of change, when it seems as if you'll never reach your goal. Take a break if need be; ask for help; remind yourself why you set the goal in the first place. When you reach the final stage of change, enjoy the ride across the finish line!

5 MEETING PEOPLE WHO SHARE YOUR PASSION

Take a deep breath. Think about all the hard work you have done. By now you are bound to feel like talking to people who share your passion. It is time to take step five: meet with people who can help you to achieve your goals, people who are excited about your passion.

Achieving your goals takes the willing cooperation of others. They share your passion because they agree with what you think is good, true, and worthwhile.

Passion Secret 5 *Network with people whose values match yours.*

Why do people help each other to achieve objectives? To answer this question, look at your top-ten want list. How will accomplishing these goals help others? Who will benefit other than yourself? Let's assume that one of your goals is to make more money, say, $10,000 more a year.

What will your increased productivity and income do to increase others' productivity and income (not to mention their sense of worth)?

Are you getting the idea that your gain will be someone else's gain, too? Can you see a connection between what you want and what others want? People cooperate with people for mutual gain. In business terms, this is called a cost-benefit transaction. What it costs me to help you must be worth the price, whether it is my time, money, or effort.

When you meet with people to achieve something you want, you will feel more confident if you remember that you have four specific assets to offer:

1. *Your family history.* Your grandparents, parents, and other relatives left you a powerful genetic and emotional legacy that you can use creatively. How you responded to your upbringing and what you got out of your particular family experience are priceless possessions that will last the rest of your life. If you see the good that came out of whatever adversity you experienced, for example, this will have a positive impact on your work, on the people who know you, and on the world you live in.

2. *Your skills and abilities.* From the work you did in chapter 3, you know your top-five strengths, such as humor, common sense, perception, imagination, and intelligence. Think how many people would benefit from these strengths.

3. *Your values.* Knowing what you value — what you think is good, true, and worthwhile — gives you the ability to assess all your choices. (You listed your values in chapter 3.) Do your values match your choices, and vice versa? Do your choices match the values of the people with whom you work and play?

4. *Your personality.* You have special qualities, mannerisms, and personal attributes that are marketable because of your unique combination of those characteristics. Movie stars and entertainers are highly paid because of their almost

magical ability to project their personalities. Perhaps you have heard of "million-dollar" personalities. Singers, dancers, actors, comedians, and leaders in every field all use a pleasing personality to inspire and entertain others. The more harmonious (that is to say, kind and thoughtful) your personality, the more you can accomplish — and better yet, the more you can motivate others to join forces with you. Remember that a self-centered, negative attitude toward others can never bring success.

RECOGNIZING LEADERS

Leaders are wonderful people to learn from. A leader is not necessarily a person who gets up in front and "leads" people. In fact, innovative people rarely want to lead; they just do what they do, and others copy them. Independent thinkers do not look to others to lead them. Instead, they follow their instincts (passion clue!).

As a head coach in the National Football League, Bill Parcells turned around three terrible teams in his career in surprisingly short order, winning two Super Bowls in the process. Parcells says that his experience taught him three basic rules of leadership. First, be brutally honest with people. The only way to change people, he says, is to tell them what they are doing wrong. If they don't want to listen, they don't belong on the team.

Parcells's second rule of leadership is to confront others with their mistakes. Confrontation is necessary and healthy, he says, a critical function of turning any organization around. If you want to get the most out of people you have to apply pressure, since most people like the direct approach. Parcells's players say what they remember most about him is one line: "I think you're better than you think you are."

His third rule of leadership is to set small goals and to reach them. As I discussed in the last chapter, realistic people set goals they can reach; they focus on immediate, not long-term, objectives. When people set small, visible goals, Parcells says, and they achieve them, they get it into their heads that they can succeed. They break the habit of losing and begin to get into the habit of winning.

To summarize Parcells's three rules of leadership:

- Be brutally honest.

- Don't be afraid of confrontation, which is necessary and healthy.

- Set and reach small goals.

In *Think and Grow Rich*, Napoleon Hill discusses eleven traits of leaders.[1] These traits are important for you to know not only for yourself but also for the purpose of assessing people you want to work for or with. Individuals who display these eleven traits are excellent models for you to learn from. By keeping Parcells's and Hill's lists in mind as you meet someone, you will know very quickly if the person you are talking to meets their criteria of leadership:

1. *Unwavering courage* based on knowledge of self and of one's occupation. No follower wishes to be dominated by a leader who lacks self-confidence and courage.

2. *Self-control.* The man or woman who lacks self-control can never control others. Self-control sets a strong example for one's followers.

3. *A keen sense of justice.* Without a sense of fairness and justice, no leader can command and retain the respect of his or her followers.

4. *Definiteness of decision.* The person who wavers in his or her decisions shows that he or she is not confident and cannot lead others successfully.

5. *Definiteness of plans.* The successful leader must plan work, and work the plan. A leader who moves by guesswork without practical, definite plans is like a ship without a rudder: sooner or later he or she will land on the rocks.

6. *Doing more than one is paid for.* One of the requirements of leadership is the willingness, on the part of the leader, to do more than he or she requires of followers.

7. A *pleasing personality.* No antagonistic, slovenly, careless person can become a successful leader. True leaders earn respect. Followers will not respect a leader who does not possess a pleasing personality.

8. *Sympathy and understanding.* The successful leader must sympathize — and empathize — with his or her followers.

9. *Mastery of detail.* Successful leadership calls for mastery of the details of the leader's position.

10. *Willingness to assume full responsibility.* The successful leader must be willing to assume responsibility for the mistakes and shortcomings of his or her followers. If the leader tries to shift this responsibility, he or she will not remain the leader. If a follower makes a mistake that shows him or her to be incompetent, the leader must take responsibility for the failure.

11. *Cooperation.* The successful leader must understand and apply the principle of cooperative effort and be able to induce his or her followers to do the same. Leadership calls for power, and power calls for cooperation.

Copy both Parcells's and Hill's lists and carry them with you when you talk with people about your interests, and when you go on interviews. Not many men and women have mastered all eleven leadership characteristics. Do not waste your time with people who do not display at least a majority of these characteristics. You will find the passionate, powerful men and women of the world in every field imaginable; the steps you are taking will lead you to these people. Better yet, measure your behavior by these standards, and you will become a leader whom others respect and admire.

On your journey you will meet people who do not measure up to your expectations; but do not let them discourage you. Do your best wherever you are; then you cannot help but succeed.

PREPARING FOR THE ADVENTURE AHEAD

As you prepare to take this step, consider how you would answer the following questions:

1. How do you want to spend your time?
2. What specific goals do you wish to achieve?
3. What type of company and people do you wish to work with?
4. Do you want to work for yourself?

So far, the work you have done has been internal, requiring you to focus on yourself. Since you are ready to venture out into the world, here is an advanced lesson on getting things done through other people: once you know the answers to the four questions above, help comes seemingly from nowhere. This happens because your mind is focused and clear. Clarity sets up a receptive field in your mind that attracts what you want and need. But clarity does not come without effort, as I'm sure you know by now. As I said in the last chapter, change is unsettling, including change for the better. We all tend to hold on to what we know, even when it doesn't work.

Think of change as though you were traveling in a foreign country. While you are in your hotel room, in territory that is familiar to you, you feel safe. As soon as you venture outside — a new place with a new language — you feel more on edge. That is because you do not know the protocol, the cultural cues, and the rules of the social road, so to speak. No wonder travel can be emotionally exhausting. But it can also be exhilarating, since everything is so *new*. Introduce newness into your life regularly. Go somewhere new for lunch; take a different route to work; try foods you've never tried before; speak up instead of keeping quiet; be bold — it will wake you up to aspects of yourself you didn't know existed.

Jane's Story

I will never forget one client who had completed her internal work. Jane knew her strengths and values, but she froze when it was time to go "out in the world." To postpone the inevitable meetings with others, she invented every excuse imaginable, from being ill to being too busy. She was so good at stalling that she derailed her personal power train for four months. Finally Jane ran out of excuses.

"I eventually told myself that if I keep on grumbling and complaining, I'm never going to get anywhere," she said. "If I don't go and talk to people, I'll do just what my father did — give up!" (She had discovered this pattern in her autobiography.)

Jane wanted to find a position in which she could use her negotiating skills. She also wanted more intellectual stimulation than she had in her present job. "I'm good at resolving conflicts. I'm always being asked to mediate between opposing factions in my company," she said in one of our sessions. Because of her natural interpersonal skills, Jane was able to resolve some problems between her manager, a fast-paced Easterner transplanted to California, and the representatives from the home office, which was in the Midwest. Jane, born and reared in the Midwest, understood the ways of business in both areas, as well as the pace of the relatively low-key Californians. She also helped to foster a more congenial atmosphere in her office.

"Our manager is never right in his approach to people," Jane told me. "He acts like he's still in New York — barking orders, wanting everyone to jump fast and work long, hard hours. And he thinks everyone in the Midwest office is a hick. Our office is not performing as it should, and he says it's because we don't know how to work. Actually, believe it or not, he's a good manager — but he hasn't changed his pace and his New York thinking.

"Fortunately, I resolved some conflicts when I was sent to the Midwest home office for leadership training. While I was there, I tactfully presented the whole scenario to the regional manager, who understood the personality problems. He flew out to California and became better acquainted with my manager. In their discussions they resolved the interoffice problems, and it was decided that in the near future my manager would fly to the Midwest office to meet the staff.

"While the regional manager was in California, I suggested that we all get together at my home to have a casual Sunday-afternoon barbecue," Jane said. "My manager relaxed and really got to know us as people. Many of the staff told him that day how much they liked the chance to get acquainted. Since then, the whole atmosphere in the office has changed. I'd like to use that negotiating ability of mine all the time. I like being a troubleshooter, particularly with people trouble."

Jane had found her passion.

She picked several industries that interested her and followed up by selecting some target companies — small, medium, and large. She studied the companies' websites, then downloaded statistics and articles about the officers and other information that she wanted to remember. Next she read trade magazines to become informed about industries and companies, products, and key people. She also made a list of people she already knew.

Most people think contacts are "what everyone has but me." When I work on this step with clients, I try to help them think of contacts as relationships. In that way, they think of them as individuals who are just like them, not as strangers. A contact is anyone who shares your interests. It takes time to build relationships, but you can easily activate new ones if you keep in mind the concept of mutuality, a similarity of interests, of passions. When you discover your pressing desire, you can be assured that others share it as well. Your gain will also be their gain.

You can build a network of contacts even if you are in a new city. It will take time, but the months and years are going to go by anyway. You might as well be making contacts! If you are receptive and alert, every person you meet can open new doors to you.

Jane made a list of her personal contacts, anyone with whom she shared an interest. She was amazed that she had listed more then forty people. "Even my therapist knows people in my areas of interest!" she remarked. Jane began with a contact list of twenty-six people, drawing from her personal list and the companies she had targeted. Her next step was to get the names of the individuals in the companies who supervised the areas of her interest — arbitration and personnel relations.

Since Jane did not know the email addresses or telephone numbers of the people with whom she wanted to meet, she looked up a list of professional organizations in her area, including negotiation and labor professionals' organizations. She called the numbers listed to find out the date of the next meetings. When Jane asked if it was all right for her to come to the meetings, the people with whom she spoke said of course, they'd be glad to introduce Jane to members of the group. Several people at the meeting were intrigued with Jane's approach; they said they wished they'd taken the time to explore career options. Many gave her their business cards.

Most professional meetings are open to guests, so if a particular area of work interests you, call the chairperson of this group and ask for the time and date of the next meeting. Once you're there, you'll have a roomful of contacts, all in your area of interest. Knowing that others share their passions helps my clients to get over their shyness.

"This process is just like sales," Jane said. "I'm rejected occasionally, but so far I'm batting .800! People are great if you're honest and open. I've had good calls with several of the people I met at the meeting. I can hardly wait to meet them again," she said.

Sometimes I suggest that my clients write an approach letter to arrange appointments. (I discuss this process in detail in chapter 8.) Written correctly, a personal letter or email to someone you'd like to meet opens the door to a productive meeting. Remember that you are in the exploration phase — you are checking the validity of your goals with people who share your values and interests. You are not yet looking for a job.

When you meet with others you have the chance to hear yourself talking and explaining what interests you. This lets you critique your approach without the stakes being so high, as they are in an interview. Any fears you have, such as the fear of failure or criticism, will come to the surface, so don't be surprised when your knees start to knock! Knocking knees is actually a good sign; it means you're taking the risks that scare you to death! And what scares you is usually your passion, since it means so much to you. It's like being in love — you are excited and scared at the same time because you love the other person so much.

Meeting people with similar interests, however, will dispel most of your fears. This is a good time to recall situations in your past about which you were apprehensive but then everything turned out well. (How about that party you went to where you did not know anyone — and wound up having a wonderful time!)

In any situation you can act from a position of confidence or of fear. We all face uncomfortable situations, times when we feel awkward and inept. Having the courage to take action in the face of our fear not only makes us grow, it also elevates our lives, making us heroic. We are all capable of reaching great heights. Sometimes it takes a crisis to bring forth our reserves. At this point, when your courage may falter, turn inward. Ask God for guidance. Prayer is a powerful tool, so use it!

Study the lives of successful men and women; read their biographies, especially those of creative people. I suggest that you read Konstantin Stanislavsky's *My Life in Art*.[2] This book is a delightful embrace of life, and Stanislavsky's perspective on life is a good alternative to the puritanical reserve most of us inherited. The Irish actor Kenneth Branagh makes it clear in his autobiography, *Beginning*,[3] that he could not last long in organizations. You will enjoy reading about the projects he initiated, the most daring being his acclaimed film *Henry V*, a study of the dilemma of leadership — and the affect of egocentric leaders on their countries. No book or person offers a perfect model — we are all human after all — but reading about another's refusal to settle for anything less than his or her heart's desire will certainly inspire you.

MEETING MORE CONTACTS

The next step in attaining your goal is setting up interviews. What to do and say is covered in detail in chapter 9. For now I would like to walk you through Jane's process so you see the result first — where you are headed with this approach. An interview is a low-keyed meeting you arrange with someone who is doing work you are interested in. Before making an appointment, you will have done the research in your field of interest. You will also have the names of several people to contact, as Jane did.

Jane wanted to use her relationship skills to help others solve problems. Every business has problems with objects, data, and people. Jobs are ways to solve these problems. Even jobs in creative fields, such as home decor, painting, acting, writing, and fine art, are solutions to problems. These fields give pleasure to buyers. Giving pleasure is definitely a solution to a problem, since we all love pleasure! Whether your marketing plan includes finding a new job, improving the job you have, starting a business, or getting involved in a creative project, the advice-call approach is the best first step. Talking to people about their work takes the mystery and glamour out of what the job requires. Then you can decide if that's what you want to do with your time every day. Many of my clients decide not to go into a field after talking with an expert in the line of work they were contemplating.

The interview makes it possible for you to get to the root of business problems, which you cannot do in a job interview. Since there is no need to impress or to hire you, the person you meet with tells you the truth about the job and the company or organization. These conversations often turn strangers into friends who are interested in your progress. As a result, they go out of their way to help you, offering you names of other people to talk to and letting you know about job openings if you want to consider the field as a career. (You hold these kinds of interviews all the time without realizing it. Whenever you question someone about what they do, you are holding an interview.)

Using the approach letter format, Jane wrote several letters to people she had been referred to, a process I discuss in chapter 8. Some of the letters she sent as emails; others she sent through the regular mail. She began each letter by saying who had referred her, then she talked briefly about her background and why she'd like to meet with the person. Four days after she mailed her letters, she followed up with phone calls. Sometimes she had to leave voice mails, since many people did not answer their phones. Some did not return her calls; but several did respond. Before she scheduled her appointments I advised Jane to avoid "stacking" the meetings.

"At first, one meeting a day, twice a week is enough," I said. "You need time in between the meetings to digest what you've learned. Be sure to call me after the meetings so that we can review them and go over your technique. With each meeting, your knowledge of the field increases. You carry that accumulated knowledge to your next meeting so that you're not always beginning again. For instance, after you meet with the first two labor specialists, the third person you meet with will see you as someone who is knowledgeable. As a result, your questions will be more focused and detailed. You'll sound more like an equal," I said.

Jane soon learned that mutuality of interest works, and her meetings went very well. She was especially excited about a company that wrote insurance policies for shipping firms — the supercarriers that keep international trade active. Jane, in her research, had chosen shipping as a category of interest.

"I've always been fascinated (passion clue!) by ocean traveling and trade. It's something about the water and boats. Even when I was very small, the fantasy books I liked best were always about big boats and long ocean journeys," she said.

Here is an example of an early natural interest, a yearning, if you will, to know more about a subject. We rarely see how these interests connect with our careers, and sometimes they don't. They are our hobbies, our spare-time fascinations. But Jane was able (by doing the same exercises you are doing) to connect an interest with her skills and experience. Although international trade is a typically male field, Jane is comfortable working with men, and they are comfortable working with her, both in a negotiating capacity and in the technical area of insurance.

Jane knew that she could succeed in shipping and insurance. She pictured herself in the job before she had it, using all the details and information she had gathered on her advice calls. The large insurance company that was Jane's target had an extensive training program. The vice president in charge of shipping underwriting met with her for over an hour, answering all her questions. He then told her about the company's training program and asked her if she would be interested in taking it.

"I think you'd have a clear idea of the career path you're on after six months of class and fieldwork. You'd be paid while you're in training, of course, but considering what you've told me, that would be just a start. We really need people with your background," he said. He understood her strengths and recognized her initiative by the thoroughness of her approach.

Before Jane made her decision, she met with two employees first — one in the training program and one who had gone on to work in the field. Well-managed companies take time to hire an employee, since hiring mistakes are costly. (If someone offers you a job at the end of one meeting, look for the nearest exit!) Similarly, you need to get to know people in a company before you accept an offer. After all, you're going to spend more time with these people than the person you marry or live with!

Every company has a culture, a way of interacting that is based on traditions and customs that emerged over time. Ask about the company's culture. What is the management style? What is expected of employees? Ask, If you were investing your money, would you put it in this company? Don't take a job until you are sure that you fit the company's culture; this is true of small companies, too, since any group develops a culture, much like a family. When someone leaves or someone new comes into the group, the group dynamic is altered. If you are comfortable with the existing culture the job will give you a good return on your investment of time and energy.

Jane kept the vice president posted on her meetings. She wrote each person a thank-you letter after meeting them, then followed up with a summary letter to the vice president, stating her impressions. In her final meeting with the vice president, she was hired, and then she began the training program, which she sees as a stepping-stone in her career.

"My goal is to be the most knowledgeable woman on the West Coast in the field of shipping insurance. I've enrolled in law school part-time for the fall program, and I plan to specialize in maritime law.

[Jane had met maritime lawyers at the meetings she attended. Hearing them talk about their work gave her a long-term goal.] I'm so excited; I can now see exactly where and how all my skills will be used," she said.

Jane is actively creating her future. She finally found her passion — her fascination with ships led her to a law career. As a lawyer Jane uses all her relationships skills. As her productivity and creativity increased, everyone benefited from her success, particularly the man who hired her. His boss told him that hiring Jane was the best decision he'd ever made.

Matt's Story

Sometimes my clients can capitalize on contacts within their own field. Matt was a successful salesman who worked hard for his company. After three and a half years he thought it was time to move on because his company did not adequately compensate the sales force, and because the president was out of touch with reality.

"We'll never meet the numbers he set this year; it's crazy," Matt said to me. "We won't make our bonuses, either."

Pressuring people to perform is not always a bad idea; remember Bill Parcells's statement earlier in the chapter? But the president of Matt's company violated Parcells's third rule of leadership: set small goals you can reach. The president had gone on an acquisition spree to impress his peers and board of directors, who should have warned him about overextending. But as we've learned in recent years, many board members are often overextended themselves, so it's a case of the blind leading the blind. To compensate for excessive expenditures, the president raised sales expectations, which cost him Matt's respect.

I suggested that Matt start talking to salespeople in his field about their companies.

"Look for a company that specializes in one of the products in your field. Remember that you're not looking for a job; you're just gathering information." I said.

While working on his autobiography, Matt noticed that he had a pattern of passivity, waiting instead of taking action. Because he was such a personable man most opportunities came to him without much effort. The idea of "bothering people" embarrassed him.

"You won't bother people when you ask questions," I said. "Most people like to talk about themselves and their work."

"I guess I think I'm supposed to do everything myself."

"Ah, I see. Where did that idea come from?"

"Well, you know, Nancy, it's a guy thing."

Many boys are brought up to believe that they are weak if they ask for help. They feel comfortable giving help but not receiving it, since they feel unmanly when they don't know all the answers. Matt's father had been the "strong silent type" who never seemed to have any problems, until Matt's mother left him because he was so uncommunicative. Then out came all of the feelings he had formerly suppressed. Matt had trouble acknowledging his feelings too, but fortunately he'd married a wonderful woman who was not afraid to confront him when he withdrew in silence. (She followed Parcells's first and second rules of leadership, be honest and confront people with their mistakes!)

Matt's story is a good example of why the personal and the public self need to be integrated before you can work with passion. To be truly successful he needed to be the same person everywhere he went. His hesitation about reaching out to others indicated that Matt had more internal work to do, primarily accepting that successful people do not have to have all the answers but that they do need to be focused if they are to connect with others. I knew that Matt had a habit of taking on more than he could handle as a way to avoid his feelings, which was why I'd asked him to slow down in his life.

"You're right, I do have too much on my plate," Matt said. "And I can see that I confuse talking to people with selling myself to an interviewer. I don't have to make that decision yet; I can just get to know them."

"Yes, many people get into a selling mode when they're looking for a job," I said. "They forget to focus on the other person. But when you're intent on making a good impression you can't get to the truth. Be assured, Matt, you make the best impression when you ask good questions."

A few weeks after our discussion, Matt was out making sales calls when he got a call on his cell phone from a sales colleague. When he asked how things were going, instead of saying everything's fine, as Matt usually did, he said he wasn't happy with his company's unrealistic goals.

His friend (a contact) then mentioned a recruiter who had called him about a job, but since he had already taken another job, he asked Matt if he'd be interested in talking with the recruiter. Sure, Matt said, give me his number.

Before Matt dialed the recruiter's number, he recalled our discussion about keeping everything low-key. So as he talked with the recruiter (a contact) Matt was relaxed and friendly, asking questions and listening carefully to the responses. The recruiter, in contrast, got very excited about Matt and his background. "I think you are just what they're looking for," he said. "Let me tell my client about you, and I'll arrange a meeting."

A few days later Matt had a long phone conversation with the regional sales manager of the company (a contact). Before that conversation took place, however, Matt called people who knew about the company in question (contacts), including the salesman (another contact) whose territory he would take, so that he would know all the inside information about the company as well as the right questions to ask. The sales manager was impressed with Matt's knowledge of the company, since nothing is more flattering than someone's thorough knowledge of your business. He said the next step would be for Matt to come to a meeting with him and three other officers in the company. Then if all went well and they all agreed that Matt was a fit, they'd extend an offer to him in a few days.

"Be sure you think about the offer overnight," I suggested. "Even if it's what you want."

The day after his three meetings John called to discuss his impressions.

"I did as you suggested, Nancy; I thought of it as a chance to get to know them," Matt said. "It's amazing how different I felt. I had a good time! They were all friendly, down-to-earth people. The human resources person was a surprise, since she was so off the wall; perhaps that was to test me, but I was myself, instead of trying to be politically correct. There were the usual situational questions from the man who'd be my sales manager and the other two officers from corporate headquarters, which were no problem. They've all carried the sales bag, so they know I know what I'm doing. My main concern is that the company might be sold. That bothers me, and I expressed that to them. Then what happens to my job? The one thing about my current company is that it is family owned, so there's no chance of it being sold."

"How did they respond to your concern?"

"They assured me that if the company were sold all the salespeople would keep their jobs."

"So were they saying it's likely they'll sell the subsidiary you'd work for?"

"That seemed to be the consensus."

"No company can guarantee permanence," I said. "After they extend the offer have them go back over that point with you. Meanwhile, do more research on the company. Check out top management — you can read their bios on their website. Ask your financial adviser what she thinks of the company."

Matt's research reassured him. When the offer was extended to him, after he thought about it and talked it over with his wife, he accepted it. "It was a really tough decision; I like my current sales manager, and I really admire the quality of my company's products, but the truth is, I've lost faith in the president," Matt said. "He's promised that things are going to get better, but promises are not the same as facts."

The next time we talked Matt told me how much he loved his new job. "It's concept selling, not just product selling," Matt answered when I asked what he liked about the job. "That's a new challenge for me. As you know, I make a great deal more money now, and my wife and I are both happy because I'm not traveling as much as I was. But what I like best about this company is that they don't try to do too much. They stick to what they know. But I would never have known that's what I needed until I stopped overextending. So in that sense, my former company and its president were a reflection of what I needed to change about myself."

Matt's astuteness is similar to the insight that many of my clients gain after they go through the introspective process in this book. When they know themselves they know all there is to know.

LOOKING BEYOND THE WANT ADS

When you are looking for a job, be aware that many opportunities are not advertised. So where are the jobs if they are not in the want ads? Jobs are attempts to solve problems, whether they are sales, marketing, warehousing, or administrative needs.

Employers often tell me that finding and keeping good employees is their most challenging task. This is why good preparation helps you to outshine competitors for any job. Employers who've met my clients say that few people present themselves as well as my clients do; nor do they ask such probing questions.

As you explore your options keep in mind that many jobs are filled through word of mouth, as was the case with Matt. His business friend knew a recruiter whose client had a sales position they did not want to advertise. Other positions are filled from within a company or organization or by asking employees for recommendations.

As stated above, hiring decisions are costly, especially in these litigious times. Most people prefer to hire someone they know or someone their friends and co-workers know. The interview process puts you in touch with many people who in turn know many other people in different lines of work. Once they get to know you, they're happy to recommend you to others. Remember that like you, most people are happy to help; helping others makes them feel good about themselves.

Decision makers have no idea that you exist until you put your body in front of them. Most people try to find jobs by referral, since there is nothing like a personal recommendation. Others read want ads in the newspaper, on websites, in trade magazines, and other media. Although these methods bring success, if you do not have the experience they're looking for, you won't get an interview.

In a low-key meeting like I describe the other person has the opportunity to assess you without having to hire you. For example, before I wrote this book I got clients by appearing on radio and television talk shows and before groups. People in the audience had a chance to assess me as I worked on air with callers or before the audience. They had a sample of me, so to speak, of what I do and how I work before they made a buying decision. Later people called to set up an appointment, saying, "I really liked the intuitive way you worked with people, Nancy. I'd like to work with you." After this book first came out I didn't need those methods to market myself. *Work with Passion* did all the work for me, since it explained what I did and how I did it.

When you use the interview approach you give people a chance to sample you by listening to how well you identify their problems. How you speak, how you think, how you handle yourself and respond to others: all speak volumes about your ability to solve their problems.

Staying alert during casual conversations is another way to make good contacts. That is how I found the producer who asked me to be a regular guest on her morning television show. While speaking about the local television scene, one of my clients said that the producer was looking for someone to discuss job possibilities for recent college graduates. I watched the show to see if the producer and I shared the same values. Then I wrote a letter to her (I include that letter in chapter 8), saying that I would enjoy talking to her audience about careers and the job search. She called to arrange a time to tape an interview. When the show aired it was so well received the producer asked me to come back several times.

Later, when the producer heard that I was writing a book, she suggested that I contact the publisher who wound up publishing *Work with Passion* (that letter is also included in chapter 8). This is the concept of mutuality at work: I helped the producer solve her problem, and she helped me solve my problem. The relationship worked because we shared the same values, using what we know to help others lead better lives.

An employer or client's problem may be (1) a position that needs to be filled or a decision that needs to be made or (2) a vague feeling that "things" are not going well. As this person talks with you he or she may realize that you are the solution to his or her problems!

Below I will offer some exercises on how to research the best companies and people to contact. But first I will offer some simple time-management exercises to help you see how to use this process most efficiently.

TIME MANAGEMENT EXERCISES

Let's look at how you are spending your time now. The "time pie" exercises that follow help you to get organized, to use your time more efficiently. If after completing these assignments you find that you are still having difficulty managing your time, consult your local bookstore, library, or book website for books on time management.

Draw two time pies. In the first pie, show how you spend your time now. How many hours cannot be accounted for? Where and how are you spending the majority of your time? Here is a sample of how one of my clients spent her time:

Sample: Twenty-Four-Hour Time Pie

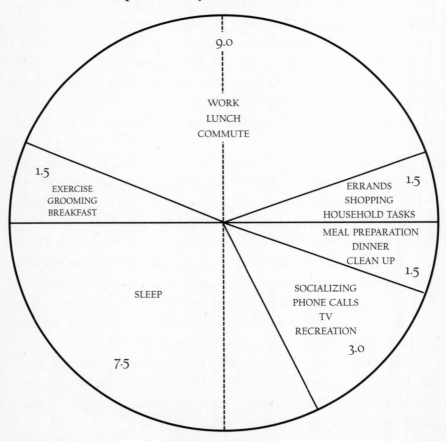

9.0

WORK
LUNCH
COMMUTE

1.5

EXERCISE
GROOMING
BREAKFAST

ERRANDS 1.5
SHOPPING
HOUSEHOLD TASKS

MEAL PREPARATION
DINNER
CLEAN UP

1.5

SLEEP

SOCIALIZING
PHONE CALLS
TV
RECREATION

3.0

7.5

Now fill in the pie yourself, charting approximately how you spend your average day.

Twenty-Four Hours as I'm Using Them Now

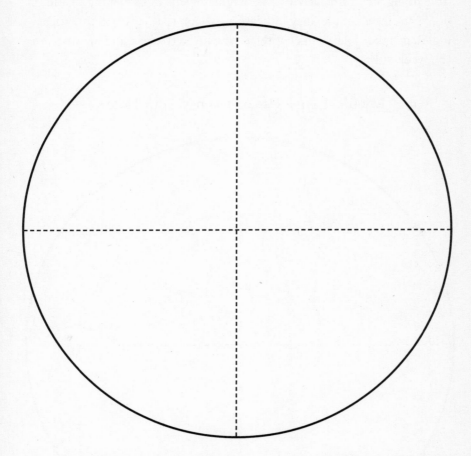

Next, draw a time pie reflecting how you would like to spend your time.

What hours would you change? Why? What would you eliminate? How many hours do you spend on self-improvement? You may find that much of your wasted time is spent socializing with people. If so, then try spending more time alone. Reflection is essential to integrating your daily experiences and to making thoughtful choices.

In addition to creating two time pies (one of your present workday and one of a balanced workday), you need to make two separate time pies for weekends. How do you spend your weekends now? Can you plan more time alone? You may discover that you spend a great deal of time doing a certain activity. Many hours spent in gardening, reading, or sports, for example, may indicate a passion that is worth investigating. Remember Joanna in chapter 3, who loved to clean and organize on the weekend?

My Ideal Time Use of Twenty-Four Hours

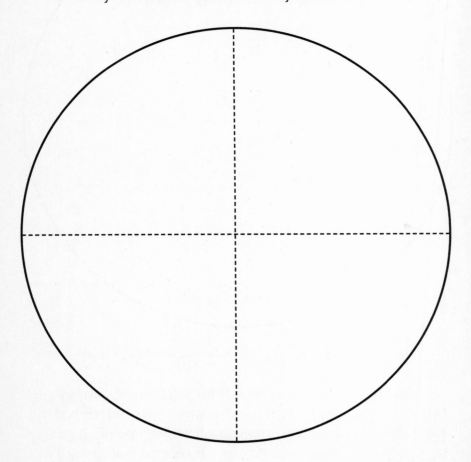

RESEARCH EXERCISES

Now that you see how you use your time, let's move on to how to conduct good research, which will lead you to the work you are interested in. After you have determined your interests, you will be ready to contact individuals whose work interests you. Let us begin like Jane did. Let your curiosity guide you as you look at broad categories of work, such as art, finance, music, real estate, and publishing.

One of the easiest and most up-to-date resources for researching categories of work is the index of your local Yellow Pages. You can also use the Internet, but *keep it local*, since you'll get distracted if you search outside your geographical area. Later, you can expand your search, if that's what you want to do. In the meantime, you can "Google" your way through the world of jobs and careers by typing in the category keyword; if you want to see what kind of jobs are in that area, then look on monster.com and other career sites. But since your phone book is updated every six months, and all the information in the book is *local*, it's best to start your search while sitting on your couch.

As you look through the index of the phone book you will be astounded by the tremendous variety of work that goes on right in your hometown. And since most job openings are in companies with fewer than twenty employees, don't overlook small enterprises; many of them have websites that are full of information. The corporate world may look attractive because it is so visible, but small businesses keep the economy going, especially during recessions. This is because they adjust quickly to changes in the marketplace; in fact, many are way ahead of the economic curve, while large companies stumble because of their size. Most of my clients prefer to work in entrepreneurial environments, anyway; many wind up as sole proprietors or in their own businesses since they value creativity and independence.

If your top-five values include independence and creativity, perhaps it's time to think about working for yourself, as a salesperson, a freelance writer, a skin care or massage specialist, or as a contractor. If you have acquired a body of knowledge and technical know-how, capitalize on it! Have a business card made and go get your first customer or client. (I'll talk more about how to do this in chapter 10.)

As you do the category of work exercise try not to think about what you could do in the fields that interest you. This is not an analytical assignment; rather, it is designed to open up your mind to alternatives. As you run your fingers down the list of categories of work, make a list in your journal of every category that holds any interest for you, including the page number. Do this exercise in two or three days. List as many categories as you desire. Eventually you will reduce your initial list to fourteen categories, and then finally to six major areas of interest.

I have included samples of finished assignments to guide you in completing your own. After you have finished the survey, go over it in your mind. Think of it: you have looked at the entire world of work! In the process, you have eliminated all the work you do not want to do. That is a major accomplishment, so congratulate yourself; you've done a good day's work.

Yellow Pages Exercise Worksheet

PRODUCT OR SERVICE	PAGE #	PRODUCT OR SERVICE	PAGE #

Break down your master list to a top fourteen categories of interest.

First Cut: Top Fourteen Categories

PRODUCT OR SERVICE	PAGE #	PRODUCT OR SERVICE	PAGE #
1.		8.	
2.		9.	
3.		10.	
4.		11.	
5.		12.	
6.		13.	
7.		14.	

Break down your top fourteen categories of interest to a top six.

Final Cut: Top Six Categories

PRODUCT OR SERVICE	PAGE #	PRODUCT OR SERVICE	PAGE #
1.		4.	
2.		5.	
3.		6.	

Note: Be sure to fill in all the blanks on all pages.

Yellow Pages Exercise Sample

Product or Service	Page #	Product or Service	Page #
airport service	41	displays, convention	480
air taxi charter service	35	entertainment	657
air tours, etc.	28	fashion show producing	679
appraisers	63	foreign trade consulting	720
beach wear	1563	fur designers	734
beauty culture school	276	fur rental	735
bed & breakfast	291	gowns, bridal	332
boat charter	306	home decorators	882
builders	824	hostess and host	480
clothing, women's	1822	introduction services	432
construction consulting	334	jewelry buyers	915
convention/escort service	659	makeup studios	996
cruises	504	party planning	1177
customs consulting	508	personal shopping service	1549
dating service	1183		
decorations, party	529	tour and travel	1703
diamond appraiser	63	trade shows	567
diamond buyer	558	wedding consulting	1798
diamond investment	560	weight reduction	1372

Yellow Pages Exercise Sample

First Cut: Top Fourteen Categories

PRODUCT OR SERVICE	PAGE #	PRODUCT OR SERVICE	PAGE #
1. tour and travel	1703	8. decorations, party	529
2. air tours, etc.	28	9. diamond buyer	558
3. appraisers	63	10. displays, convention	480
4. beauty culture school	276	11. fashion show producing	679
5. clothing, women's	1822	12. hostess and host	480
6. cruises	504	13. party planning	1177
7. dating service	1183	14. weight reduction	1372

Final Cut: Top-Six Categories

PRODUCT OR SERVICE	PAGE #	PRODUCT OR SERVICE	PAGE #
1. decorations, party	882	4. hostess and host	480
2. fashion show producing	679	5. diamond buyer	558
3. tour and travel	1703	6. weight reduction	1372

The above samples are the work of one of my clients. Do you see the passion that emerged in Gina's work? She narrowed her interests to several areas. Then she was ready for the next step — talking to people in these areas of interest.

After a round of interviews, Gina got a job as a tour guide for tourists and convention attendees. She loves her city and she loves sharing it with others. As you can see from her final six choices of interest, she is an extrovert who enjoys the "show biz" aspect of working in front of the microphone on the tour buses. In addition, she is doing research on starting her own singles' introduction business. Not surprisingly, affiliation was one of Gina's top-five values!

The other categories on Gina's list turned out to be personal interests: fashion, diamonds, weight reduction, and decorating — all were what she wanted for herself, but not as a full-time activity. Another of Gina's top-five values was recognition, and Gina's customers give her plenty of that! She, in turn, gives them an entertaining tour of the city she loves. Here you have the concept of mutual passion that brings people together.

FINDING A SUPPORT GROUP

You may want to spend time with other people who are also finding their passion. Joining "job clubs" — groups of people who are looking for the right work — can be helpful. You can form your own group with several friends, or you can find friends on the Internet to talk with about the job search process. Look on job websites for chat lists.

It is best to focus on local people for support, for all the reasons I've mentioned, so check community announcements in your local paper for groups that you can join. State employment development departments have programs that are free to the public; they offer interviewing workshops, lead generation, résumé-writing services, and other feedback resources you can use. Joining a group will keep your spirits up when you get discouraged; however, bear in mind that any group has its share of negative people. So be selective in your choice of companions — not everyone is a "foxhole buddy."

SUMMARY

Passion Secret 5 *Network with people whose values match yours.*

1. How do you really want to spend your time?

2. What specific goals do you wish to achieve?

3. What types of companies and what kinds of people do you wish to work with?

4. Be patient with yourself as you begin to change. Exercise, get plenty of rest, and eat a balanced diet. Avoid watching the nightly news. Don't worry; someone will tell you if there is a crisis that needs your attention.

5. Change is scary at first, but it is also enlivening!

6. Implement your plan in the proper order; don't interview for or take a job before you get accurate information. Remember the old saying: "marry in haste, repent in leisure."

7. Explore your categories of interest; allow your "free spirit" to direct you.

8. Treat everyone you meet with respect, friendliness, and courtesy.

9. Mutuality of interest runs the world.

10. Keep tabs on your fears; be aware of the ones that interfere with your enjoyment of the process.

11. Affirm your worth to yourself.

12. Marketing yourself is based on solving problems. What problems do you want to solve?

13. Most jobs are not advertised; they are in the hands of the employer, client, or customer who has a problem your top-five strengths can solve.

14. Enthusiasm activates curiosity.

15. Look at the world of work comprehensively.

16. As you do the exercises at the end of this chapter, allow your natural interests free play. Do not be afraid to couple the familiar with the unfamiliar.

17. Make a list of the people you already know who share your

passion. Ask them if they know others who feel as strongly as you do.

18. Join with others who are doing what you are doing; join a community support group or chat sites on the Internet, or talk with friends and family members who are encouraging and supportive.

6 FINDING YOUR NICHE

Passion Secret *6 Know your niche; always follow your passion.*

Now that you have a good understanding of your strengths, values, and interests, you are ready to take step six in finding your passion: discovering the right work relationships and the best company size and structure for you. This chapter will help you find both. When your work allows you to be true to your preferred type, you will grow to your full potential. First let's take a look at the types of relationship that brings out your best.

THREE TYPES OF WORK RELATIONSHIPS

Just as flowers flourish in certain environments, people do their best when they are in compatible relationships. Before you meet with people, it is important to know your personality type, that is, whether you will flourish in a partner, team, or solo relationship at work. Below I describe the characteristics of these three types.

The Partnership Type

Would you be happiest in a partnership? Working in tandem with another person in an equal give-and-take relationship requires two people with great sensitivity. Any relationship is an organic process that works when both people share values. It also helps if they are mature, self-confident, and happy to see their partner become successful. The partner type:

1. Loves and needs give-and-take feedback in conversation and in decision-making ("What do you think?").

2. Forms intimate, long-lasting friendships with a select few. Is equally balanced between liking to be alone and with one other.

3. Finds that creativity increases in the confines of a trusted relationship.

4. Is self-reliant (paradoxical, but true).

5. Is an excellent listener. Enjoys hearing the partner's ideas and concepts.

6. Likes pooling resources: money, ideas, property, knowledge; feels more powerful with shared riches.

7. Sees relationships as shared independence between equals. Is uncomfortable with authoritarian relationships.

8. Thrives on encouragement from the partner (not necessarily from others).

9. Likes to share risk taking with the partner.

If the above profile fits you, and your present occupation requires that you work alone or with a team most of the time, you are not in the right work relationship. Your partner can be your customer or client;

the point is that you need interaction with another person to stimulate your imagination and creativity.

Other clues that indicate the "partnership" personality: you married early; you have always had one close friend, even as a child; you share easily with a trusted individual. You are happiest when paired, in romance, in sports, at dinner, and so on. Also, you are fascinated with duos of any kind, in love, work, or play. Famous teams intrigue you, and you would like to be part of one yourself. (Remember, these are simply clues, not hard-and-fast rules.)

A successful partnership involves not only willingness but also a strong desire to include the other. In fact, you perform at your best when creating with another. You blossom into a rare and beautiful flower when you find the right partner.

The Team Type

The individual who flourishes in the team environment is a specialist at whatever he or she does. The team type enjoys the camaraderie and give-and-take of a group, in which decision-making is spread around. Plenty of discussion, consensus agreement, and the group's benefits are all highly regarded by the team type. Think of a sports analogy: If you were a professional athlete, would you prefer to play on a team, with a partner, or by yourself?

A team can be a powerful force when each member is willing to play his or her part and play it well. The team player needs the structure of an organization. He or she enjoys the rivalry between and among other departments and companies, valuing individual contribution within the larger framework. The team type:

1. Loves competition and rivalry as a motivator.

2. Forms many friendships easily. Is gregarious and outgoing.

3. Responds to a good leader. Feels comfortable with competent authority figures.

4. Finds that creativity increases with abundant praise from teammates and leader.

5. Sees relationships as cooperative units within a larger structure.

6. Is conscientious and loyal.

7. Is sociable; likes to belong to clubs, groups, and organizations.

8. Likes to be alone only about 20 percent of the time.

9. Likes to share risks with the team and its leader.

As a team type, you wilt without comrades with whom to share your defeats and victories. Loneliness is your biggest fear. You are right at home when your career fills your need for stimulation and excitement. Other clues for determining whether you're a team player: as a child you played with a group of friends; you came from a large family, or you had early positive experiences with large families; you can maintain several relationships at once: lovers, friends, and so forth. You love team endeavors — in sports, in success stories of large corporations. You prefer to use your talents to help a team win.

The team player thrives in cooperative, competitive, and stimulating environments. You are a hardy, cheerful flower when you are on the right team.

The Solo Type

Are you happiest when you are completely in charge? Do you like to make all the decisions? The solo type likes to say, "I did that." "That" can be the company he or she built, the sale made, the book written, or the house constructed or remodeled. The common trait of this personality is the desire to wear all the hats.

The solo type prefers to make up his or her mind and is therefore resistant to outside influence. This type can make an invaluable contribution to teams or partnerships because he or she will not give in to group pressure. Since solo types are inner directed, outside pressure makes them even more introspective. The solo type:

1. Is resourceful and self-contained. Prefers to make up his or her mind. Needs and likes privacy.

2. Is highly creative, finds that creativity increases when alone and with other creative people. Inventive, imaginative, artistic; possesses a thinking, contemplative mind.

3. Is fiercely independent and a risk taker.

4. Carefully chooses friendships; selects other independent types as associates and friends.

5. Strongly resists any authority — the more freedom, the better.

6. Enjoys and needs to work alone; time to process thoughts and ideas is the solo type's number-one objective.

7. Sees all relationships as unique. Functions best in small groups or in one-on-one situations.

8. Becomes energized by the creative process. Takes praise for accomplishment with easy grace. Surprisingly, the more talented the solo is, the more grateful he or she is.

9. Picks an independent marriage partner — another solo type.

You can see from the above descriptions what a tragedy it is for the solo type to be in a large, highly structured company or organization (unless he or she is the president!). If you are a solo, you like to make up the rules as you go along. Other clues: as a child you were extremely imaginative, daydreaming a great deal; you had imaginary playmates and pets; you had great powers of concentration; you love nature — being alone in the woods is your idea of heaven; you were on stage alone as a performer; you are drawn to individual sports; the singular, the unique individual, the star fascinates you; you made your own money early. You are the flower with a deep taproot.

These three types — partnership, team, and solo — are not mutually exclusive. For example, a solo can be in a partnership if the other individual is independent. The team type can work with a solo or a partner when both are willing to listen to alternatives. Clashes occur when people do not know their types, or when they project their needs onto others. We are all a combination of the three types. However, one type will be our preference, particularly when we are under pressure.

You can discover what type you are by watching what you do when you feel stressed. Do you retreat from the world to process your thoughts and feelings? Then you are a solo. Do you talk about your concerns with a spouse, friend, or trusted co-worker? Then you are a partner type. Or do you talk things over with many people to relieve your stress? Then you are a team type.

Another way to determine your type is to pay attention to your body. Do you get tired when you are alone too long? (You're a team or partner type). Or do you feel your energy waning after being with people a couple of hours? (You're a solo type.) You can also ask those who know you well which type they think you are. Their answer may surprise you!

Now that you know your personality type, or the type that best describes you, it is time to pick your right niche.

FINDING RIGHT LIVELIHOOD

In his book *The Seven Laws of Money*, Michael Phillips, a former banker and president of POINT, the Whole Earth Catalog money-giving group, stresses the importance of a balanced approach in dispersing money: "Right livelihood is a concept that places money secondary to what you are doing. It's something like a steam engine, where the engine, fire, and water working together create steam for forward motion. Money is like steam; it comes from the interaction of fire (passion) and water (persistence) brought together in the right circumstances, the engine."[1]

Phillips suggests two questions to ask yourself to see if you are integrating your most desired activities with your livelihood. Powerful people (remember the definition of power — the ability to take action) achieve right livelihood. First of all, do you think you can undertake your work for a long time? Right livelihood could be spending your whole life as a carpenter, for example.

One of the qualities of right livelihood is that the constant perfecting or practice of it will give you a view of the whole world, similar to the old man in Hemingway's story whose life as a fisherman gives him a connection with a "whole world of experience."

Right livelihood brings its own rewards: it deepens the person who practices it. When she is twenty years old a woman who is in her right livelihood is a little different from the person she will be at thirty, and she will be even more different when she's forty and fifty. Aging works for you in the right livelihood. It's like a good pipe or a fine violin: the more you use it, the deeper its finish becomes.

Another question you can ask yourself about right livelihood is whether the good intrinsic in your livelihood is also good in terms of the greater community. This is a hard question to answer when you are asking it about yourself. It can often be hard to establish the criteria, especially when your job isn't in the helping professions, but a carpenter can certainly be doing good for the community in a very powerful way. All this is by way of saying that you shouldn't separate the idea of doing good from your livelihood; they can be integrated. With the right livelihood you would not be saying, "I'd rather be a nurse, I would rather be head of the Red Cross." That kind of dichotomy would not be necessary. What you would be doing, in your eyes, would be as beneficial to the community as any other function.

The stories in this book are about people who have found right livelihood. My clients envisioned their prospective job or business. They worked hard, giving their plan the necessary time to come to fruition. It can take eight to ten years of dedication to right livelihood before full achievement, full recompense. If you are to succeed you must be patient: maintain clarity of vision, accept yourself as you are, see the journey as fun, implement your plan, pick the right niche, continually gather information, enjoy the research, make and keep lasting relationships, have self-discipline, and finally, always trust your instincts.

The passion secrets discussed so far in this book are reflected in the concept of Phillips's First Law of Money: Do what you love; the money will come when you are in the right niche. Productivity is the result of genuine interest. Some people produce no matter where they work because they are internally motivated. They like to complete what they set out to do. They think of a task as meaningful in itself. However, the commitment to completion only goes so far with anyone. Beyond the end result we all want other rewards, such as financial compensation or personal recognition.

Have you noticed how productive you are when you love what you are doing? For example, if you love to cook aren't you always on the lookout for a good recipe? Do you count the hours you spend in the kitchen? How about when you are doing something you dislike? Don't the hours seem like days? Enjoyment is the key to any successful endeavor. For example, did you ever wonder why people who are financially independent continue to work when they don't have to? The answer is that they are having fun. (Passion clue: ask yourself what you do when you are having fun.)

Let us assume you presently hold a position in a company but are not totally satisfied with your working environment. You have three alternatives: (1) you can decide to remain where you are, either in the same position or in one with more responsibility and challenge, if it's available; (2) you can choose another company or job; (3) you can decide to start your own business, whether in a partnership or on your own. The ideas and techniques discussed in this book will help you to become successful on whatever path you choose — as long as you are on the path to passion!

The Trend toward Entrepreneurship

Now more than ever, people are choosing to work for themselves. This trend is largely due to the tremendous upheavals that have taken place in the work world over the last several decades, instability that forced people to be more independent. Gone are the days of the job that lasts until retirement, and (happily) the fear that you are a job hopper if you move around in your career.

Changing technology is another factor that keeps many workers on their creative toes. Yesterday's hot trend is today's obsolescent model. Remember when the Japanese way of doing business was all the rage? And look what happened when time, as time will do, revealed the ineffectiveness of that model.

In addition, competition in the global marketplace forces workers to think like entrepreneurs, which means they have to act as if they own the business in which they work. Shedding an employee mentality requires that they be concerned with customer satisfaction rather than with personal gain. Focusing on the customer stimulates creativity, since an ownership mentality encourages workers to come up with ways to do a better job for the customer, which improves their overall problem-solving ability. Employed people work smarter when they think like entrepreneurs because they assume more responsibility than they are paid for and, ironically, that consumer-oriented attitude only increases their marketability.

Taking responsibility for your company's success is the best way to move forward in your career. Doing this can seem overwhelming at first, but remember that your creative self thrives on challenge, not predictability. Companies need you to pay attention if they are to stay competitive in today's market. If you act as if you are an owner you will survive when others flounder, since you are in touch with what customers want. As a result, you sense the market's direction and adjust accordingly, to its ups as well as to the downturns.

Since I began my work in 1976, the trend toward entrepreneurship has increased at an exponential rate. Women especially are starting their own businesses five times faster than men. There are several reasons for this trend. First, women are not afraid to start small. Many women were the first to have home-based businesses, now a popular way to work. Women are more apt than men to take risks that may make them look foolish, as Joanna did when she walked away from a prestigious, high-paying medical career to start a janitorial business. Women are less likely than men to need the ego boost that comes from size and appearances, such as a big, fancy office, an impressive job title, high-powered associates, and a large income. Although Joanna could have had all the accoutrements of success when her business grew, she preferred to live modestly.

Second, many people believe that women are genetically designed to respond quickly to changing circumstances in the environment. They easily pick up on danger signals, a survival trait designed to help them protect their children when they're in danger. Third, women are less likely than men to sacrifice their mental and emotional health for money, since most women measure their value by the quality of their relationships, not by how much money they make. Many women want time to relate, time to just be, and time to spend with their families. They do whatever it takes to find work that helps them to achieve these goals. And because of their influence and buying power, many companies do their best to keep female employees happy.

Finally, women have never expected much of themselves, since throughout their history they have been expected to support men. This is a sad truth, yet this conditioned humility can actually work in their favor when they start businesses. Like Joanna, they are unassuming and modest so they set goals they can reach. Women tend to share knowledge with each other freely; they are also open to correction, willing to admit and learn from their mistakes, the most important factor in any successful business.

Conversely, men are conditioned to compete with other men. As a result, some find it hard to share information, to admit mistakes, and to say what they think and feel. They are honest in private but they hold back in public since not having all the answers is interpreted as weakness. Men judge each other harshly when they fail, which is not always bad, since men learn to "take it on the chin" and bounce back from criticism better than some women. Men who start their own businesses, however, display the same traits as women entrepreneurs: they are open, flexible, and independent.

For both men and women, starting a business in today's world is easier than it used to be. Cultural values have changed, especially after the fall of the corporate model of success. The "Ceonistas," as one humorous article described the bandit-like behavior of chief executive officers, are on the way out. Greed will always be with us, but working for money and possessions is no match for the satisfaction that comes when you do what you love for a living.

Every client I work with is the venturesome type. They are risk takers. You are a risk taker too, or you would not be reading this book. Think of how you could use your talents and skills to serve others. What work would be a pleasure for you to do? Don't be afraid to start small; serving the needs of one customer or one client puts you in business. You can develop your business or creative project on the side while you bring in money from your current job. Many of my clients get started this way. Remember that finding your passion is a process.

If you work for a company, whether large or small, you can use the structure of that business as an entrepreneurial training ground, whether you are on the way to the executive suite or into your own enterprise. You learn about what works wherever you are, even in a failing business, and what works in business is to serve your customers' needs. Serving customers' needs turns profits, and profits make stockholders happy. Profits, wisely invested, produce business expansion that creates more jobs. So here is your first lesson about niches: pick one that serves its customers well. Stay away from dying industries.

Warren Buffet's letters to the stockholders of Berkshire Hathaway are an excellent example of how entrepreneurs think. Buffet says that if he can't understand the business, he doesn't invest in it. He spends most of his time researching companies and their management teams, hard work that doesn't seem like work because making money for his investors is Buffet's passion. Many stockholders have gotten wealthy following his wise advise.

You can understand the company or business that interests you by visiting websites and adjoining links. Are these companies responsive, do they serve their customers well? You can also read weekly business journals to learn about up-and-coming companies and industries, such as any business connected with self-improvement, homes, health, and families, as well as the ones that are on the way out, such as industries that are strike-ridden and burdened with cumbersome tariffs, rules, and regulations. In your city, however, you can find small- to medium-sized companies whose owners run their organizations with passion!

Make some inquiries at your chamber of commerce. Remember that serving customers' needs is the key to a successful business, as it is to a successful you. Companies that overextend or spread themselves too thin lose touch with their customers, who go elsewhere for the service and products that make them part with their dollars. In these turbulent times smart companies stay with what they know. The more responsive a company is to its market segment, the more likely it is to survive. This includes educational institutions and government organizations; consumer orientation is the name of the game in today's market.

A well-managed business teaches you about *pragmatism* — a word that is a fancy way of saying "it works." You will also learn about marketing — how a product is packaged and presented to the customer. Remember the business truism: nothing happens until a sale is made. Then comes the service of that sale, which keeps your customer loyal to you.

Additionally, in any job you learn about timing, the ability to wait for a new product to prove itself. You learn to be patient with the delays, failures, and setbacks that are part of any business. After all, it's people who run businesses, not computers. People get sick; they get cranky; they have problems at home; they forget; they change their minds. I'm amazed that anything works at all, given the frailties of human nature. That the mail comes every day, buses run, phones ring, and people by and large are polite and helpful are all minor miracles.

Since impatience is the number-one problem in business, as one executive told me, the next time you get impatient with the process of finding what you want to do, recall a time when you got in a hurry. What was the outcome? Then recall a time when you were patient. What was the outcome of your willingness to wait? As you no doubt learned from your experience, impatience is the kiss of death in business and personal relationships. Patience, on the other hand, wins lifelong friends and customers. A well-managed business is like a well-managed life: both teach you that you'd better be patient if you want to reach your goals.

STAYING IN THE NICHE YOU LOVE

Being patient can apply to staying right where you are, even when what seems like a good opportunity appears on the horizon. For example, sometimes a promotion is not what's best for you. A classic example is when you perform superbly at a task and then are promoted to supervise others who do what you used to do. Managing others requires an entirely different set of skills, not necessarily natural for you if you like to perform.

Let us say that you make the best hamburgers in a restaurant, and because you are so skillful it is assumed that you should supervise the other hamburger makers. You do not get to do what you love anymore, and supervising others drives you crazy. You may make more money and have more responsibility, but managing others is not what you want to do.

Most people are told to be upwardly mobile: "Keep moving, be a comer, get your MBA so you can get on the fast track." Most people want the prestige of a new title and the opportunity to earn more money. But what if the job does not satisfy their top-five values? Remember that no amount of money and possessions can make up for emotional dissatisfaction. So when you are tempted to move out of your niche ask yourself if you are productive where you are. If the answer is "yes," do not leave! Instead, think of what you can do to improve the situation. Perhaps you need more time to yourself, or you need to teach others what you know.

Problems can often be solved by getting bigger or smaller, either contracting or expanding your activities. Which of these solutions applies to your current situation? Do you need more time, or do you have too much time on your hands? Stay where you are until you have the answers to these questions. Be patient; in time, you will see how to make better use of your niche.

Jim's Story

Jim was a product-marketing manager in a large corporation. For years he had followed the corporate path, moving into greater positions of responsibility. But Jim's flaw was his inability to read others' hidden motives, largely because he did not know himself. (Jim needed to develop emotional intelligence.) One day, a difficult and conniving associate woke Jim up from his self-imposed slumber.

Jim told me, "I couldn't 'read' him. He was friendly to my face, he said I was doing superb work — which I knew I was — and he seemed very happy with me. Then I'd overhear phone conversations where he'd run me down and blame me for every failure in the region." Jim became so ill from an ulcer that he began looking outside the company for a new job.

"Anything was better than being around him. Then I learned he'd been setting me up to be the fall guy in some very unethical dealings he was involved in. That's when the light went on for me. Guys like this are very manipulative. They make you question yourself. It was devastating."

Once Jim "read" the other man's game plan he was able to outmaneuver him.

"It gave me great pleasure to turn the tables on him — not because I wanted to 'get' him, but because I found that when my self-esteem returned, I was already one step ahead of him. I could predict what he would do. That felt great!" Jim said.

After one too many unethical moves, the destructive manager got fired. (Don't count on this to happen; corporations are slow to fire people, and most people are afraid to expose abusive people because they fear retaliation.) A year after the incident Jim decided to leave his company to start a partnership with an old friend who worked in the same company. To his dismay, his partner did not hold up his end of the bargain, which forced Jim to end the partnership and go out on his own.

Jim was blindsided by people because he was afraid he could not make it on his own, and so he compromised his values for the illusion of support. Jim was a solo type masquerading as a partner type, which was why he could not succeed.

"Now that I look back on it, that experience with the manager — and the partner — was worth the ulcer. Both taught me more about myself than ten personal growth workshops!" Jim said. Here you have a good example of how to turn failure into a learning experience.

For Jim, finding a partner seemed the logical choice, but that choice was based on fear, not reality. The truth was, Jim needed his partner's money to help him buy an existing business. In the corporation where they formerly worked, he and his friend went through many trials together, but Jim's real desire (his passion, if you will) was to be in complete control. Since he didn't have the money he needed he asked his friend to go into the business with him. Then the problems started. After Jim decided to take the risk of buying his partner's share of the business he succeeded. As I have stated earlier, honest self-scrutiny can be scary, but the payoff is finding the right niche for you.

As you can see from Jim's story, staying true to your values is the key to self-respect and success.

MATCHING YOUR VALUES WITH BUSINESS SUCCESS

In the first edition of *Work with Passion,* I quoted from Richard White's book *The Entrepreneur's Manual.*[2] Because what White wrote is still valid after all these years I want to include his thoughts about values and business success in this edition. Everyone who has read White's book treasures his timeless advice. (Check out the enthusiastic star reviews on amazon.com!)

White says that the person who succeeds in business must have intellectual honesty — the ability to see things as they are, not as she or he wants them to be. (This was the rule that Jim ignored because he needed his partner's money. But recognizing his true values gave him intellectual honesty.) Moreover, as we discussed in chapter 3, White says our values must be in harmony with the venture or it is doomed to failure, no matter how good the product or service. For example, if the owner of a fine art gallery does not value aesthetics, he or she is unlikely to make the gallery a success.

When White wrote his book he worked as a consultant to venture capitalists, businesspeople who invest capital in start-up enterprises (largely but not exclusively in technology). Because good management of these young companies is crucial to their development, venture capitalists want a handsome return on their investments, which is why they research the management team carefully. They often hire top-tier recruiters to find these people for them.

Before investing in the venture, the backers evaluate the personal values and maturity of the management staff — if the staff is felt to be unsuitable, the venture capitalists replace them or add other people. Venture capitalists need to be good at spotting when a person's values are at odds with his or her work, or they risk losing their money. If candidates value money and status they will not make good chief executive officers. The best leaders focus on what they can do for the company, not what the company can do for them.

Because work opportunities are so plentiful, talented people have many choices. Sometimes they have difficulty making a choice precisely because they are able to do so many things. That is why the work on your strengths and values (from chapter 3) must be continually reviewed. As you grow older your values may change, but your strengths become even more solid. Again, stay in the niche that's right for you; longevity, experience, and talent will take you to the top of any profession.

Once you start the process of finding your niche you become inundated with possibilities, which should remove any fears you might have about scarcity. There are basically two ways to look at life: (1) Opportunities are contracting and shrinking — therefore my chances are scarce. (2) Opportunities are expanding and growing — therefore my chances are based on abundance. Give the process of finding your niche the time it needs to develop. Finding the right job is a lot like romance. You may have to give it several tries before you get it right.

Ed's Story

"The day came when I said to myself, enough is enough," recalled Ed, formerly a personnel executive with a major bank. At the age of forty, Ed realized he was not having fun anymore — the thrill was gone.

"At first, you think it's the bank's fault, the institution. Now I know better. It was me who was the problem; my values had changed. Once I loved being part of a team; it was fun and exciting. But as time went by, I got tired of waiting for others to make decisions; I wanted to control my own destiny," he said.

Here we have an example of what happens when values change. Ed once valued affiliation and status, so he was happy to be part of a team in a bank. But when he started to value independence he needed a niche that reflected that change. Ed recently celebrated his twenty-fifth anniversary in his human resources consulting business. Even after the first year in business he said he knew he would never go back to the corporate world. The change was not easy, because Ed had to give up the security of a paycheck and the society of his comrades.

"I planned for over a year to go out on my own. I've been in personnel work most of my working life, selecting and directing people. I felt I had the ability to do whatever I wanted, but I had to structure the economics first. Giving up a secure income without a replacement takes some thought," he observed. And his first months were rough and lonely.

"The hardest thing for me at first was the lack of a team. On your own, you are the resource," he said. (See the solo type outweighing the team type?)

Ed says that discovering what motivates him has been the most exciting part of starting his own business. He says his management-consulting activities allow him to solve problems in a variety of ways. And variety (one of his top-five values) really turns him on.

"Just knowing that you can't be sure of the outcome of the meeting with a management team is exciting. (Not surprisingly, creativity is another of Ed's top values.) Sometimes there are so many problems you hardly know where to begin. I started one project to recruit some staff and wound up structuring and implementing the management team's career path strategy: timing, income, training, everything," he said.

Ed admitted that he had remained in the wrong slot for too long. "The bank is better off with people who want the structure, the security, the organizational backup. That's not for me, not anymore."

Ed said that his main problem now is turning down business.

"Saying no is hard, since I really like helping people solve their problems," he said. "But selectivity is one of the chief reasons I risked starting my own business. When a prospective client contacts me I listen to my intuition. If I hear no then no it is."

Ed's urge to be his own boss gave him the chance to follow his intuition instead of the directives of upper management. He is happy now because he makes all the decisions.

When Your Needs Change

Richard White once told me, "A creative worker is troubled when his organization no longer rewards his innovation. Profit maximization is great for the stockholders but can be restrictive for the creative, do-it-yourself-a-different-way types. They get restless, start thinking about change, and usually quit or get fired with fireworks."

"It doesn't matter how much money they're making, either," White added. "If they're not getting their needs met on the job, they'll try to meet them some other way, not always constructively."

Ulcers, heart trouble, drinking, using drugs, overeating, and other escapes: it is tragic what people do to themselves when they do not like the work they are doing. Emotional problems assume reasonable proportions when you love your work. It is amazing how many problems disappear when my clients finally find their niche! Both Ed and Rich White advise that you remain in your present position as long as possible while you are researching new opportunities, absorbing new ideas, and implementing new goals.

"You learn patience working in an organization. Business is a game, and a good one compared to some others. Your decisions and plans may take months, even years. When you get enough confidence in your own decision-making abilities, you'll venture out into no-man's land," White said to me.

Kevin's Story

As we saw above, your right niche may be right where you are. If you are not happy it may be because you are at war with yourself, as was the case with Kevin. At twenty-seven years old, Kevin was successful in his job, selling top-of-the-line outdoor sporting equipment. From my perspective everything looked fine.

"What's the problem?" I asked.

"I'm running out of time. It seems like I need to think more about the future, and I've noticed I'm not enjoying my work anymore," he said.

Kevin's desire to leave his niche as a salesman did not make sense to me. But as he wrote his autobiography, it became clear that his dissatisfaction was the result of childhood experiences. He was still angry with his parents for what they had done to him, although this was not conscious on Kevin's part. This is why I ask my clients to write their autobiographies: their stories reveal the inner demons that sabotage their happiness and success, conflicts that never show up on a résumé.

The theme in Kevin's story was that others controlled him. That he *let* them control him was the real problem. For example, he said that he was "not allowed to pick out the college" he went to, and that he rarely had the opportunity to make important choices in his life. Thus Kevin saw himself as a victim, which was the position he took in all his relationships. He did not see that he let others make decisions for him in order to avoid responsibility. He preferred to think of himself as an independent person, yet his actions did not match his image of himself.

During his childhood Kevin's wealthy parents had assumed he needed to be cushioned, and so they made nearly all his decisions for him. Kevin complied because he believed that his parents knew better than he did, as most children do. It was also true that Kevin gave in to avoid conflict, a pattern he repeated as he grew older, which was the source of his anger.

Sometimes well-meaning parents take away the opportunities children need to develop character. Children who do well as adults have early experience in making decisions. First, they learn how to make a decision. Second, if their parents do not criticize them when they fail, they learn to accept failure as a learning experience. Third, they learn that no matter what decision they make, more good than bad comes from it. Making decisions teaches children to trust their judgment, to enjoy the process of learning.

Kevin was still angry because he had not yet separated (emotionally) from his parents. He still called them to discuss his decisions, which infuriated his wife. Most of their arguments were based on Kevin's refusal to break free from his parents. His dependence on them was rooted in the belief that they knew what was best for him, and on his interest in the large inheritance that would come his way when they died.

As we discussed his dependence on his parents' money and the times when Kevin made good decisions without them, he realized that he knew what was best for him, and that calling his parents was a habit he needed to break. I suggested that he imagine that he could get along without the money they would leave him, and to let some time go by when he was tempted to call them.

"Think it through first," I said. "Then if you still want to call them, do so."

The next time we met Kevin said he'd cut back on the phone calls to his parents.

"After you and I talked, Nancy, it was as if a light went on inside of my head," he said. "It was hard to hear what you said, but then I started thinking about a customer I have trouble with. Suddenly I knew what the problem was, and the solution: I was letting him control me. That knowledge was there all along, but I'd been too stubborn to let the truth in."

Kevin said his shift in attitude had also affected his marriage.

"My wife says I'm like a new person," Kevin said. "And both my parents treat me with more respect. At some level, they must know that I don't want anything from them except a relationship."

"Growing up solves most of our problems, Kevin," I said, and we both laughed.

Kevin's niche was right where he was, and he stayed there. He is happy now because he is independent. Like Kevin, many people think they need to change their jobs when what they need to do is change their behavior. When they do they move forward into a better future. This is not easy, since it takes the intellectual honesty that Richard White talks about.

Before you make any change, stop and look at yourself for the source of your discomfort. If you are angry and resentful, ask yourself if you are replaying an old childhood scenario that keeps you in the victim role. If you want to move out of this role, take responsibility for all your choices, including the ones you are making now. Taking responsibility is not the same as blaming yourself for what you did in the past; at the time, you thought you had no other alternative. But today is not yesterday. You can decide to let go of behavior that does not work. Then you'll move into a better future.

Jo's Story

A job that matches your relationship type will also need to match your values. In other words, you can't be happy in a solo niche if you value affiliation more than you value independence. When this happens, your values are in conflict. Since you feel lonely you are likely to sabotage the niche (spending too much time on the phone or out with friends social-izing) unless you figure out how to fill your need for companionship within the niche. Or maybe you're not a solo, as the following story shows.

Jo, a vice president in a large telephone company, is an example of matching up one's type and values. She says the corporate world satis-fies her inner needs, her values, and her personality type (the team). Jo likes her job — supervising thousands of telephone operators — because she gets to take the risks inherent in management, and at the same time she gets to work with a team.

"If I had my career to do over again, I'd take a lot more risks a lot earlier. It took too long for me to realize how good I am," Jo said to me. Jo gives the credit for her enlightenment to a supportive boss. For that reason, and others, the company has been right for her.

"I had helped many fast-track male managers move up the corpo-rate ladder. When my boss asked me how I'd feel about helping a woman move up over me, I reacted by deciding that it was time to put myself 'out there.' Suddenly everything was different. I realized how competitive I am. The company wasn't keeping me back; I was keeping myself back," she said. After that conversation with her manager, she went after an upper-management career.

Jo encourages self-scrutiny, especially for women on the way up. She thinks women should understand how much time it takes to become an effective manager.

"I spend an enormous amount of time for my company — dinners, meetings, conferences. It suits me, but it may not be worth all the effort for some. You need to continually ask yourself some searching questions," she observed. (Her love of the team, the chance to shine within the large structure, means that she willingly makes the necessary compromises. Solo and partner types are less inclined to do this.)

Jo's "searching" questions are:

1. How much time do I want to devote to my job?
2. How will I feel when important personal plans conflict with business obligations?
3. Do I really want to keep doing this job?
4. Do the benefits outweigh the liabilities?
5. Do I belong in this company?
6. Do I like this product or service?
7. Am I doing all I could do, using all my potential?

Much of Jo's work involves establishing work environments that meet employee needs for on-the-job training. That challenge is highly rewarding, she says. Since one of the basic purposes of her company is to foster human communication, the corporate values are in harmony with her own. There are abundant opportunities for advancement and recognition, which are major needs of Jo's.

"Each of us has the opportunity to make change happen if we're willing and able to begin the change within ourselves. Once I realized that I was standing aside for men, I found plenty of opportunity to advance. There are always problems to solve," she said.

Jo likes to encourage women to take more risks, to learn how to be powerful and forthright. "Most of all, women in business need to know that it's okay to laugh. I sometimes think today's career woman takes life too seriously. If you can't laugh at yourself, as well as at events, the trip won't be worth the fare," she commented.

Jo is beginning to think about her future alternatives. When her corporate role ends, she says she might have to try her hand at her own business. "I'd make a heck of an entrepreneur. It would be fun to take those kinds of risks."

Most people want the chance to make a contribution to their organization, but sometimes they have simply picked the wrong type of organization in which to achieve recognition. Your niche might be a "where" problem, not a "what" problem. Jo says that when you are fed up with your job, have the courage to leave and find something else. She says the security of the telephone company keeps many people there who would be better off in another job. For her, the first choice, over thirty years ago, was the right one.

Change is scary. There is tremendous internal and external pressure to maintain the status quo. But security is no match for the rewards that come with doing what you really want to do. You will have all the security you want when you use your talent in the right career.

CONSIDERING THE PUBLIC SECTOR

Perhaps your values are not in harmony with the corporate culture, as Jo's are. For many people, work in nonprofit or government fields is a fulfilling niche. Unlike the private sector, where businesses generate their own income from sales, the public sectors, such as universities and colleges, rely on donations or taxes (private or government funds) for income. The amount of income delegated to any project depends on political judgments about the *social value* of the programs and the competition for available funds.

The fields are vast — health care, the arts, libraries, law enforcement, and all government at the city, county, state, and federal levels. Good, solid, beneficial, and satisfying careers are available to those who wish to be part of a public organization. In spite of budget cuts, there are numerous opportunities even in a small city for public service.

Adrian's Story

One city manager told me that her job was like being an orchestra leader. She did not have to know how to play all the instruments, but she had to know how to get them to play together. This function fascinated her. She had been active in politics since she was a teenager and had studied political science in college. Her passion was consistent with her work.

During her senior year in college, Adrian interned with city managers. She was fascinated by the dynamic interplay between and among competing interest groups. She particularly liked the city council and city manager relationship because it kept her in touch with local concerns. Another factor that appealed to her was public relations work — talking to the members of the press and to other media representatives. Since the job was close to the roots of local government, she was able to maintain a close circle of contacts in her community.

Additionally, Adrian found out that the real function of a city manager is to act as an advisor. This position was a perfect personality fit for her. A student of human nature, she was challenged by the daily problems that related to the political decision-making process.

"We're all just human beings trying to gain what we see to be our fair share of resources. Tax money is limited. I perform a balancing act to oversee the distribution of those resources. It boils down to the question, What's the fair distribution of resources?

"Government service can be extremely rewarding. Recently I helped persuade city residents and the city council about the benefits of constructing low-income units for older adults. This project is close to my heart because I've seen what the cost of housing does to those on fixed incomes. We need to do what we can locally to help seniors. Communities must take the initiative and assume the responsibility for solving their own problems," she insisted.

As you can see, Adrian is a team type. Her job as a city manager is in harmony with her values, ethical harmony and altruism. She uses the vehicle of political action to create results that are important to her. Her long-range goals include more in-depth work with the aged.

"I feel that one of our greatest resources is the wisdom of the older person, and that is ignored by many people. I want to educate the community about the value of the years that come after the age of sixty-five," she said.

Government and agency work require a special kind of leadership, someone with vision and patience. The opportunities are there for those who have the tenacity to work through the maze of committees and appointed officials — otherwise known as the bureaucracy. Yet the rewards are well worth it, a fact that Adrian would confirm.

James's Story

"It's worth it if you can keep your eye on the results. They may not be exactly what you had in mind, but change does occur, although slowly," commented James, who is a director of finance in a health systems agency, with a PhD in public administration. Like Adrian, James was drawn to government work through his studies in college. His field of interest was budget management. He enjoys organizing, forecasting, and distributing government funding. James's work is at the county level. His job brings him in contact with state and federal agencies, funding sources, and hospital administrators.

"Health care is a growing field, and I like being involved in helping the providers (hospitals and nursing homes) achieve their objectives. The problems revolve around cost containment, so I use my strengths in budgeting, providing financial information that is vital to any program's success. I also teach public administration courses at the master's level to health care specialists. In this way, I stay informed about the latest developments. I love teaching, and the health care field is full of opportunities. New blood, pardon the pun, is always needed," he laughed.

According to James, the practice of medicine will become more entrepreneurial in the future. This is because insurance companies and government sources of funds will seek the most competitive price for medical services of all kinds. Alternatives to expensive hospital treatment are already cropping up. Small outpatient clinics are replacing hospital stays, for example, and the tremendous advances being made in medical technology are cutting costs and eliminating personnel.

James advises those who pursue health care as a passion to research the industry thoroughly before investing years of training into what may become obsolete in the future practice of the healing arts. "Talk to hospital administrators, physicians, technologists, nurses, and other health practitioners in your area. There will be opportunities, but only for those who are able to adjust to the idea of health care as a business. Actually, though the changes are disruptive now, the consumer will benefit economically from a more efficient, less wasteful system in the future," he said.

Both Adrian and James agree that the best way to determine whether government work is for you is to meet with public service professionals first, using the advice-call approach discussed in the last chapter.

"People in public service are very approachable, perhaps more so than those in the private sector," said Adrian. "I met with many city managers, mayors, city council members, and city employees before I decided that this field was right for me. I began as a staff member, did more than I was asked to do [a key to success], met the editor of the local newspaper, and asked questions about the city. All were pleased that I was so interested in their interests. Mutuality of interest is the key."

"Government jobs are filled in a different way than the private sector, through eligibility lists and tests. However, you still need to inform yourself and know 'who's who' so you can enter at the level you want. Attend city, state, and other government meetings, write letters, and meet good people," James advised. "We all have the same objectives, whether or not we are elected. Our job is to respond to the public interest."

The public sector may be your niche if you like the service aspect that these jobs provide. Get familiar with the people and activities and see if your enthusiasm and interest are piqued. Remember, you will know your niche if you are fascinated by it (passion clue!).

The following two exercises will further clarify your personality type and niche, as well as the choices that worked for you. Use your journal to do the second exercise. Be spontaneous when you fill in the blanks; don't think too hard before you come up with your answers.

DESCRIPTIVE TRAITS EXERCISE

In this exercise you are asked to describe yourself. Notice wether your choices match your self-image and the insights you gained from writing your autobiography and the work on yourself that you've done in the other chapters. You can also have family members, several close friends, and business associates evaluate you, using a copy of the chart. This can be helpful and revealing, as it is a source of additional information about how others view you; and it can be compared to the self-image work you did at the beginning of the autobiography. Before you begin, make a few copies of the blank chart.

My clients' self-images change as they do the work in this book. After each step, they are much more self-aware and much less self-critical. Circle the word from each of the comparisons listed under Descriptive Trait Choice that most aptly describes you most of the time. For example, are you more agreeable or more resistant?

After you have completed this, then rate yourself for each word you have chosen on a scale from 1 to 10. Again, keep in mind that selecting number 1 on the scale would indicate that you feel this is one of your more minor traits, selecting number 2 indicates a greater degree of intensity, and so on up the scale, with number 10 indicating you feel this is one of your major traits. Again, don't stay in the middle; choosing low or high ratings means that you are definite rather than indecisive. To get an idea of how this works, use a copy of the blank chart and complete it for someone you know, such as your spouse, child, or a friend or family member.

Descriptive Trait Exercise

DESCRIPTIVE TRAIT (circle one)	MINOR TRAIT ——————————➤ MAJOR TRAIT								
Agreeable/Resistant	1	2	3	4	5	6	7	8	9	10
Modest/Conceited	1	2	3	4	5	6	7	8	9	10
Courageous/Timid	1	2	3	4	5	6	7	8	9	10
Controlled/Impulsive	1	2	3	4	5	6	7	8	9	10
Emotionally stable/ Easily upset	1	2	3	4	5	6	7	8	9	10
Flexible/Rigid	1	2	3	4	5	6	7	8	9	10
Energetic/Slow	1	2	3	4	5	6	7	8	9	10
Introvert/Extrovert	1	2	3	4	5	6	7	8	9	10
Leader/Follower	1	2	3	4	5	6	7	8	9	10
Objective/Subjective	1	2	3	4	5	6	7	8	9	10
Passive/Proactive	1	2	3	4	5	6	7	8	9	10
Quick to anger/ Slow to anger	1	2	3	4	5	6	7	8	9	10
Reflective/Superficial	1	2	3	4	5	6	7	8	9	10
Self-assured/Insecure	1	2	3	4	5	6	7	8	9	10
Sociable/Loner	1	2	3	4	5	6	7	8	9	10
Sophisticated/Naive	1	2	3	4	5	6	7	8	9	10
Tolerant/Disapproving	1	2	3	4	5	6	7	8	9	10

Next, use another copy of the blank chart and select the numbers that reflect your balanced self-description that you wrote in chapter 2. For example, if in your self-description you described yourself as self-assured, then circle "self-assured" and a value of 9 or 10. You can use this description as a model to follow.

How Do You Feel about Yourself?

In your journal or on your computer, answer these questions quickly, without too much thought. Notice how far back in time your successful experiences go. If your success is recent you are on the right track. Watch for passion clues in what you choose to write about

1. I felt really good when

2. I was most successful when

3. It felt good to me when someone said to me that

4. The most successful part of my past was

5. The best thing that ever happened to me was

6. I was happiest when

7. The best period of my life was

8. I did my best work when

Passion Clues

Now, also in your journal or on your computer, answer the following for each of the occasions you described above:

1. Were you alone most of the time, with one person, or in a small or large group?

2. Were you physically active or quiet — were you indoors or outdoors?

3. What about the event is a pattern for you now?

4. What qualities were you expressing (perseverance, determination, self-control, self-confidence)?

Study these events carefully. Look for symbols; what do your answers say about you?

SUMMARY

Passion Secret *6 Know your niche; always follow your passion.*

1. Relationships are the foundation of business.

2. What is your relationship type: partner, team, or solo?

3. The key to productivity is to do what you love to do.

4. Stay in the niche you love.

5. What size company do you feel comfortable in? Small (fewer than twenty employees)? Medium (twenty to five hundred employees)? Large (five hundred or more)?

6. Spend thirty minutes a day reading about various niches, jobs, or companies in which people have fun. You can learn about business by reading websites, newspapers, magazines, books, and newsletters.

7. See the world of work for what it is: abundant with problems to solve — people problems, data problems, and object problems.

8. Spend a few minutes a day reflecting on your past choices. Did you think about your personality fit before you took your current job? Are you drawn to entrepreneurism? Do you want to work for yourself? If so, study entrepreneurs and talk to local business owners and discover how they got into their businesses.

9. Are you blessed with intellectual honesty? Can you see things (people, places, events) as they are — not as you want them to be?

10. What about the public sector? Do you like politics? Can you be patient with politics and a slow decision-making process?

11. Adjust your plan as you learn more about the fields that interest you. Keep daily tabs on your feelings. Self-scrutiny is like fine-tuning a precision instrument — you!

12. Do you feel confident about your decisions? Do you like making decisions? Are you happy with your past decisions? What would you change if you could go back in time?

13. What could you do to solve problems right where you are?

14. Do you think that because you are a woman you must make way for men?

15. Do you think that because you are a man you have to compete with others?

16. Do you laugh frequently — with good, open humor?

7 DOING RESEARCH BEFORE TAKING ACTION

S tep seven focuses on gathering information about your six categories of interest, using resources like the Yellow Pages, websites, and your local chamber of commerce. The research in this chapter builds on the research you've conducted in previous chapters.

The purpose of doing research before meeting anyone is that it prepares you for the unexpected. Before Matt (from chapter 5) met with representatives of a company that was interviewing him for a sales position, he learned the company was in the process of being sold. Had he not discovered this before his interviews he would have felt betrayed once he accepted the job and learned the truth, particularly after he had given up a secure job. But since Matt knew what was going on in the company and he felt confident in the meetings — since he did not think of them as job interviews — he felt free to ask his future boss and company officers questions about the prospective sale.

A $15,000 EMAIL

After his meeting with the president, the vice president of sales, and the district sales manager of the company, I suggested that Matt research the company even further by looking on the website for bios of the officers, particularly of the president, since he set the tone for the company as a whole. When Matt couldn't find any bios, he called the district sales manager for this information. The manager gave Matt the officers' email addresses and suggested that Matt write directly to them.

Matt worked carefully on the email he sent to the president, following the guidelines provided in the next chapter. First Matt said how much he'd enjoyed meeting him; then he wrote about one time during their meeting when the president had seemed the most excited. Next Matt said that he'd like to know more about his background before he made his decision, specifically why he chose this particular company and what he liked most about his job.

Both Matt and I were surprised by the president's response. He wrote a long, informative email about his background, the company, and what he enjoyed most about his job, which was finding and developing good people and marketing a quality product to customers. He went on to reassure Matt that the sale of the company would be best for the company in the long run because he could focus on a niche in the market, rather than being part of a corporation whose products were in a different field.

"It is very unusual that the president would be so forthcoming with information before you're hired," I told Matt. "That must mean he trusts and respects you, and he truly wants to answer your questions. What a good communicator he is. I'm very impressed. So what did the vice president of sales have to say?"

"He said his management philosophy was to hire talented people and give them all the support they need to succeed," Matt said. "Then he said he hoped I'd join the team. He also attached a press release that described his background. I've heard from a rep that worked for him that he's tough, but I think what he meant was that he cuts to the chase. But he's fair."

Matt wrote a thank-you email to both men (again, following the guidelines in chapter 8), making each note personal. To the president, he said how much he appreciated his thoughtful reply and the information about himself, the company, and its impending sale. He said that had helped him to decide that this was the right company for him. To the vice president of sales, John said that he was impressed with his background and management philosophy, and he thanked him for encouraging him to join the company.

Matt had only one final concern, which he discussed with the district sales manager. "In the worst case scenario, what happens if the company's sold, sales plummet, and I'm out on the street? I have a secure job now, so I'd like to ask if the company would be willing to give me a few months' severance, just in case things don't work out," he asked.

The district sales manager said he'd get back to Matt. A day later he called to say that since the company was going to be sold they didn't want Matt's severance pay on the books, but would he accept a $15,000 sign-on bonus?

"This offer comes directly from the president," the district sales manager said to Matt. "He wants you to feel comfortable."

After Matt got over his shock, he said, "Of course, I accept. Thank you very much, I'm excited to join the team!"

The sales manager added that if Matt were ever interested in moving up into management that option would be open to him. "You and the president are a lot alike, Matt," he said. "You're both straight shooters."

"Matt, I'm so proud of you," I told him. "How does it feel to write a $15,000 email?"

"Well, it really pays to get accurate information," Matt said, and we both laughed.

Be honest, direct, and sincere; it works. And take time to become aware of the current developments in the fields that interest you. Locate specific individuals within those organizations who will be helpful to you, using as a foundation your top-six categories of work from the exercise you did in chapter 5.

Passion Secret *7* *Enjoy doing research; then act on the information.*

You do not have to be certain before you act on the information you have. (Certainty comes *after* you act.) You will learn from every experience, regardless of the outcome, so if you still have questions your research didn't answer, don't worry; you'll get more information when you meet with people. Trust in the process; that will give you the security you need, just as it did for Matt. He did not know everything before he went to his meetings, but he knew enough to ask the right questions.

Sometimes you have to reconnoiter before you can take action. For example, do you remember times when you went shopping before you knew what you wanted? Because you did not know what you were looking for you may have been overwhelmed by the choices of so many brands, styles, and colors. But once you got home you thought about what you had seen, which helped you to narrow down your choices. The next time you went shopping you knew what you wanted so you went right to the store that had the item you were looking for.

Research is like shopping; you look and look until you discover what interests you. Then you act on that information. My point in this discussion is that looking can be fun too, so don't rush the research process. Once you know enough, and you will know when this is, you can act on the information you have. Be sure to pace your acquisition of information, remain conscious of how you feel and what those feelings tell you to do, or not do. Sometimes this means waiting until you get an intuitive signal. Listen to the "still, small voice" inside of you. When you're in doubt, this voice is your best guide.

Keep in mind that you do not have to know all there is to know about any field before you meet someone in that field. All you have to know at this point is if you are fascinated by this activity and you want to learn more.

The truth is, you're probably already living your passion but you're not aware of that fact because you're not getting paid for it. Remember Joanna who cleaned her neighbors' garages on the weekends? She learned how to clean professionally, and then she got paid for it. Ask yourself if you would be willing to do what you do in your spare time until you are good enough to get paid for it. Is the process of getting to the top as interesting as the top itself? Would you take the journey anyway because of what you'd learn? If the answer is yes, then you are on the right path.

Conducting thorough research is what you do when you are interested in something. You can't get enough of the subject that fascinates you. Your appetite for learning gives you the confidence to talk with people who are fascinated with the same subject, such as fashion, computers, or landscaping. You share the same interests. Notice when a group of mothers are discussing their children. They are all fascinated with their kids, and with others' kids. Although this interest may or may not translate into a career involving children, more than one mother has gone into a children's clothing or toy business, has written a children's book, or has come up with a new way to entertain, educate, or transport children.

When you are interested in what is going on in a company or organization you can't help but ask probing questions. Your curiosity holds until you get the right answer. Your intensity (passion) makes a positive impression on the person with whom you are interviewing, since interest is the sincerest form of flattery — as is thorough research.

Rather than winging it, do your homework first. You want to know about everything this person knows so that you can make a good choice. You want to know about the quality of his or her company's products and services, as well as any hidden problems in the company. Certainly you want to know if you can make the money you and your family need, so you'll want to find out if the company or organization is financially stable. When you get straight answers, you are relieved of the anxiety that comes from making choices before you get the facts.

FOUR PRELIMINARY STEPS: A REVIEW

In chapter 4 you read about Jane, who wanted to find a job as a negotiator. I touched briefly on how she implemented her plan (which led her to her passion — a career in shipping and maritime law). Let us review these four preliminary steps:

1. Identify your values and your strengths.

2. Identify your relationship type.

3. Research the fields that interest you.

4. Call companies or individuals for information.

Step One: Identify Your Strengths

Jane identified her top-five strengths, then she memorized these strengths until she knew them as well as her telephone number. She also memorized her values, both of which she listed on a three-by-five card she carried with her in her purse. Jane knew her requirements for a work setting, and the kind of people she wanted to associate with. This is what you do when you go shopping. You make a list so that you don't forget anything.

Remember that the people you want to work with share your values. When you work with people with very different values, there will be endless conflicts. For example, if you value creativity and you take a job in a large, bureaucratic organization like the post office, can you imagine your frustration with the daily routine? On the other hand, if you value security, that is the perfect place for you to work, since security is what the post office sells to its customers (remember the motto "through sleet, snow and rain, the mail comes on time"?).

Other security-based businesses and organizations are insurance, banking, education, and city, county, state, and federal government positions. You discovered your strengths when you wrote about your pleasures in chapter 2. Your strengths are most effective when you are intensely interested in what you do, since that is what you think is important, true, and worthwhile.

Step Two: Identify Your Relationship Type

Jane was a partner type who liked to use her strengths to create workable compromises. Since she had very little ego she could have done a good job anywhere, but she chose law, a good field for people who seek compromise rather than perfection, since the law is about resolving conflicts of interest.

Since Jane knew that she would spend more time with her colleagues than with her spouse, it was important for her to assess her co-workers and boss before she accepted a position. Similarly, you need to examine future co-workers, bosses, and partners with a discerning eye, not trying to impress them but doing your best to see them as they are, not as you would like them to be.

For example, if you are an extrovert and like to talk, ask yourself if your boss is an introvert who feels drained when people talk a great deal. Conversely, are you an introvert who needs uninterrupted time and a private space? Or perhaps you are a mixture of the two temperaments; you need to spend half the time alone, and half the time with people. Is this temperament similar to that of the people you are meeting? Of course, depending on the function you perform, the importance of these dynamics will vary, but still, it is always a good idea to get a sense of the company's persona.

Most people accept a job offer based on two or three interviews. That is like the person who looks and looks for a "soul mate" and finally accepts one without any serious thought. That is a crazy way to pick a life partner. And your work is essentially a life partnership between you and your colleagues. Naturally there are times when your intuition tells you that you have made the right choice, that you needn't look any further; but if you examine how you came to that quick conclusion, you'll see that a great deal of past experience is behind the choice. We rarely think that we have much intuitive power. But you do, you can, and you will make a wise choice, once you know and trust yourself.

Step Three: Do Your Research

When researching a potential job, you need to know the answers to the following questions: who, what, where, when, how, and why. When you can answer these basic questions, you will be ready to consider an offer.

1. *Who.* Who leads in this field? What personality type describes these people? Are they partner, team, or solo types? If the best in the field are team types, and you are a partner or solo type, then this is not your niche, unless you do the work in an introverted way, such as working one-on-one, doing research, or writing a book about the subject.

2. *What.* What business activity generates the income? What is the organizational structure? If you hate to travel and this company requires that you travel more than a third of the time, forget it! If you love chocolate and they sell chocolate bars, on the other hand, you'll love the place! What customer need does this business meet? Is it social, economic, philosophical, pleasurable, practical, aesthetic, intellectual? Is the product or service a combination of these? Does the product or service match your five values?

3. *Where.* Where is this enterprise located? Think of Goldilocks; is this business too big for you, too small, or is its size just right?

4. *When.* When was the business started, and by whom? Are the founders still there? Is it a seasonal business, or is it steady year-round?

5. *How.* How is the product or the service marketed? Do they target a special niche or sell to a wide variety of people? Would you buy what they sell? How do they advertise their existence? How important is the Internet to sales and service of the product? How and by whom are the products created? Are they in foreign markets? How are the services performed? Who does this work?

6. *Why.* This is the most important question of all. Why does this organization exist? What makes it special and unique?

Take out the Categories of Work exercise that you did in chapter 5 and look at the areas that sparked your interest. Look at the final cut — the top-six categories that interested you. Take category one and think of all its facets. Let's say your top category is finance. How many different jobs are there in money? Well, there are literally dozens. Finance means many things, including the circulation of money, the granting of credit, the making of investments, and the provision of banking facilities.

You can see from this simple definition how many avenues exist in every field. Now that you know how finance is defined, do this with your top-six categories. With a clear picture in mind of the ways to work in finance, think about the function you'd like to perform in this category. For example, do you want to sell financial products? In fact, you might want to think of all the categories in terms of "would I enjoy selling this?" Or are you exchanging money, circulating it, granting credit, making investments, or researching financial information, designing websites about money issues, such as trends in the stock market? Are you working in a bank? Are you a stockbroker, a financial analyst, an accountant, or a controller?

One of the most effective ways to discern your ideal working environment is to do the simple exercise I use when I work with a group of people. I ask the members of the group to close their eyes and take several deep breaths. Then I guide them down a flight of stairs one step at a time, from step ten down to one, reminding them as they descend that they feel quite wonderful and excited about what they are going to see. This guided meditation engages their imaginations.

"Now you are at the bottom of the stairs," I say when we've reached step number one. "Keep walking down the path you are on until you come to a door. On top of this door is a plaque with your name and an inscription written in beautiful print that says, 'the perfect work environment.' Now open the door and walk in. Are you indoors or outdoors? Is this an office in a city, a home office in the country, or is this a place you use only as a base?

"What else is in this place?" I ask. "What are the colors, the furniture, the smells, the view? Are you by yourself, or are there other people with you? What have you come here to do? Why are you doing this? Take all the time you need to imagine this place, since you can come back again and fill in the blanks; this is your personal space, the place where you are the most creative and content. Now let's go back out through the door. But before you go through the door, look up over the door, and you'll see a number. This is the amount of money you make doing this work. Take one last look at the room, and then walk through the door, close it, and then go back up the stairs, slowly, very slowly, one step at a time until you reach step ten. Then, take three deep breaths and open your eyes."

The contentment and excitement on the faces of the group members are astonishing. Many have tears in their eyes, as if they've found a lost treasure, and so they have. Try this exercise and see what is behind your magic door. Remember that you can always go back to this place until you get it just right. In time, this wonderful picture will be a reality. In fact, it may already be on your collage, as was the case with Michele in chapter 4.

When one of my clients did this exercise she discovered that she was in a small, suburban office with other creative people nearby, helping to promote the books of authors she admired. So she wrote an extensive analysis of all the jobs involving the production and marketing of books. Based on the amazing amount of detail in her list, Janet will leave no stone unturned in order to promote books! She is a fountain of ideas, so promoting a product is the right path for her. I insert the list she wrote here to show the innumerable opportunities in the world of books, just to name one subcategory that falls under the general heading of communication. Janet's work will inspire you as you make your own list.

Janet's List: The Jobs behind a Book

Here is Janet's written description of the many jobs behind a book:

Begin with the tree: jobs connected to trees are as follows: forester, plant geneticist, lumber worker in various categories, support for lumber workers (real estate sales, construction, civil engineers, heavy construction equipment — drivers, superintendents, sales, manufacturing, and so on). Industrial engineers, trucking (drivers, managers, sales, manufacturing thereof), entrepreneurs, financiers, banks, and credit institutions. Then there are the furnishers of food and housing for all these types, legal services for all these types, and local, county, and state or federal government agencies.

The tree is now on its way to the mill: buyer, paper engineer (paper chemist, civil engineer, industrial engineer), plant designer, various mill workers (skilled and unskilled), marketing specialist, clerical support services; financial, legal, and political support and/or regulatory in-house and outside systems; product designers working with customers and engineers to produce new and improved products, to maintain quality in current products, and to develop new production systems. To market everything you have the sales organizations, in-house and outside advertising agencies (artists, account executives, copywriters, management, and support services).

Meanwhile, back at the typewriter, laptop, or the computer or notepad, we have the stimulus for all this activity — the writer(s). Researchers, librarians, typists, literary agents, stationery and office supply stores (and all the buying and selling that involves), magazines, and all the support systems that produce these books — other writers, editors, publishers, sales forces, subscription services, artists, printers, type designers, and so on. You have graphic support (artists, designers, typographers); support in necessary computer hardware and software; editors, publishers, sales and promotional support, TV and radio programming. Financial, legal, and clerical support systems for all this. Public relations and marketing specialists, trade publishers and publications, salespeople for the publisher, bookstore, Internet book sites, library and book club buyers (decision makers), book reviewers.

Customers — lots of them with money in hand, an avid interest in the subject, and an abiding interest in telling other people to buy the book.

And, alas, we have the entrepreneurs who buy and sell or destroy publishers' remainders; the destroyed ones go back to pulp and into the cycle again.

If the book makes money enough for people involved along the way, we add travel agents, investment counselors and brokers, CPAs and tax specialists, real estate brokers, interior decorators, and all their support systems. And legal — the legal people are always with you, win or lose (contracts, copyrights, lawsuits, and so on; even until the end of the world, when they probably are in charge of arrangements with St. Peter).

As you can see, Janet has a great sense of humor, a strength that is helpful in any job or profession.

Locate Companies in Your Interest Category

As you make your list you can become so bombarded with words that their precise meanings sometimes become obscured with time. Try this exercise. Turn on your computer, open your word processing program, and type the name of one of your categories. Highlight the word, then select thesaurus from the tools menu. Study the definitions of each of the six categories this way. Next, go to a search engine and type in these words. The list of options will open your mind to the thousands of possibilities in the work world in just one of your categories.

Next, apply one category of interest to a specific company or entity that is shown as a link on your search engine's references. You can also use the Yellow Pages to reference your category back to the page numbers of specific businesses and organizations that are in that field, such as a specific art or consulting or health organization or practice; remember that the phone book is updated every six months, so this data is current. Most websites are also frequently updated.

Study the websites your search engine directed you to. Select six favorite sites. Then select six companies or organizations from that same category in the Yellow Pages. (You will eventually select six companies or organizations in each of the six categories so that you begin with what is called a "marketing sample" of thirty-six organizations — small, medium, and large. For now, however, I want you to concentrate on just one of your categories.) At this point you may not know much about most of the companies. Just pick any six at random.

Let us use finance as our example again. The six companies could include your local bank, an investment organization, stock brokerage, or the financial functions within an organization, for example, treasurer, controller, or accountant. Include the professional organizations these people belong to, since contacting these groups could prove to be excellent advice calls. Make sure you vary your selections by choosing small, medium, and large organizations. And don't forget the sales aspect of whatever product and service you choose. Nothing happens in any business until a sale is made, and made, and made.

This is an excellent time to email everyone in your address book and to call friends and associates to ask for ideas or names of organizations and people in your categories of interest. Ask them to email you any name (a person or a company) that comes to mind as a good advice-call candidate. Say that your purpose is to arrange a conversational meeting with this person, not to ask for a job interview.

Step Four: Contact the Companies for Information

The next step is to contact the companies for information available to the public. You can do this on their websites by selecting "contact us" or "about our company." Download the information that interests you so that you can refer to it as needed. For local companies or organizations, feel free to walk in and ask for brochures, annual reports, or advertising material. A good part of any company's budget is spent on advertising. You can freely reap the benefit of these advertising dollars.

When you contact a company for information, you are looking for the answers to who, what, where, when, how, and why. Sometimes the marketing department sends these answers to you, other times it is the treasurer's office, the communications department, or public relations, depending on the size of the company Many times, the company has a catalog that proves to be a gold mine of information.

If the company is publicly held — that is, if its stock is traded on one of the public exchanges — an annual report will be available. Two of my favorite websites are morningstar.com and motleyfool.com.

Morningstar is a well-respected company in the financial community. The Motley Fool's criteria for good management are fascinating, well written, and humorous, as are their summaries of what to do and what not to do when looking for a place to invest your money. You can get on their email list for future insights on business trends.

If the company is privately owned, although the financial information will not be available, websites will most likely be available. In any case, some kind of Internet data is available about any organization that serves the public, such as sports teams, foundations, government, and educational institutions. Many have job openings and career paths links you can peruse to see if those jobs use your top-five strengths.

Be sure to look for the names of people on the website who are doing what you want to do or who can be helpful to you. If you walk into a company or an organization, ask the receptionist for the name of the person you'd like to meet and how best to contact him or her. If you are asked why you are doing this, say that you want to know more about their work and that you'd like to send them an email or write them a letter. This approach is like making a cold call in sales. Be relaxed and friendly; after all, what you want is information, not a job. Your purpose is to establish new contacts (that is, relationships). If your inquiries are met with hostility or suspicion, watch out! This reaction is a red flag signaling that this organization has something to hide.

After you gather reports and other data, read through everything carefully. You should be checking on the organization's sales volume, expenses, philosophy, and presentation of product or service. How sophisticated is the presentation? What is the quality of the visuals and the writing? These are all clues about this company's culture and expertise; note how well they stack up against their competitors.

Sometimes just reading a catalog, a brochure, or an annual report indicates that this is not a good company to contact. If your interest increases as you read, however, use a marker to underline items of interest, and make notes. Imagine yourself working for this company. Would you be pleased with their image? Does it match yours? If not, maybe you can help them do a better job!

After studying your research data, you are ready to approach a representative of one of these companies or organizations. The most up-to-date information comes from talking in person with experts in all areas. Many successful people are in small organizations as well as large ones. It is not always true that bigger is better. The best opportunities for personal and professional growth come from exposing yourself to the right kind of mentality and philosophy for you. Many innovative and dynamic teachers and mentors can be found in small- to medium-sized organizations. Generally, people in smaller companies like to wear many hats. They tend to be generalists, not specialists. For example, they like to know what's going on in sales, as well as long-range planning.

RESEARCHING AN INTEREST CATEGORY

Let us continue with our example of finance and review the entire process involved in researching one interest category, primarily establishing new contacts. This process can be broken down into eight steps:

1. Identify six banks, investment houses, or other financial institutions.

2. Read your research data; there's much more available on the Internet. If you do not have a computer or you are not online, your local librarian will be glad to help you.

3. Select a person to contact. Ask your friends, co-workers, and others for the names of appropriate people.

4. Write the person a carefully composed letter or email that is designed to arrange a meeting between you. (Chapter 8 will provide guidance in this area.)

5. Follow up with a telephone call no more than four days after sending the letter or email. When you leave a voice mail, speak slowly and clearly in a pleasant tone of

voice. I cannot overemphasize the positive impact of a well-modulated voice. If you growl, cough, mumble, or rush through your message, don't expect a return call! Nothing is more frustrating than playing back a message over and over as you attempt to decipher a phone number. You have only one chance to make a first impression; so don't waste the opportunity. If need be, practice speaking in front of your bathroom mirror before you make any call.

6. Schedule an appointment (for an interview, covered in chapter 9).

7. Go to the appointment with three objectives in mind: to make an accurate self-presentation, to gather information, and to ask for referrals.

8. Write a thank-you letter or email to the person no later than the day following your meeting. Good etiquette is the mark of a professional.

Selecting a Person to Contact

In this section we will discuss step three above: selecting a person to contact. But first I would like to ask you to look at your list of affirmations, your "ten most wanted" list that you made in chapter 4. One of those affirmations should include a "want" that describes your future career. Did you describe in detail the kind of person or persons you want to work with? Now that you know what relationship type you are, write your affirmation again so that you are even better prepared to find your target. You can use the following as a guideline to describe your ideal work environment:

My associates are compatible with my personality type. We recognize each other's special abilities. We encourage, inspire, and support one another's personal growth. I use my _____, _____, _____, _____, and _____ (top-five strengths) and fulfill my _____, _____, _____, _____, and _____ (top-five values). I discover my niche with ease. It is fun to look, learn, and complete the process of research. Next, describe your associates: They are _____, _____, _____, _____, and _____. (Enter the desired characteristics of the people you work with.)

It is useful to read this affirmation aloud every day, changing it to suit your needs. After the picture is clear, you will be ready to take some steps to locate the people you want to meet in your area of interest.

This part of the process makes most people apprehensive because it brings up images of the future meeting. You may not be sure yet what you are going to say, even though you will be well prepared for your encounters. The only attitude that works here is simply to go ahead and be scared. You will get over your apprehension after you have completed a few meetings. Then you will be more confident about the process. Remember, at this point I am just walking you through the process — just relax and let me guide you.

Whatever work category you have selected, chances are good that you already know someone in that area, or that you at least know someone who knows someone. Remember the concept of mutuality? That is what contacts are, people who share your interests; your success is their success. It is very helpful to practice the interview technique with people you already know.

For example, if you are researching the finance area, set up an appointment with your branch bank manager. He or she knows the community very well, since part of the job of manager is to belong to clubs or organizations in order to bring new customers into the bank. Remember to ask your friends for the names of people they know in finance.

How do you select a person to write to when you do not know anyone in the company? First, decide on the department or area of interest. Do not write an email or letter to the president of a large company. Focus on the section of the company that interests you and identify the person who is most knowledgeable about that section.

Let us continue with our finance example. Call or contact the company by email and ask for the name of the person who knows the most about, for example, mortgage lending. Do this in each category, whether it is the arts, sailboats, food, or photography. Receptionists and other assistants are usually helpful if you keep the right tone in your voice (self-confident, warm, and polite). Always ask for the assistant's name. Next, ask for the name and correct title of the person you want to meet. If the assistant asks you why you want to know, say that you are writing a letter or email and you want to verify the correct name and title.

Once a client of mine called a company for the name of a person in her area of interest. After she had waded through all the options, a receptionist came on the line. My client had such a stimulating conversation with the receptionist that my client invited her to have coffee with her to talk about the company. Not only did my client get the name of the right person to send her approach letter to, but she also got the email address and inside information about the company. She also made a friend she has to this day.

In another instance, my client's follow-up phone call went right through to the person he wanted to meet! Though he was unprepared for this, he kept his head and explained the reason for his call. His contact agreed to meet with him, and asked when he would like to come in. Naturally, he did not have to write an approach letter, since he had already spoken with the other person by phone. Be flexible — use the process in your own way and to your own advantage. Don't be surprised by success!

Some of your attempts to contact people will not go well. Your contacts won't respond to your emails. They won't return your calls, in spite of many attempts. Keep your good humor, and do not take rejection personally. Remember, the person ignoring you does not even know you, so it cannot be personal. Probably they are too swamped to think about you; maybe they'll call you later. Or maybe they are shy, so they are reluctant to talk with someone they don't know. Maybe they hate their job and don't want to talk about it with you! Many of my clients go on interviews thinking the other person is the expert, and they wind up being that person's guide. "I wish I'd taken the time to do what you're doing," one interviewee said to my client.

When you are not treated well by representatives of a company, or by any individual you contact, it usually means the company is in trouble and the employees are reflecting that situation, or that the individual is not doing well in his or her job.

Conversely, repeated failure to establish contact may be a signal that, unconsciously, you may not really want the contact to occur. This is a good time to look at your pleasure assignment from chapter 3 and see if you have gone off track. Don't underestimate the tendency to relapse to old ways of thinking, particularly when you get impatient. Chances are you'll go right back to what you know, even if it doesn't work, such as taking a job because you have given up on the process. You will be tested about whether your interest is genuine, so if you are disciplined and you take setbacks as opportunities to reassess your approach, the right doors will open for you. If they are not the right doors they won't open, no matter how hard you push. Some will slam shut.

If the first person you talk with is not the right one, he or she will refer you to the person who can best help you. Stay relaxed. If you find yourself getting nervous, irritated, or tense, take a break. Come back to the process another day or even another week. It has been said that genius is perseverance in disguise.

Writing an Approach Letter

Now let us discuss step four from the above list: writing a letter or email to the person you want to meet. Many people receive emails, but few receive a handwritten or perfectly typed letter on great stationery, so think about using this approach before you hit the send icon. Yes, it takes more time, but think how you'd feel if you received such a carefully crafted letter.

This letter or email should be based on your knowledge of the person and the company you want to know more about. (In the next chapter, I go into much more detail about how to write this letter or email.) The title of the person you write to will vary, depending on your interest. Usually the president or owner of a small firm is most knowledgeable about the overall picture of the company. In larger companies, select the manager in the area of your particular interest, such as the sales manager if you are interested in sales of that product or service.

I encourage clients to use interviews internally — within their own company — before going outside. Sometimes opportunities are right in front of you; all you have to do is show interest. A client who came to me thinking he needed to change companies found that his real opportunity lay under the same roof; all that was necessary was a shift in his attitude.

Philip's Story

Philip's story shows how writing an approach letter can initiate an exciting journey. In his case, the letter led him out of his company and back to where he started. By then his personality had been completely transformed.

Philip was angry because he thought he was the token minority in his company. He felt unappreciated, underpaid, and overworked. He had owned a small business, but he closed it because of a slump in the economy. Now he worked for a large forest products company. His work was good, but his attitude troubled not only him but also his supervisors. Philip's dissatisfaction with his company permeated his work space like a bad odor. (Of course, sometimes the company is the problem. An objective analysis will help you decide if this is the case.)

Philip went through the eight steps I just outlined. As he met with his peers in other companies, he discovered that he was extremely marketable, based on their positive reaction to his entrepreneurial background, such as the time Philip increased sales 50 percent in one year because of a new marketing idea. One of the men he interviewed asked, "Why aren't you in sales, Philip? I can't imagine that you'd be happy crunching numbers all the time." Philip's confidence rose with each meeting. As his self-esteem grew he noticed that things got better where he was.

"Everyone seems to be so cooperative these days," Philip said. "My supervisor spent a great deal of time with me yesterday explaining her situation and the pressures she was under. I didn't know the company was contemplating so many major changes. She said she'd noticed a shift in my attitude, and then she expressed appreciation for how cooperative I'd become!"

Philip and I both laughed.

"Yes, everything looks better when we like ourselves," I said.

This situation is not uncommon, since positive external change is the result of internal change, as Philip experienced. The end of his story proved to be a new beginning. His self-esteem took a big leap when his company gave him a $10,000 raise and a new title. He accepted the promotion, and then he sent each of the people he had met with in other companies a brief letter thanking them and letting them know the outcome of his search. In this way Philip kept the relationships intact.

Philip's appreciation for the people he met paid handsome dividends. A few called to say how glad they were for his success and to stay in touch. A few years later, one of the men came to Philip for help, which Philip was glad to give.

Accurate feedback is very valuable, but unfortunately it is rare. A form of mental and verbal blockage is at work in our culture that causes parents, spouses, supervisors, friends, and even lovers to withhold praise from us. In case you doubt this, ask yourself how recently someone told you what a good job you are doing — in specifics that meant something to you. Sadly, it seems that many people are more inclined to offer criticism instead of praise.

Some people just don't feel good enough about themselves to praise others. This habit of withholding praise also has its roots in the fear that praise will inflate the recipient in some way. Praise is therefore considered detrimental to the development of character. However, I find that human beings become miracle workers when they receive kind, generous encouragement. I have yet to see genuine praise create an egotist. Rather, it is the scarcity of praise and the abundance of criticism that creates egotism.

People who give praise easily understand the value of recognition. At some significant stage in their growth and development, they received encouragement from others that inspired and uplifted them. If your life is devoid of praise and encouragement, it may be because you don't ask for feedback. Or perhaps it's the result of a failure you experienced a long time ago, from which you have yet to recover. Once Philip realized that experiencing failure did not make *him* a failure, he regained his confidence and became optimistic about the future.

Philip's story continued long after the first big raise. He devised such a good accounting system for his company that the controller in the parent company became aware of his talent. She called Philip one day to ask if he would consider a move back East. He talked with me about the offer, since he was not sure that he should leave a stable position. He was apprehensive about the disruption the move to the East Coast would cause to his family and home life. I asked him what he felt like doing.

"Inside, I really want to take it on," he said. "In two years I could come back, in line for a controller's job out here on the West Coast. There may be drawbacks in the new position, though. I'd be overseeing many people, and I haven't done that before."

"Are you comfortable with the adjustment your family will have to make?" I asked, knowing his wife had an excellent job with a major retailer.

"They're very flexible and have no qualms," he said.

"Then what is the problem? I hope it's not your old negative self-image giving you trouble!"

Philip smiled. He said he had carefully considered all his fears, and one kept popping up. "I guess I haven't conquered my fear of criticism yet, Nancy. I'm afraid if I don't do a good job, I'll disappoint everyone," he said.

"If you don't take the job, who do you think you'll disappoint?" I asked.

He thought for a few seconds and then took a deep breath. "Me," he said.

"And who's most capable of assessing your worth and evaluating the situation?"

"Me!" He laughed this time.

After we spent another twenty minutes or so developing the strategy to negotiate for his compensation, Philip made up his mind to take the position. He had taken another giant step. A year and a half later, he stopped by to tell me he had secured an even better position than that of controller. He had just been promoted to the position of vice president of finance. We had a fine reunion. Six months after that he came in, excited and smiling, with a plan for his own business.

"You've come full circle, Philip," I said.

Philip agreed. He said that this time he knew exactly what he wanted; and better yet, he understood what the experience of the last several years had meant for him.

"I finally realized that I was blaming everyone for the problem inside me. I kept trying to change everyone else to be what I needed to become: appreciative of myself. I guess you could say that I was the racist, but man, that was hard for me to admit. You can't be successful in business or life with that attitude. The good Lord just took me on a journey to teach me that I needed to grow up and take responsibility. Now I know I'll succeed in my next venture because there's no ego involved. I was too arrogant and angry before, and I was mad at the world. Now I see how wonderful people are."

"Including yourself, Philip," I said.

If you are contemplating a change, do not quit until you look outside your organization to make comparisons. You may find that you are better off than you know! And it could be that your present job can become more to your liking; or maybe the job is fine — it is you who needs to change. Everyone gets bored from time to time with any job, even your passion; it's just human nature to need a break from any activity. Take a vacation when that happens, or take on a new challenge. If you are like Philip, your biggest challenge will be looking in the mirror.

Take a good look at your present environment. Write a short paragraph about all the people surrounding you in your daily life. Who inspires you? Who needs your praise and inspiration? Who uplifts you, informs you, and makes you think? If you are unable to think of anyone, you can see why your life is stale and joyless. It is time to find some inspiration. Ask for feedback. Be prepared to hear what you don't want to hear, as well as what will encourage you. That's what competent people do all the time.

SUMMARY

Passion Secret *7 Enjoy doing research; then act on the information.*

1. Remain open to new information.

2. Remember that powerful people are not the same as power-motivated people. The former are competent because they are open to positive and negative feedback.

3. Thorough research prepares you to take action.

4. Know your strengths and values as well as you know your address.

5. Learn how to find information about the organizations you are considering — get the answers to these questions: who, what, where, when, how, and why.

6. Learn everything you can about your top-six categories of interest.

7. Use research materials well. A vast amount of data is available on the Internet and in the business section of any library.

8. Talk to experts — people who do their work well. They will tell you what you need to do to succeed, which will save you a great deal of time, energy, and money.

9. Remember that this process is a process.

10. Call or email companies for names of possible contacts. Read your local newspaper, journals, and so on to determine the names of people you want to meet. Ask your friends and associates for names.

11. Genius is perseverance in disguise. Take it easy. Time is relative; you always have enough of it. The complete process will normally take a number of months. But since the months are going to go by anyway, you might as well be doing what you want to do.

12. Gather data to write your approach letter or email (covered in chapter 8).

13. Look inside your company. How would you change it if you had the power to change it? What costs could you cut? Could you increase sales? Could you increase efficiency or improve communications, such as the presentation of your company's products or services?

14. Stay with your present job, in commitment and attitude, while you consider other opportunities. Yet do not be afraid to voice your discontent to the appropriate person. Maybe you can improve the situation.

15. Inspiration comes more quickly to you if you inspire others first. We all need to give praise to others. Do it! Have a generous heart.

16. Ask yourself who makes you think, who inspires you to take action in your life. Where are your sources of strength and encouragement? For whom are you that source? Do you have a spiritual home, such as a church, synagogue, or mosque to go to for refreshment? Do you pray regularly for guidance and direction? Do you invest in self-development courses, seminars, speakers, and books — whatever will assist you in developing your confidence?

17. Remember the results of the survey in chapter 4 — only 8 percent of the people in the study were wise enough to get rich by first investing in themselves. The other 92 percent tried to make money so that they could do what they wanted to do, the reverse of those who work with passion. Note: Ideas can come from the most unexpected sources. You may be casually reading an article in a magazine or newspaper that gives you the information you need, or the name of a valuable prospective contact. If you get excited during your reading or during a conversation with someone, pay attention! The excitement (passion) lets you know that you are on the right track.

8 WRITING AN APPROACH LETTER OR EMAIL

The eighth step on the path to finding your passion is to approach the person you want to meet. This can be done in a conversation, a phone call, a letter, an email, or through people who know the person you want to meet. Approaching someone in person can be as simple as introducing yourself while at a social or business gathering, such as a party, a religious service, a company conference, or during a sports event or a parents' meeting.

Once you have finished with your internal work you start to see contacts everywhere. As I've stated earlier, blockage in the outside world is often a sign that your inner world needs your attention. One of my clients had many interviews and no luck until she resolved a complex that was based on her belief that she was worthless.

Suzanne was a feeling type who had been invalidated by people who did not understand the value of feelings. This dismissive attitude toward feelings is common in a culture that values achievement. Since the end result is all that matters, many have no tolerance for the process of getting there or (heaven forbid) for failure, thus the rampant addictions people use to numb uncomfortable feelings. Everywhere Suzanne worked she had conflicts with bosses who expected too much of her. Once Suzanne realized that perfectionists were the problem, not her, she found a job with a boss who thought Suzanne was terrific.

Remember the law of interest, that what you concentrate on increases? As long as Suzanne doubted herself she ran into people who validated her low opinion of herself. This self-fulfilling prophecy determined all her relationships, at home and at work. She was married to a man who measured success by material possessions. When he refused to acknowledge the value of his or Suzanne's feelings, she had no choice but to leave him to protect her sanity. Similarly, her bosses were hard-to-please individuals for whom nothing was ever good enough.

At the core of many complexes lies a decision (or series of decisions) a young person makes while he or she is under great emotional duress. In Suzanne's case, this decision was made in reaction to her parents' perfectionism. Since she was too young to know that her parents were trying to live up to unrealistic standards, she assumed there was something wrong with her because she felt her emotions so intensely. Suzanne's belief that she was wrong or bad got activated when someone criticized her performance. Then she went into an emotional tailspin. Stepping aside and observing the emotional power of her complex helped Suzanne to gain objectivity about her highly charged reactions.

Writing your autobiography, identifying your strengths and values, knowing your personality type, setting goals, and making your collage are all ways to identify and change beliefs that do not work. If you find that you are still blocked at this point, stop and reflect rather than "push the river." There may be something that you do not see clearly yet, an attitude or perception that needs to be changed.

Unconscious conflicts are just that; they are not conscious on your part, so don't interpret failure as "your fault." Resolving internal mysteries is so difficult it often requires professional help. So don't hesitate to hire an objective ear, or if you can't afford a counselor, work with a support group. We are all too close to our problems to be objective; a dispassionate viewpoint gives us the clarity we need to settle our inner wars. Then you'll move forward in your career and life.

For example, the same week that Suzanne uncovered the origin of her belief that she was worthless she had an interview with the man who later became her new boss.

"I felt so different in that meeting," Suzanne said. "I didn't feel self-conscious at all. Maybe it's because we are on the same wavelength."

"How would you have felt about this man before?" I asked.

Suzanne thought for a moment, then she said, "I would have thought something was wrong because he didn't ask me a lot of questions."

"In other words, he was too accepting?" I asked.

"Yes, I've always had to explain why I do things the way I do them. But this man just kept nodding as I spoke. He validated everything I've always felt. But it feels very odd, not having conflict, I mean," Suzanne said.

"Yes, imagine what life will be like when it works," I said, and we both laughed.

TURNING FROM THE INNER TO THE OUTER WORLD

Suzanne's story is an example of how the outside world shifts as we change the way we think. As the philosopher Krishnamurti said, if we want to transform the world, we must begin with ourselves. Transformation can be a subtle, gradual alteration in the way we think and feel, or a sudden realization, as Suzanne experienced in our conversation. But we had done a great deal of work together before Suzanne had her breakthrough, so I don't want you to think that enlightenment occurs overnight. Changing your point of view is the result of many hours of reflection.

As you turn your attention from your inner to the outside world, keep in mind the function that is right for your temperament and personality type. For example, are you more comfortable in a staff or line position? Do you want direct contact with the customer or client, or do you prefer to work behind the scenes producing or fine-tuning a product or service? Or perhaps you like to produce the product or service, sell it, and service the sale.

The niche that is best for you may be a small, specialized activity called a boutique business, such as designing jewelry, repairing items, running a massage or physical therapy practice, counseling, or consulting, either as a legal, business, or creative consultant. This kind of business is usually formed after you have worked with partners or for others for several years and now you want to do the business your own way.

What is unique about a boutique business is that you are the person who services the sale. You want to "hold the baby" as the saying goes, to be present during the process and when the happy ending takes place. This is great for your customers too, since they want you and only you to meet their needs. If this is what you'd like to do, meet with someone who has taken this route so you can discover the pitfalls and rewards of sole proprietorship.

The second way to approach people who are doing what you think you want to do is to write them a letter or email. When done with care and enthusiasm, the letter or email makes a good impression on people. Don't confuse an approach letter or email with a job search cover letter that accompanies a résumé. That latter asks the recipient to make a decision about hiring you; the former puts no pressure on him or her. Some of my clients feel more comfortable calling people, but I encourage them to write anyway, since writing helps them to get their thoughts in order.

Like Suzanne, all my clients have a Niagara of long-stored feelings about events in their lives that must be released if they are to express themselves clearly. After the initial emotional flood of feelings, then comes the still, reflective tone of voice that is characteristic of good writing. The approach letter or email paves the way to an effective meeting because the tone is thoughtful and respectful. This causes the other person to read the letter with interest. A well-written letter is magnetic; it draws people into your world. Like all good writing, a letter or email that comes from the heart has a powerful effect on the reader.

Transmitting Your Thoughts

An electrical current is a good metaphor for the phenomenon of mutuality in relationships. It takes the combination of positive and negative energy to turn on your lamp. Electrical wiring shorts out when too much strain is put either on the positive or negative energy. Good relationships are composed of a harmonious balance between two electrical beings. When they are not on the same wavelengths, as was the case with Suzanne and her former husband and bosses, conflict erupts.

A master electrician once told me that when she is hired to solve a wiring problem she always starts at the meter and works her way back to the perceived problem. I told Carolyn that her business was just like mine. I, too, start at the source of my client's perceived problem by asking them to write an autobiography. In this way I see the origin of my client's inability to focus, a negative conclusion they made about themselves when they were too young to know better. Writing their stories and talking with me about them, as Suzanne did, helps my clients to identify and change this decision.

To comprehend the power of your mind, look around you. Everything you see was once a thought in your mind. Perhaps you eliminated certain possessions and relationships from your life to be where you are now. If so, your thoughts repelled what was outmoded, and so these possessions and relationships left your life. Of course you are always free to resist change; you see this phenomenon in the houses and offices of people who are "pack rats." They never throw anything away, which leaves no room for anything new to come into their lives. In this case, the fear of the unknown takes precedence over the need for creative change.

Leaping into the unknown takes courage, but when you hold on to what is dead and gone it is as if you turned off the electrical current in your brain. Meeting with new people will wake up your feelings. Some of them will be uncomfortable, but at least you will know that you are alive! You'll find that by and large people want to help you when you approach them with courtesy and respect. So don't let fear of the unknown stop you from taking the next step, writing a letter or email; your courage will open doors for you.

As you write pay attention to your thoughts and feelings. Are you excited, curious, scared, ambivalent, indifferent? Your thoughts transmit themselves to others through your writing, particularly if the other person is intuitive: he or she reads between the lines to see what is really on your mind. Let your feelings direct you. Identify any fear that comes up as you write, and deal with it constructively. Fear is the barrier between you and your mastery of the next passion secret.

Passion Secret *8* *Speak and write clearly.*

Many people fail to do the simple things in life — arrive on time, give a word of praise, write a thank-you letter, make a phone call, invite someone to lunch or dinner, or return generous favors. By contrast, successful men and women have an ongoing appreciation of those who helped them get where they are, and they do not take relationships for granted. (They also end relationships that need to end.)

Copy the behavior of people who relate well with others. Yes, relating takes effort. But learning how to connect with people will save you years of trial and error. A well-written letter or email helps you to make an emotional connection with the recipient because you are not trying to be anyone other than yourself. You are also informed about the person you are writing to, which makes a positive impression. The letter or email is based on mutual interest. Once you master this concept your self-confidence will soar since you will know who to approach and who to avoid. You'll meet so many interesting people, you'll wonder why you never explored this simple avenue to success.

Remember that when you are yourself you are interesting to everyone who meets you, since nothing is more magnetic than honesty. You connect with others who are also grounded in reality. Napoleon Hill calls this phenomenon the "master mind concept." Minds in harmony, with similar objectives, create a mastermind, he said, an entity that is far greater than the sum of its parts.[1] Your letters, emails, and follow-up meetings bring you into the presence of people who would like to meet you too.

By now you have lists of people you would like to meet. You have studied websites, read annual reports and articles, and read about people in the field that interests you. Now you need a face-to-face verification of your interest. Is this truly your niche? Is it a good fit? Or is it a hobby or a fantasy? Who you write or talk to will depend on where you are in the process. If you know exactly what you want, then approach the people who can help you achieve your objectives (remember that your success helps them succeed too!). If you are a bit shy or concerned about your self-presentation then send your first three letters or emails to people you already know as a way to practice the process of interviewing.

Even if you can pick up the phone and easily arrange to have lunch with people, try writing an approach letter or email instead. When you write a letter beforehand you will be more relaxed when you meet. The other benefit of writing first is that the letter or email gives the other person a chance to think about what you've written without having to make a decision then and there. Most people are busy, so they appreciate a succinct, explanatory note prior to a phone call.

Think of three people you know. This could be your banker, real estate agent, a teacher, a lawyer, a friend whose work you respect, or a businessperson whose products or services you buy. Think carefully about each person. What does he do? What does she like? Sketch out a paragraph on them and their work, their successes, accomplishments, or hobbies. This exercise will cause you to focus on the other person, rather than on yourself. If his or her interests match your interests, then you are on the right track.

WRITING TO SOMEONE YOU KNOW: PETER'S APPROACH EMAIL

One of my clients, Peter, liked to go sailing with a friend. Peter's friend worked for a major bank in the leasing department. Since finance was one of Peter's top-six categories, I advised him to write to his friend Jack as a way to start the interviewing process. Peter asked how to approach his friend, since they were so well acquainted that even an email might seem odd.

"True, except that you want his advice on your career change; that's a conversation better handled in a more formal setting rather than on your boat when you are distracted by the demands of sailing," I replied. "You want to learn more about what he does. Jack's office is the right place for that."

Sometimes you can invite people to coffee or lunch, but it is best to meet with them first without the distraction of food or drink. That way, you can both concentrate. After the meeting you can go to lunch or have coffee or a drink together. Of course, what you decide to do is up to you; as always, trust your instincts.

Peter was a salesman who worked for a pharmaceutical firm that sold medical testing services to physicians. He did very well in his position until a bigger company acquired his company. The home office then shifted from the West to the East Coast, which caused considerable delay in getting medical results back to doctors. This damaged the fine relationships Peter had built with the physicians in his territory.

"I'm going crazy; all those years of work went right down the drain!" Peter moaned.

Peter was conscientious, so he told his doctors about the changes in his company, but even though they were sympathetic with Peter's predicament the doctors were concerned about the negative effect of delayed results on their anxious patients. After a few months, Peter decided that he no longer wanted to be a scapegoat for company decisions he could not control. The time was right to change course, so we worked on the email to his friend, concentrating on the bank, its future, and his friend's function.

"What has your friend accomplished there that he's excited about?" I asked. (Passion clue!)

"He told me that his biggest success came as a result of competing with a much larger bank. His competitor uses the Chinese army technique. They have so many assets that they flood the competition. My friend Jack developed personal relationships with customers who want him and only him to handle their accounts. His bank's standing is almost secondary in consideration to how his customers feel. (Here you have an example of the power of emotional connection. Customers buy from the salesperson they feel comfortable with; the product or service she sells is often secondary.) Several customers told Jack that even though the bigger banks were stronger financially, they lacked Jack's personal touch.

Personal service is the key to staying competitive in today's markets. The bigger a company, the less personal it tends to be. Although many companies say they put the customer first, customer service depends on the individuals who work for them. Peter and his friend Jack succeed wherever they work because they focus on the customers' needs.

"Remember when you told me the doctors selected you over bigger competitors because they knew and trusted you?" I asked Peter.

"Sure, Jack and I have a lot in common, that's why we like each other," he said.

"Let's put that in the first paragraph," I said.

Here is the opening Peter and I came up with:

Dear Jack:

You may wonder why I'm writing an email to ask you about your work, since I've known you for years and we have so much in common. I've always admired your ability in your work — the bank is more profitable because of you, just as I am better off having you for a friend. You know how to listen, analyze, and come up with sound advice, both for your customers and me. No wonder your customers choose you: they see what I see. [Wow. Can you imagine the smile on Jack's face as he reads this email?]

This first paragraph is very personal and full of genuine appreciation. You cannot fake this approach. It is individual and focused. As you write your own email or letter, read it aloud to see if it sounds like you are talking in a friendly and casual manner. (In a letter to a friend, it is acceptable to use the pronoun I as much as Peter did.)

In the next paragraph, Peter talked about himself. A few brief sentences described his background and what he has accomplished. Even though Jack knew Peter, he would need a phrase or two to get the gist of Peter's approach. I asked Peter what his top strengths were.

"I'm an excellent salesman, I know how to listen, and I get along with high-echelon professionals as well as with most other people," he answered.

"Okay, what else?" I asked.

Peter paused and said he could put his skills into five phrases — he is a hard worker, a quick learner, attentive to detail, good at communication, and he has good organizational skills.

"What you left out is your great sense of humor, Peter," I said, smiling. "But I'm sure Jack knows that. Because you understand the concepts of marketing you know that Jack's job is basically the same as yours. You sell medical services, and he sells money, true?"

"Exactly. So I should say that I know how to do what he does. Isn't that presumptuous?" he asked.

"Only if you say it the wrong way. Try the second paragraph."

As you know, I've been considering a shift in my career since the buyout of my company. I've spent the last few months thinking about what I do best. I've had considerable success in selling. I've been effective in varied sales situations, from leading my platoon in the war (yes, sales is like leading a platoon!) to convincing doctors I could solve their testing problems. I'm organized, I communicate well, I learn quickly, and I pay attention to detail. Like you, Jack, I enjoy helping my company make a profit. Because I respect you and your field, I'd like to ask you some questions about how you market your financial product.

That is an example of effective communication. It is honest and direct. Most business letters miss the mark because they don't get to the point. The writer is usually wishy-washy because he or she lacks confidence, or because a return is expected. Have no expectations when you write letters or emails. Instead, think of it as an adventure, a chance to learn what you need to know.

While you need to write without expectations, you can still have an attitude of expectancy. There is a subtle difference between expectation and expectancy. With the former others know that you have an agenda. You make a contact, but because you want predetermined results the other person picks up on your expectations and backs away. It's the approach-avoidance syndrome. You come in too close to someone, and he or she backs away. You let them be and they feel free to approach you.

All relationships founder on the rocks of expectations. Expectancy, however, is the foundation of healthy relationships. In other words, when you are receptive to what actually happens it turns out to be better than you could have planned! Let go and let God, as the wise saying goes. Remember passion secret 4: getting there is all the fun. Be relaxed yet prepared for whatever comes.

A well-written approach letter or email prepares you to hold a mutually beneficial meeting between you and the person you meet. So what does the recipient get from you, you may ask? Your attention, interest, and the chance to talk about themselves are three benefits you give them. What to do and say during this meeting is covered in detail in the next chapter. For now, keep in mind that the letter or email plants the seed for that meeting. Although face-to-face contact creates an electrical exchange, the letter or email is the initial conduit through which your personality makes itself known to the recipient.

Peter's last paragraph contained these words:

> I'll call shortly to arrange a meeting. I realize you are busy, so I'll take no more than thirty minutes of your time. I'm looking forward to seeing you.

Most people mail a letter that ends with, "If you're interested, call me." This passive approach makes them do all the work, which is why they rarely call you back.

If you plan to write a letter, use fine stationery. The correct weight and color of stationery is important, since quality is a sign that you care. Crane makes beautiful Monarch-sized stationery in ecru that is appropriate for these letters. This stationery elicits a favorable response because it is aesthetically pleasing. If your handwriting is good, you can write the letter in business style — including the date, the inside address, the body of the letter, and the signature. Put your return address on the outside of the envelope in the upper left-hand corner, and use a commemorative stamp. This applies whether you are writing to a friend or someone new.

Since Peter knew his friend very well, he decided to write him an email. His entire email looked like this:

Hi Jack,

You may wonder why I'm writing an email to you about your work, since I've known you for years and we have so much in common. I've always admired your ability in your work — the bank is more profitable because of you, just as I am better off having you for a friend. You know how to listen, analyze, and come up with sound advice, both for your customers and me. No wonder your customers choose you: they see what I see.

As you know, I've been considering a shift in my career since the buyout of my company. I've spent the last few months thinking about what I do best. I've had considerable success in selling. I've been effective in varied sales situations, from leading my platoon in the war (yes, sales is like leading a platoon!) to convincing doctors I could solve their testing problems. I'm organized, I communicate well, I learn quickly, and I pay attention to detail. Like you, Jack, I enjoy helping my company make a profit. Because I respect you and your field, I'd like to ask you some questions about how you market your financial product.

I'll call shortly to arrange a meeting. I realize you are busy, so I'll take no more than thirty minutes of your time. I'm looking forward to seeing you.

Warm regards,

Peter

Peter followed up with a phone call a few days after he sent the email. Jack was delighted with the approach. "I'd really like to talk to you. Thanks for the email; I was surprised but pleased!" he said.

Peter and Jack had a very productive meeting in Jack's office. Peter asked all the right questions (I cover these in the next chapter), keeping his attention on Jack and his work. I had asked Peter to imagine himself as a business reporter whose task was to write an informative piece about bank leasing after his meeting. He surprised Jack with his knowledge of leasing. Peter had read all the leasing material he'd gotten from the large competitor bank's website, as well as from websites of other banks. He was interested, informed, and enthused — and his attitude of expectancy paid off.

"Peter, I never knew you were so interested in financial packaging. What about considering our bank for your career change? I know you're a hell of a salesman, and we need marketing experts. Few of our financial people understand sales like you do," he said.

"Jack, I know sales, but finance is new to me," Peter replied.

"I could teach you that. Believe me, you know more than you think. In exchange, you could work with our staff on improving sales. This is a highly competitive field. Banking is really competitive; it's not like the old days when customers used to walk in to give you their business," he explained. "Now they carefully evaluate a bank before deciding to be a customer."

Jack introduced Peter to four other people in the bank that same day. But he made sure to set up meetings with each person rather than trying to cover everything during a casual introduction. Peter also met with representatives of Jack's chief competitor. We worked on that letter very carefully.

WRITING TO SOMEONE YOU DO NOT KNOW

When writing an approach letter or email to someone you do not know you need to be friendly, but don't be as intimate as you would when you have prior personal contact. In the first paragraph — as you write about your contact, his or her company, and the field — be a bit more distant than Peter was with Jack, but choose words that convey enthusiasm.

As you compose your letter or email try not to use the personal pronoun *I* in the first paragraph. Sometimes you must, but with a little practice you should be able to manage four or five sentences without. Most letters that people receive are trying to sell something. You don't want to be categorized, so use language that makes your purpose clear.

An effective approach letter or email reads as if you are having a conversation with the other person. As I mentioned earlier, clear thinking is essential to good writing, and clarity usually takes at least three attempts before the letter reads well. In time, your personality will emerge. Do not be afraid of informality. (We are all just people.)

Peter decided to write a letter instead of an email to the head of the leasing department in another bank. He began with an acknowledgment of the bank's fine reputation, since he knew that bankers are sensitive to their banks' images in the market. Here's the first paragraph of Peter's letter:

Dear Mr. Jones:

Your bank's reputation for excellence is well known, as are your leasing activities in agribusiness. You are a model in this state for others to follow. You provide a service for your farming customers that works well for both small and large enterprises. You must feel considerable satisfaction.

The approach is both complimentary and knowledgeable. The recipient is intrigued and ready to read more. He knows that Peter knows his business. You can use similar wording for almost any enterprise, whether it is agribusiness, airplanes, or art. If you are following your passion and you did your homework, the right words will come to you. If the language feels forced after several tries, you may be off track. Rethink your objective. You cannot hide lack of interest or poor research; both will be glaringly obvious to anyone.

The second paragraph begins with a brief description of yourself and why you are writing the letter. Peter said:

> I am a marketing professional with a background in all facets of sales. For some time I have been interested in the kinds of activities your company pursues [notice that he gets right back to the recipient]. I would like to learn more, particularly about agribusiness leasing and the corresponding developments in related industries. I'm excited about the future of leasing, so your observations would be helpful to me. I would like to meet you in person and ask some questions. At this point, my visit is for information, not a job.

In paragraph two you write about yourself and why you want to meet. The recipient is usually flattered that you have singled him or her out as an expert. Rarely do we receive recognition for our achievements; a complimentary (not obsequious) letter makes us feel good about ourselves — as it did for Peter's friend Jack.

The third paragraph of Peter's letter said:

> I will call in a few days to arrange a meeting with you. I appreciate the value of your time, so be assured that I will take no more than thirty minutes. If I don't reach you by phone I'll leave a voice mail with my number and the best time to get back to me. If I don't hear back from you in a few days I'll call again to make sure you received my letter and phone message. Thank you very much for your time and attention.

Peter's entire letter looked like this:

Dear Mr. Jones:

Your bank's reputation for excellence is well known, as are your leasing activities in agribusiness. You are a model in this state for others to follow. You provide a service for your farming customers that works well for both small and large enterprises. You must feel considerable satisfaction.

I am a marketing professional with a background in all facets of sales. For some time I have been interested in the kinds of activities your company pursues. I would like to learn more, particularly about agribusiness leasing and the corresponding developments in related industries. I'm excited about the future of leasing, so your observations would be helpful to me. I would like to meet you in person and ask some questions. At this point, my visit is for information, not a job.

I will call in a few days to arrange a meeting with you. I appreciate the value of your time, so be assured that I will take no more than thirty minutes. If I don't reach you by phone I'll leave a voice mail with my number and the best time for you to get back to me. If I don't hear back from you in a few days I'll call again to make sure you received my letter and phone message. Thank you very much for your time and attention.

Sincerely,

Peter Johnson

People's writing styles vary, of course. The more individualized your letter, the better. If your letter or email sounds as natural as your speech (excluding slang or colloquialisms, of course), it is well written. (At the end of the chapter you will find more samples of approach letters and emails.) You can write these letters and emails to any person in any field. They work well for artists, musicians, or other people in nontraditional work settings, too — do not think this approach works only in the corporate world.

If you are a singer and you want to appear in a certain nightclub, for example, go to the nightclub first so that you can observe the quality of service, the audience, and the content of the shows. Then, based on what you learned, write the letter to the owner or the person who selects talent. Who knows, after that meeting, you may not want to work with this person or sing before that audience! (You will also find a sample letter for creative artists at the end of the chapter.)

Many times we become stiff and formal when we write, so the letter sounds like it was written by formula or rote. There is no *feeling* in such a letter, and so it falls flat. When you finish your first draft, read it aloud to someone you trust. You will hear the tone better, and get feedback. Rewrite the letter or email until it sounds like you when you are speaking informally. Ask yourself how you would feel if you received your letter. Is this letter a reflection of you? Do you talk like that when you're enthused about something?

When you write to a busy person to request a meeting, he or she will naturally want to know what you want. People do not enjoy having their time wasted or having pressure put on them to make decisions they are not ready to make. Your letter or email makes it clear that you want the person's perspective, advice, and knowledge — none of which is threatening in any way or requires him or her to do anything for you.

When you approach people thoughtfully they are glad to share their knowledge with you. They will listen to you and refer you to those who can further your search. In this way you tap into the circle where you can hear about needs, problems, and trends in your area of interest. You are face-to-face with the reality of the job or business situation. During these low-key meetings, people often ask you to get back to them if you have more questions and to let them know when you know what you want to do. These are signs that you've made a positive impression.

This method of researching first and approaching later works because you take the initiative. You familiarize yourself with aspects of the field you are interested in so that you don't waste people's time. Doing your homework increases your self-confidence and earns the respect of the person you are contacting. The more thorough your research is the greater the likelihood that you will make the process work for you.

Once you master the techniques of self-marketing, you will use them the rest of your life. You will no longer be the passive reactor; you will take action — which, as you may recall, is the definition of power.

When you're writing letters in anticipation of meeting your contacts, send at least ten letters or emails at a time. If you send only one or two letters or emails, chances are that the recipients might not be available to meet you, for one reason or another. Then you may doubt the process. (There are exceptions to every rule. One of my clients fell in love with one company, wrote just one letter, and had several subsequent meetings that cemented the match!)

The ten letters or emails should be sent after the initial three you send to friends or acquaintances. You should also wait to send the ten letters until after you have held the three practice meetings. You will be more aware then of what you are doing and why. It also helps to enlist the aid of a friend, counselor, or coach during this process. We are social creatures, and we need praise and encouragement as we take the risks that make us grow.

MAKING A FOLLOW-UP PHONE CALL

After you have written the approach letter, the next step is making a follow-up phone call. Make a list of the names of people that you will be calling. Allow a space for the assistant's name, if that is applicable. Make your call fairly early in the morning, at the beginning of the workday. Remember these basic facts regarding human nature:

1. People like to be treated with respect and courtesy.

2. The person you are calling has many things on his or her mind.

3. You are last on his or her list of priorities. Don't take this personally; it's just the way it is.

Assume consent when you make a call. Smile as you tap in the phone number of the person you are contacting. You are only one person, and you need only one career position out of all the thousands that exist. If you can't reach the person, leave a voice mail (practice your response before you call, since it's likely that you'll get a voice message rather than the person).

If the person doesn't call you back right away, don't interpret that as lack of interest. Sometimes people are out of town, they are ill, or they are busy with a project. Be persistent. Continued problems at this step are sometimes connected to fear of failure; that hesitation comes across in your voice mail or letter or email. Perhaps your contact is afraid to talk with you. You may want to reassess this contact to see if talking with that person is what you really want to do — what he or she does may not be a match to your top-five values.

Most firms have recorded messages that give you extension options to select. If you don't know your party's extension wait for the live person to come on the line, then ask for the extension number of the person with whom you wish to speak. Make a note of that number on your list. If you reach an assistant, your conversation will go something like this:

"Hello, my name is _____, and I'd like to speak with _____."

The assistant may give one of several answers:

"Let me connect you; that extension is..." or "He/she is not in, would you like to leave a voice mail?" "He/she is in but is busy, may I take a message?" or "One moment, please." And then you are connected.

If your contact is not in, say, "Fine, I'd like to leave a voice mail." If he or she is busy, say, "Fine, is there a better time for me to call back?" Always ask for the assistant's name. He or she is a person, too! When you call again, use the assistant's name — remember that everyone likes to feel important. Phone calls are a good way to test your communication skills. These days people are more relaxed about business; it has become more human, and everyone has an extension number and email address. By telephoning and leaving voice mails you will learn to use your voice to establish rapport. Some examples of my clients' experiences may help.

If the assistant asks: "What is this concerning?" your response should be truthful and concise. "Mr./Ms. _____ is expecting my call." And that is true. Remember the last paragraph of your letter or email?

In some cases, the assistant thinks you want a job, so he or she says, "Let me put you through to the personnel department." You respond, "That won't be necessary, since I'm not applying for a job." And you are not. You are investigating, not applying. Not yet. (You have not even "dated" yet.)

The personnel department screens applicants for companies that are large enough to need that function. Unwittingly, they often screen out qualified applicants based on the résumés they receive. If the résumés don't match the job, they go in the reject pile. Had Peter sent his résumé to his friend's bank, for example, the personnel director would have rejected him because he did not have banking experience. By talking with Jack, however, Peter got to the decision maker.

Personnel people handle the necessary legal and internal paper-work for their companies. Some of my clients are in the personnel field, and they love their work, but they didn't get their jobs by talking with the Personnel Department. Like Peter, they established relationships with the people who had the power to hire them. Interviews with personnel people or recruiters can be effective when you are looking in a field with which you are already familiar. But they can be discouraging when you are still in the stage of searching for what you want.

Elaine's Story

Elaine had visited four or five companies and talked to a dozen recruiters (her interest category) before she decided on her target contact. He was the owner of a small but growing group of home-improvement retail stores. Any product or service having to do with the home is a growing field, since home represents security. The horrible events of September 11, 2001, and subsequent terrorist attacks increased everyone's need for the security of hearth and home, no matter where they lived.

Elaine called the owner five times, but he was always in a meeting or out of the office. She talked several times to his assistant, so she felt comfortable enough to jokingly ask, "Betty, is there a good time to reach this man?" Betty laughed and said, "Call him at 8:30 A.M. sharp tomorrow. He'll pick up the phone. That's about the only time this week someone won't be on the phone with him or in his office."

Elaine called the owner of the company the next morning and explained briefly who she was. He said he was not sure what she had in mind even though he said he'd read her letter, but he was willing to meet with her.

"Do you prefer the first part of the week or the last?" Elaine asked, giving him a choice.

"Tuesday is fine for me," he said.

"Morning or afternoon?" Elaine asked.

"How's 10:00 A.M. for you?" he asked.

"Perfect. I'll be there at 10:00 sharp," she replied.

A self-directed person is irresistible to a decision maker.

Elaine had already designed a proposal that combined career development as well as recruiting. Her areas of interest were design, decorating, and fabric selection, but her strengths were selecting, training, and motivating people. Elaine identified the problems she wanted to solve, then she located a person who had those kinds of problems. Next, she persisted through five phone calls, finally enlisting his assistant's help in making the contact. Her approach to him was well thought out, personal, and focused. His reaction was open and receptive, and a few months later, she got the job!

Elaine knew she could select good employees and motivate them enough to stay on the job. She also knew the owner was too busy with expansion demands to stay on top of this problem, so she made it easy for him to hire her. Like Elaine, you can use your strengths to solve an entrepreneur's growth problem. Or as was the case with Peter, you can approach someone you know whose organization needs your skills. Peter's story ended with a job offer from his friend's bank.

Today Peter is a leader in the bank-leasing industry, specializing in agribusiness. He continues to advance in his career by applying the principles of mutuality. He compared his new position with his old one at the pharmaceutical firm: "The difference is that now I wade through fields of produce rather than doctor's offices to make my sales. I love it!

My customers are so proud of their farms and vineyards; they treat the land as a precious commodity. I've learned a lot from them. They often ask me to stay for dinner after we conclude business," he said.

Peter and Elaine built relationships that were based on the concept of mutuality. Like all relationships, they will last as long as there is mutual interest.

SAMPLE LETTERS AND EMAILS

In this section I provide a few more sample letters and emails. They are not meant to become your actual letter or email, just to help you write more effectively. The first email was written after my client met with a respected employee in the personnel department. In this situation, contacting the personnel department was the way to begin his search. The second email is another referral from the same employee. Insiders can put you in touch with the right person in their companies. My client spent quite a bit of time making each letter to the individuals within the same company a little different. This effort is well worth the extra time.

Dear Mr. Lane:

I heard about Computers Inc.'s reputation for quality products and decentralized management from Jay Jones, in your training division. He said you were the person with the most up-to-date information about your marketing program.

For the past four and a half years I've worked in scientific application of programming. I'm making a transition to software sales and technical sales support. Your perspective will help me take the right steps and avoid the wrong ones! Please understand I am not asking you for a job. At this time, I'm just researching the market.

I'll call in a few days to arrange a day and time to meet. If I don't reach you I'll leave a voice mail with my number and the best time for you to reach me. If I don't hear from you in a few days, I'll call again to make sure you got my email and message. Thanks so much for your time.

Sincerely,

Clark Jones

Dear Mr. Smith:

Jay Jones in your training division said you were the person with the right information when it comes to matching individual talent with your company's needs. He said you would be available for an information meeting to discuss marketing and sales positions in your company. Please understand the purpose of the meeting is not to get a job, but information.

I've been in scientific application of programming for the past four and a half years. I'd like to use my technical experience in software sales and sales support. Your perspective would be valuable to me. I know you're busy, so I'll call in a few days to arrange a brief meeting. Thanks so much for your time and attention.

Sincerely,

Clark Jones

When Clark and I first started working together, he was so stiff in his communication that I finally suggested he enroll in an acting class. He did, and he discovered a new "act," honesty. An acting class can be a wonderful tool for opening up emotions. Clark would never get a job in sales until he was comfortable with his feelings. That was hard for him to do since he'd grown up with older parents who did not express or acknowledge their feelings, with the exception of anger and frustration. Sadly, suppression of emotion is an all too common experience for many of my clients and their parents. As I said in the introduction, hacking through the fears that surround our passionate selves takes great determination.

The woman who wrote the following email met the recipient while taking a class from him. Instructors of university extension courses are great resources, since many of them work by day in the business world and are on top of current developments and opportunities.

Dear Mr. Lee:

I took a course from you recently and found it to be very useful. You made it clear that a financial planner has to be comfortable with emotions as well as money if he or she is to be successful with clients.

I am interested in starting my own personal financial planning practice, but I think I need a transition job before I take that step. I am currently employed as a systems analyst on a project to develop an accounting and reporting system for the Supply and Distribution Department of a large oil company. My master's degree emphasized finance and quantitative analysis, while my undergraduate degree prepared me for a career in clothing and textiles retailing. I have a creative side that is restless with crunching numbers. I am currently considering a career shift that will make use of my creativity, and I believe that may be the financial planning profession.

I would like to meet with you to see if I'm on the right track. At this point I am gathering information, not looking for a job.

I will call shortly to arrange a meeting at your convenience. Because I appreciate the value of your time, our meeting will take no more than thirty minutes. Again, thank you for a stimulating and informative class.

Sincerely,

Jenny Webster

In the following letter, Jenny used the resources in her own firm — the Women's Forum — to find individuals who share her interests.

Dear Ms. Jones:

Although it was well over a year ago, your presentation at a dinner meeting of my company's Women's Forum made a distinct impression on me. Your humor lightened what can be a heavy topic (money!). You also gave excellent advice on finding a financial advisor. You mentioned that a large firm offers the advantages of a good reputation and recourse for unsatisfied clients. I am interested in my own financial planning but, more important, I think I'd be effective as a financial planner. I am currently employed as a systems analyst on a project to develop an accounting and reporting system for the Supply and Distribution Department of a large oil company. My master's degree emphasized finance and quantitative analysis, while my undergraduate degree prepared me for a career in clothing and textiles retailing, so I have a creative side that is restless with crunching numbers all day. I want to make a career shift that is more in alignment with my natural interests and talents, and I believe that could be the financial planning profession.

I would appreciate your perspective on that future, and so I'd like to meet with you to ask a few questions before I make a decision. At this point I am gathering information, and am not coming to you for a job.

I will call shortly to arrange a meeting. I appreciate the value of your time, so please be assured that our meeting will take no more than thirty minutes. Thanks so much for your time and attention.

Sincerely,

Jenny Webster

In the next letter, Jenny picked up an idea for a contact from her reading. In this case, the woman she wrote to was too busy for a meeting, but she arranged for her associate to see Jenny. The meeting went even better than Jenny expected, since the other woman was more her equal. Jenny's tone in the letter reflects the comments of the woman who was interviewed for the article in *Money* magazine.

Dear Ms. Jones:

You were quoted in the April issue of *Money* magazine as saying that "sensitivity to people's needs is as important as putting numbers together." [Note how this quotation tallies with what I've said about the need for emotional intelligence.] Your approach combines intuition, empathy, and financial savvy — an unbeatable combination!

I am interested in my own financial planning but, more important, I am fascinated with the financial planning profession. I am currently employed as a systems analyst on a project to develop an accounting and reporting system for the Supply and Distribution Department of a large oil company. My master's degree emphasized finance and quantitative analysis, while my undergraduate degree prepared me for a career in clothing and textiles retailing, so I have a creative side to my personality that is restless with crunching numbers all day. I'm ready to make a career shift into a job that uses my natural talents, and I believe that may be the financial planning profession. Since you are doing the work I think I'd like to do, I'd like to meet with you in person to ask a few questions before I make a career change.

I'll call shortly to arrange a meeting. I appreciate the value of your time, so please be assured that our meeting will take no more than thirty minutes. Thanks so much for your time and attention.

Sincerely,

Jenny Webster

The meeting with the associate turned out to be a turning point in Jenny's career. She encouraged Jenny to complete her degree in financial planning and to keep in touch with her, since she knew a firm that was planning to hire women like Jenny the following year. In the meantime, she suggested that Jenny join the financial planners' association, which Jenny did. In addition to our work together, I suggested that Jenny work with a therapist to help her to get in touch with her feelings. A year later, Jenny got her financial planning degree and was hired as an associate in the firm her new friend recommended. The following year, she began to meet with clients.

Like Clark, Jenny could not succeed in what she wanted to do until she developed people skills. It was not enough that she know how to manipulate numbers and information; she needed to empathize with others to be a financial planner, although she was not aware of that when we began our work together. As the woman who was interviewed by *Money* magazine said, connecting with people is the key to success in any helping profession.

In the next email, my client Phil sets up a meeting; in his second email he follows up after the meeting.

Dear Ms. Edwards:

As head of your company's financial planning department, you know the importance of profitable product/service mixes and cost-effective distribution methods. Strengthening Clothing Unlimited's position in the international market must be a rewarding challenge.

I am a financial planning professional with a background in international economic evaluation. The expanding role of your company into nonclothing product/service lines is of keen interest to me. I would like to learn more about your approach to these new areas. I'm especially fascinated with your efforts to expand into world markets. Because of your knowledge of the industry's direction, I would appreciate your perspective and I'd like to meet you in person to ask you a few questions.

At this point, my purpose is not to look for a job, but to make sure that my research matches the facts. I'll call shortly to arrange a meeting. I appreciate the value of your time, so please be assured that our meeting will take no more than thirty minutes.

Sincerely,

Phil Steele

In the above letter, Phil combined his natural interest in a company's products with his fascination for strategic planning and expansion. He is a long-range thinker, and so he likes to take on projects that take time to complete. He set up a meeting with his contact. This is his follow-up email:

Dear Joan:

Your explanation in our meeting yesterday of Clothing Unlimited's organization, planning approach, and areas of business interest was most informative for me. Your concepts for incorporating nonclothing product lines into existing operations are being pursued in an imaginative and vigorous fashion.

Your expanding activities in international trade are timely from a strategic standpoint. It is obvious that you are spending much time in planning a long-range structure that will allow Clothing Unlimited to expand its business, especially in the nonclothing product line. This strategic planning is an exciting project for you.

I enjoyed meeting you and truly appreciate the quality of our discussion. You have been most helpful to me in gaining an understanding of the nature of your company and its innovative ideas. Since our conversation, I've had some ideas on Clothing Unlimited's business expansion. When I draft a brief strategic plan, I'll give you a call and see if you are interested in seeing it. And if you believe there is anyone else with whom I can explore these topics further, I'd be grateful for your referrals.

Sincerely,

Phil Steele

Notice how in his follow-up letter Phil summarizes what was covered in the meeting, and he requests the names of others he can talk to about his areas of interest. In addition, because Phil got excited about the company's proposed expansion, he intends to draft a strategic plan and present it at a later date to the vice president of finance.

Ironically, as Phil worked on his proposal he realized that the large clothing company was violating a basic business principle: they were expanding into markets with which they were not familiar, while neglecting their customer base. So Phil decided not to pursue another meeting with the vice president since he knew she would not be open to his critique, or, more accurately, because she did not have the power to change course. The company ran into big trouble a few years later, and the stock plummeted to a low point before the company shed its overly ambitious plans and got back to their core business. After several shaky quarters, the stock price went back up to its former level. Phil turned his attention to finding small- to medium-sized businesses that needed his insight to help them develop strategic marketing plans.

Meeting with people gives you a chance to assess them before you commit your time and talent. Of course you can also do this in job interviews, but it is less stressful when there is not so much at stake (like your paycheck!). As Phil learned, people in positions of power are human just like him; they get carried away with plans of expansion while their base suffers from neglect. Soon those customers go elsewhere, then it's hard to get them back. Phil felt validated after his meeting since it removed his fear that he needed to be perfect to succeed.

"What matters is how you handle mistakes, Nancy," Phil said to me. "Are you open to correction, or do you deny what you don't want to hear? I want my clients to want the truth."

Not surprisingly, Phil's top value was ethical harmony.

Approach Letters and Emails for Creative People

Approach letters and emails are just as effective for creative and performing artists as they are for businesspeople. People involved in the media, show business, and the arts are receptive to this approach.

"Right livelihood" for artists is preceded by years of their supporting themselves while mastering their art form. After all, Renoir did not hesitate to paint porcelain in a factory while studying and growing. He and Monet ate beans for weeks on end, and yet Renoir looked back on that time as being full of happiness and excitement.[2]

The artist, like the entrepreneur, is primarily a solo type. Their values are not like the values of the majority of the population, which tend to be security and money, not creativity and freedom. While money and security are enjoyed, they are not as important to creative people as freedom, friendships, and the chance to innovate.

It is crucial that creativity be seen for what it is: a vivid imagination that is linked up with a desire to express oneself; in other words, creative people have to find an outlet for their feelings and thoughts. This is probably because from an early age they have been in tune with collective forces that urge them on. It follows that the creative artist as well as the entrepreneur have a great deal of energy and capacity for hard work. I have already discussed how important friendships are to all of us. They are vital for artists and entrepreneurs for the cross-fertilization of each other's creativity. The word *friend* is used in its true meaning, not carelessly, as we do when we call acquaintances our friends.

Sometimes the only people who can understand a creative mind are other creative people. Conventional people tend to misunderstand creative thinkers since they don't fit into categories. Do you remember teachers and other authority figures that stifled unusual behavior? For them, obedience was more important than spontaneity. Were you married to or "friends" with people who thought you were too strange, too imaginative, and so on? The creative person is usually "too" something. Like Suzanne, who suffered until she found a creative boss, passionate people feel as if they are on the wrong planet until they find kindred souls.

Your approach letter or email can help you to develop artistic and entrepreneurial friendships. It follows the same format as all the other approach letters and emails. Focus on the recipient. Do not overestimate people in the arts, media, or small businesses. Television especially tends to glamorize people.

Remember that creative people value their time more than any other commodity, since time is vital to their creativity. Do not write your approach letters or emails until you have done your homework. For example, if you want to talk to a television producer, watch the show. Study it. Make notes. Compare it to other shows. Go to classes in television production — a good way to meet the right person. Work. Nothing impresses other creative people like the willingness to work. Then write your letter or email. You will have no trouble figuring out what to say!

Bear in mind that television (and other media) is most interested in what is already successful. Think how a hit show usually generates a succession of similar ones — most of them mediocre imitations of the original. Radio is a more intimate medium than television and therefore more approachable, but listen to your favorite shows before you approach anyone who is connected with that show.

Artists and other creative people such as writers and painters often teach classes at your local community college or university. Go online and check out the classes that are available on your local campus. Taking a class from these people will help you to discover if you have the talent and desire to succeed. If you want a personal critique from these experts, pay them, if need be. The money spent will save you years of struggle.

If you are well along in your art or craft and you have something to offer to the media, the approach letter still follows the same outline: the first paragraph focuses on the recipient, the second paragraph on you, the last paragraph suggests a plan of action. In this case, enclose materials that substantiate your qualifications, such as brochures or tapes — some evidence that shows why you would make a good guest on their show.

The following is an approach letter I wrote to a television producer. The host of the show had given me the name. This letter was written before I wrote this book, thus the emphasis on job hunting, as opposed to finding one's passion (it would be another year before that concept occurred to me).

Letters to people in the media should always be typed. They get so much handwritten fan mail, you'll want your letter to look businesslike by contrast.

Dear Shirley,

Nancy Fleming suggested that I send background information to you since you are in charge of booking her guests on the show. You must feel pleased to be the producer of such a fine show. Nancy thought the area my business covers would be of interest to her viewers.

I've been a career consultant for many years. I work with individuals who retain me as their advisor to help them solve all kinds of career problems. My clients run the gamut, from first-time job seekers, re-entry men and women, to those who are employed and self-employed. They all want more satisfaction and personal growth.

Nancy said that the focus for the show could be on two topics, college graduates and re-entry job seekers. I'm happy to talk about both. I've enclosed a brief bio, some pieces I've had published, and an outline of the service I provide. I'm looking forward to meeting both of you.

Sincerely,

Nancy Anderson

I had listened very carefully to Nancy Fleming while we talked about the show and her needs, and I took that into account when I wrote my letter. As it turned out, the producer invited me to appear on the show. The audience response was so strong that I was invited back several more times. The experience gave me exposure to the world of television and a steady stream of clients, as was the case following my appearances on local radio talk shows.

My editors at New World Library suggested that I include the approach letter that accompanied my submission to them of the first chapter of this book. They contacted me right after they received it and said they were very interested in seeing the entire manuscript.

Dear Marc:

The first law of money is: do what you love; the money will follow.

Most Americans are not in the right work and haven't the tools to discover their passion and how to make money at it. For over seven years I've worked as a career consultant in my own business in San Francisco helping individuals find the work they love. Before this business I was a journalist, interviewing and writing about subjects from hard news to features. I've combined my two passions, counseling and writing, to inspire others to achieve what I have. The result is my book, titled *Work with Passion.* This book fills an ever-present need — to find happy, productive work. The audience for this book will be all who earn their living and who want the satisfaction of a career they like so much they'd do it for nothing, but don't. They get paid, and well.

I've enclosed an outline, preface, and first chapter for your perusal. The book is finished.

I've selected you because of the work you've done with Gawain's *Creative Visualization* and Ross's *Prospering Woman.* The layout, editing, and design are exactly what I want. I think my book is a next logical step for you, from visualizing, to prosperity consciousness, to working with passion. Thank you for considering my book.

Regards,

Nancy Anderson

P.S. I've enclosed a tape of a recent KGO Radio guest spot to give you an idea of how I come across. Promotion of the book is very important to me. I want very much to be involved in marketing the product I believe in so strongly.

The letter was obviously effective. You are holding the results in your hand!

SUMMARY

Passion Secret *8 Speak and write clearly.*

1. While you are making appointments, be aware of people and events that "accidentally" present themselves — old contacts that tell you about an opening, a friend's suggestion, or a phone call that comes out of the blue. Do not think of the process in terms of a rigid plan. You never know how the process will work for you — but it always does, sometimes disguised as a chance happening. Be assured that when your inner work is done the outer world will change to reflect your new sense of self. Thus, the results you want do not have to happen in a linear way; most often, success comes when you are open to what life brings to you.

2. Your thoughts are electrical currents that connect (or disconnect) you with other people. Similar minds create a "mind trust," an entity that is greater than the individual mind.

3. A well-written approach letter or email is a powerful communication tool.

4. Your first three letters or emails should be directed to people you already know. Through these contacts, you can observe how mutuality works.

5. You cannot "fake" passion or poor research.

6. Your strengths can solve big problems.

7. Expectations demand certain specific results, and they often lead to disappointments. Expectancy, however, is creative and open, and the results are always better than what you could have planned.

8. Write your approach letter on fine stationery, such as Crane's ecru Monarch-sized stationery. Write or type the letter flawlessly. Send ten letters at a time. Emails follow the same outline, three carefully composed paragraphs that begin with what you know about the other person, a description of yourself, and a request for a meeting.

9. Make your follow-up phone calls four days after you mail your letter or send your email.

10. Be natural with any assistant you encounter. Always ask his or her name, and be friendly and polite. Be sure your letter or email has been received and read. If it hasn't, say that you'll call back in a few days after they've had a chance to read it.

11. If you are referred to someone else in the firm you contact, get the person's name and write an approach letter or email first, even if your original letter was passed on to them. Personalize each contact. Many of my clients have had referral meetings when their original choice was absent, too busy, or not interested. Turn obstacles into opportunities.

12. Do not be surprised by success. When agreement to meet comes, do not hesitate. Make firm plans, keep your appointments, and always be on time or even a bit early. Do not let fear of failure suddenly sabotage you with sickness or other problems.

13. Every man or woman with business problems is hoping that a solution will walk in the door. They have no idea you exist. So walk in — and enjoy building a new relationship!

9 INTERVIEWING, FOLLOWING-UP, AND RECEIVING OFFERS

Passion Secret *9* *Trust your instincts.*

You are now ready to take step nine on your path to finding your passion: holding interviews. There's nothing mysterious about these meetings. You have them all the time — you just haven't labeled them informational interviews, as Richard Bolles calls them in his book *What Color Is Your Parachute?*[1]

When I say that you hold interviews all the time, I am referring to those seemingly casual conversations that occur when you are gathering information about a person or subject that interests you. These conversations can occur while you're shopping for a television set or for some other service or product. You ask questions, listen carefully, and when you have gathered enough information, you make a decision. Or they happen when you meet someone you like, or whose work is intriguing. The difference between your "casual" interviews and those that I discuss in this chapter is focus. Let me illustrate how the concept works with the following story.

Brian's Story

Brian was a thirty-year-old Latino who wanted to become an attorney. He received his undergraduate and graduate degrees from good schools and then set out to pass the bar examination, meanwhile taking a job as a contracts administrator in a government agency. He took and failed the bar exam six times! I met him after the sixth round, while I was working as a consultant with city government.

Brian had pushed himself to his limit, as he had done his whole life. He came from a family in which few members had high school degrees, much less the Juris Doctor. He was proud of his achievements in school, in sports, and as an up-and-coming leader among his people. He was recognized by his peers as a man to watch. Yet he could not pass the exam.

The day we met, I knew from his answers to my questions about life and work that his quest for the law degree reflected a need for status, not a passion or an urge to practice law. It took several meetings before his entire story emerged.

"I've never failed at anything I set out to do in my life. I am determined to be a lawyer. I know the law, yet I can't pass the bar," he said, the wounded pride quite obvious in his face.

"While you're waiting for the results of your last attempt, why not take a look at other alternatives?" I asked. He agreed.

During our meetings, I observed that Brian was a conceptual person, intense and serious. He had a form of mental "tunnel vision," focusing on only one way to do something. I felt he had the capacity to pass the bar exam from the work he had done on his exercises. I also felt that at a deep level he did not want to practice law — and that explained his failure to pass the bar. The source of his problem obviously was a conflict of values — which was not conscious on his part. He was a fighter in a battle he had set up to lose.

When you are at odds with your authentic self you experience defeat. Your attitude during these times is crucial. Are you reaching too high? Do you need to take an interim step first? Are you sure this is the right path for you? If not, your unconscious mind will block the achievement of what you think you want in order to focus your attention on what you need, as was the case with Brian. Remember that a goal has to be authentic for you to accomplish it.

Brian wrote approach letters and emails and conducted follow-up interviews flawlessly. He mailed twenty-three letters and emails and had twenty-one meetings. In the process Brian discovered why he had failed the bar exam. His early attempts at his approach letters and emails, as well as the follow-up thank-you letters, were stiff, legalistic, and boring. In trying to sound like an educated man, Brian was not making sense. No wonder he could not pass the bar exam! He used pompous words and phrases and bureaucratic jargon. Brian had to learn to speak from his heart.

When Brian climbed down from his position of superiority (a compensation for feelings of inferiority) his writing and speech patterns simplified. As a result, he got to the point. Over time, a quieter, more self-assured person emerged as Brian shed his false persona. He learned that success came when he was relaxed. He also discovered in his interviews that the higher up in the hierarchy he got, the more tolerant people were. Brian explains what he learned from his interviews.

"An interview is like a racquetball game. You have to play the ball as it comes to you. You're a challenger, developing your job search differently than others, beating the system by using these improved methods. You have meetings with people you choose, playing a spontaneous match where you have to learn to trust your natural reflexes, your instincts. It's the most challenging set of matches I've ever played.

"I finally realized that I would never have been happy practicing law," Brian adds. "I thought being a lawyer would give me status as a minority person. I now know I wanted the legal information and mental discipline of a law study program, and automatically assumed my next step was passing the bar. Not true — not for me. The job offers I've received in my two areas of interest, finance and merchandising, require the use of all my strengths, those I already have. I thought I could never get what I wanted unless I was an attorney."

How did twenty-one meetings with individuals in his areas of interest teach Brian in six months what he did not learn sitting in the classroom for seven years? Brian talked about his insights.

"When you're in college your focus is on the next set of exams and papers, on getting good grades, on taking in and analyzing information. The most important thing — how your training fits into your life as a whole, and into your passion — gets lost in the scramble to finish school and start your career. On campus you're isolated from the world so that you can think and study. Formal education is not an integration process; at least, it wasn't for me. I was so caught up in proving myself that I never took the time to reflect, to ask myself, 'Why am I doing this?' I just did it!" he laughed, no longer the overly serious Brian of old.

Brian failed because he thought in stereotypes. He had rejected his culture, prejudice he had projected onto others. He did not know that power in any culture comes from the ability to blend in without losing one's identity.

Be proud of your cultural origin, but be sure to master the language of society. Learn to speak and write clearly and succinctly. Good communication skills reflect your status more surely than a bank account or title. Look at powerful people from all walks of life. They are articulate, and at the same time, they cherish their roots, whatever their heritage. Failure forced Brian to reassess his goals, which is the purpose of failure. Law school was not the problem, nor was the bar exam, since success in both require the ability to think and write clearly. Brian needed to drop legalistic jargon and affectations and just be himself. But he could not do that as long as he thought he was not good enough as he was.

Brian's aggressive, competitive nature makes him a fit for his new job in sales. He spends most of his time talking to corporate treasurers and individuals with large sums of cash, convincing them to purchase his company's certificates of deposit ($100,000 and up). His willingness to work on his written and verbal skills got him the job, and his new-found confidence led to a remarkably fast start in his new company. He says: "I love the environment, the competition [notice the team personality in Brian's language. He likes to be part of a group]. Our company is the challenger in the investment field — an upstart, a maverick. We're hitting our competition hard with a quality product. There's a scoreboard in the office with everyone's name on it and the weekly results of our production written for all to see. It's inspirational when someone scores!"

The following is a summary that Brian wrote about his recent career experience (and his work in the eleven-step program outlined in this book):

It is extremely difficult to get where you want to be in a career while feeling defensive. While on the defense, one is influenced by the expectations of society, colleagues, family, and friends. Does the system dictate that I be a teacher, lawyer, or a computer programmer? If I do not achieve what I perceive that others covet, am I a failure?

Doing the work on myself made me realize that my life is in my own hands. It is not what society dictates or covets that makes the difference between success and failure. It is what is generated from within each one of us that allows us to move forward — and we all do it differently, in our own way.

The ultimate challenge, in moving through this process, is to have the courage to look consistently within yourself and visualize those attributes that make you a winner. Courage brings confidence, which in turn generates passion.

Like any source of energy, passion needs to be stoked and nurtured because you never remain the same. When you've completed the process, the glow from within will have only begun.

A few years later, Brian accepted a job in commercial real estate sales, where he was able to use his knowledge of property law and contracts. Brian has now come full circle. He is in the right niche with teammates and leaders who inspire him. He now sees that his minority background is an asset, not a liability, and he is proud of it. Brian had been ashamed of his humble roots, thinking they kept him out of the "in" crowd in society. But now he appreciates his origins, and his father's down-to-earth wisdom.

"My father is an unusual man. I now realize that I learned about love of work by watching him. He is proud of what he can do with his hands. Nobody tells him who to be; he is his own man."

Before we turn to the process of holding an effective interview let me remind you of passion secret 6: Know your niche; always follow your passion. Simply put, love your work. Money is important, but not as important as satisfaction. To repeat what I've said before, when satisfaction is your priority you will choose work that meets that need, and then you will make the money you need. Money will come *because* your work is in harmony with your values. The logical mind understands this concept, but your unconscious beliefs about work and money may undermine your common sense.

On an unconscious level, Brian knew that he was not in the right niche, so he was unable to pass the bar exam. Yet since he thought law was the route to power and money, he was too stubborn to admit that he was off track. Refusal to drop what was obviously not working interfered with Brian's creative self, which knew that he would be happier in the business world.

Imagine how Brian felt when a relative made thousands of dollars every month selling her patchwork kitchen aprons to eager gourmet cooks, and the attorney he knew who developed much-in-demand (and high-priced) seminars for labor negotiators. You too may hear or read about others who "made it" and wonder what you are doing wrong. You think you are doomed to keep hitting your head on the low bridge of frustration. Like Brian, your frustration will come to an end when you know you are on the path that works for you.

YOUR FIRST INTERVIEW

Okay, you've sent out a letter, followed up with a phone call, and now the appointment for an interview is set. As you prepare for your first interview, keep in mind that many people you meet will not be in their right niche. You may threaten some of these people; a few may even discourage you. You will know that you have had a good meeting when you feel good about yourself and the other person after you leave — regardless of the outcome.

If you feel uncomfortable during an interview, do not always assume there is something wrong with you. The other person may be insecure. When people love what they do, their eyes sparkle and they are very supportive of whatever you want to do. Conversely, when the person is unhappy or is in the wrong job he or she may use you to vent frustration, to show off, brag, or play the "see how well I'm doing" game.

Sometimes the other person may rationalize unhappiness by saying, "I tried to do what you're doing, but I finally decided that I was better off where I am. The money's good, and retirement isn't that far off." When this happens, be thankful that you are not settling for a ho-hum life. An occasional destructive interview can leave you feeling deflated. If so, talk with a counselor, friend, or support group. Most of the time you'll meet people who are kind and helpful. So just ignore the few who settled for less than their best effort.

My clients have interviewed hundreds of men and women in all kinds of jobs and businesses. Like Brian, after several calls they say, "Wow, there are so many unhappily employed people out there! I feel lucky to be taking the time to get it right. One person I met with said he envied me — he wished he had done what I'm doing."

You too are giving yourself the opportunity to "get it right" — or you would not be reading this book. Statistics abound on job dissatisfaction, and you know from your own experience that most people are not doing what they love. This knowledge will remove any fear that the people you want to meet are in any way superior to you. They are not. Most people — friendly, interested listeners who are thoughtful in their approach to life and work — will be happy to talk to you. Once you hold at least three meetings, you will discover an ability you did not know you had: you can meet and interview with anyone! As your awareness grows, you move up on a learning curve that otherwise would take years.

Now that your first appointment is set, you may be a little nervous because you have never done this before. You can reduce your anxiety by rehearsing with a friend or trusted advisor. Many of my clients say that admitting their nervousness to their contact helps to break the ice; and it makes both of them feel much more comfortable.

As with any performance, stage jitters are normal but tremendously motivating. Your instincts are forced to take over, and your instincts are your best guide. Even clients who have been in sales or in theater get nervous about their first few interviews. That is because it is so personal. The opportunity to test your skills as an interviewer soon becomes enjoyable, however. Many clients have told me they enjoyed the interviewing process so much they were sorry to end the process and go to work! It is like Brian's racquetball analogy: if you like to play, you want to get on the court. Keep in mind that you can continue the interviewing technique even after you are on a new job. Meeting with people keeps you fresh and informed, and interviewing is an excellent business-development tool.

The interview "script" begins with greeting the receptionist. Notice your surroundings. Is the office organized or confused, quiet or noisy, aesthetically pleasing or ugly (maybe they need you to redecorate the place)? Use all your senses to assess the situation. Can you see your-self working here? Are you comfortable? If yes, why? If no, why not?

In a few moments your new relationship (contact) greets you. Shake hands warmly and firmly. Look directly into this person's eyes and smile. Eye contact is best made if you remember how you look at someone when you are intrigued. It is not a staring gaze, but a consid-ering one. Tell yourself (silently, of course) that this person is going to enjoy the meeting — and she will. You want to hear what she has to say. Think about it. Who does she have to talk to about her work, her successes, and her concerns? Is it her boss, her friends, her spouse or lover? All those people have a vested interest and are therefore not very objective. *You* are objective! What a gift you give to this person just by showing up.

Take a few minutes to refresh his or her memory and to set the tone.

"John/Jane, or Mr./Ms. Doe (whichever is appropriate), I want to thank you for taking the time to meet with me. I realize the value of your time. As I said in my letter [or email] I'm looking seriously at your field and want to know more about the way your business works and how your job fits into the whole picture. I've spent the last few months thinking about what I want to do. I'm a good communicator; I speak, write, and listen well. I'm organized and thorough, and I enjoy all kinds of people and get along well with them." (The introduction varies with your own combination of abilities, of course.)

In three to five minutes you have given the person a wealth of information, "handles" he or she can hold on to. Your approach is reflective and self-assured, not pushy or arrogant. You have thought about your skills. You do not always begin your meetings with all these words, but somewhere in the conversation you will express your strengths and values. Remember, all the self-knowledge you gained from your work in preceding chapters is meaningless if you do not take action. Now you are ready to express yourself. How do you feel now? Do you like what you hear? The interview is as much for the other person as it is for you. As you speak, he or she will be making mental connections: thinking about his job or business, people he knows who are like you, places he could use you.

Next you say, "I have been researching the kind of work that interests me. I read all available material (you can get specific here — what did you read?) and picked several people to talk to about what I've learned. And that's why I'm here now, John/Jane. You are one person I really wanted to meet, so I'll begin with some questions and ask your opinions. At the end of the meeting, I'd like to know if you can refer me to other people who would be helpful in my search."

You have given him your agenda. He knows you do not have a "surprise" for him, such as, "Do you have any openings?" This last statement is the reason why many people dislike interviewing. A person comes in with a résumé in hand and puts the pressure on. No one likes this approach, even if there is an opening. Why? Because selecting people is painful. You have to make a personal judgment under stress. It's far better to get the chance to look at someone without having to hire him or her. Then you can really listen and observe.

How many times have you met someone casually and considered hiring him or her, or thought about what a good co-worker he or she would make? Most good jobs are filled just this way. Someone knows someone, as a friend or former co-worker, as was the case with Peter and his friend Jack from the last chapter. The entire recruiting world operates on the age-old question, "Who do you know?" Word of mouth, networking, call it what you will, but it is the way companies fill the majority of their positions — on personal recommendation.

The interview works equally well whether you simply wish to change positions in your field or within your company or you want to explore an entirely new option. If you are already familiar with the field, obviously you adapt what you say to the situation. In any case, the approach brings you face-to-face with people so that you hasten the word-of-mouth process. You are becoming known, in a way that is quicker and easier than waiting for an outside chance of recommendation. The best part about interviews is that frequently you are talking to decision makers who are planning company changes and forming new objectives. They have yet to write a job description because they are still busy defining the problem that needs to be solved.

Eric's Story

One client, who picked transportation as his top interest, talked to five people in the trucking industry, his favorite area. Eric spoke with leaders in several areas — private business, labor, and government — so he developed a full understanding of the industry's problems. Deregulation, labor, and competition — all these were crucial issues to the people that Eric interviewed.

"The labor leaders told me that the old tough-guy image was on the way out. They were now thinking about new personality requirements for the labor representatives who work with management. I asked them exactly what was needed to be a labor negotiator in the years ahead," Eric said.

Here you see the early stages of job definition. As it turned out, Eric was helpful to the man he was talking to. The question had provoked a thoughtful analysis of the needs of the labor leader. Eric was able to make intelligent observations because of the thoroughness of his research and his experience in previous meetings with other industry leaders. His quiet, unassuming, but firm manner made a good impression on the labor leader, who stopped to reflect.

"You've certainly been thorough in your approach. You said as you began our meeting that your top strengths included a down-to-earth ability to communicate and excellent organizational skills. Those are two of the qualifications that any negotiator must have. Have you decided yet about whether you want management or labor as your career?" he asked.

He had started thinking about Eric as a potential employee because of Eric's personality and background. "Labor needs professional, well-balanced, and dedicated people," he said to Eric, "not someone who's out to get the boss. Rather, the ideal is a commitment to strong representation of the employees' position. You seem to have an understanding of that position."

Eric had gained some of that knowledge by driving a truck before he attended college. He was now close to completing his bachelor's degree in industrial relations. With graduation pending, Eric needed to find the right job, which is why he asked me for help in locating the right niche for his talents. Before Eric held his first interview, he had to know what questions to ask. Asking the right questions can make the difference between accomplishment and frustration — as I am sure you have discovered in your own career.

Copy the following Research Interview Data Sheet into your journal and use it as an outline to keep track of your interviews, as Eric did. Fill out the page as soon as possible after the meeting. Otherwise, you will forget important points. Writing while the information is fresh is best. In addition, you will find that the Factor Evaluation Work Sheet at the end of this chapter is a useful tool for weighing the alternatives that will lead you to choose one position over another. You may have other job characteristics to add in measuring your requirements when selecting a company to work for.

The Research Interview Data Sheet

Date of Interview _____

Company _____

Main Product/Service _____

Name of Person_____

Title _____

Comments: Salient Points

1. What did you learn about this person?

2. What did you learn about the industry?

3. What did you learn about the company?

4. What referrals did you obtain within the company? Outside the company?

5. What problems seem to be of most concern to this person?

CREATING YOUR AGENDA

You determine the agenda in your interview, not the person to whom you are speaking. You have three objectives:

1. Presenting yourself — your strengths, values, and what you have defined so far as your objective.

2. Gaining information — you ask questions, probe for problems you would like to solve.

3. Asking for referrals — "Who do you know that would be helpful for me to meet?"

Your interview will stay on the right track if you ask questions that fall into three categories: personal, industry, and company. Give the questions pluses and minuses. The "plus" questions are designed to draw the person out as well as to elicit information. The "minus" questions probe for problems.

Begin by asking the individual to tell you about his or her experience; why this field, why this job? That is a "plus" question. Don't start with "minus" questions like, "How does competition in your field affect your ability to attract good people?" (However, sometimes your sympathetic ear will elicit surprisingly frank discussions of problems early on in the meeting. Again, there are no rules for these meetings. What happens depends on you and the individual you are meeting with.)

Examples of "safe" industry questions are: "What are the trends in your field? What changes in the market have occurred that have set these trends?" Since a person cannot speak in generalities forever, the interviewee will begin to connect your questions with his or her circumstances.

For example, a person who is in the beauty business may reply, "The trend in the cosmetic industry is toward total personal care. More women are taking better care of their bodies by eating properly and exercising frequently. That's why we've introduced a vitamin supplement packet to go with our basic skin care products. I use this all the time and have found it very helpful." "Oh," you reply. "How have you found it helpful?" Take the last word a person says in a sentence and then form it into a question. Remember that they wouldn't have used the word if they didn't want to talk about the subject.

Then you can ask some company "plus" questions. When she or he has given you all the information you need or appears reluctant to go further, move to another safe "plus" question, in either the personal or industry categories.

The following are examples of plus and minus questions to ask during your interview. You will not have time to ask all the questions, of course. However, several will be crucial in getting the information you need. Let us begin with a list of plus questions. These are generalized questions that will give you some ideas about the scope of your questioning and establish the proper tone and approach. Your questions will be more focused and refined, appropriate to the individual situation.

Plus Personal Questions

1. What is the most significant contribution you have made to your firm in the last year? The last five years? What fascinates you?

2. What person (or persons) have you recruited who has gone on to fulfill the potential you recognized in him or her?

3. What attributes are necessary for success in your position?

4. How have you changed the nature of your job?

5. What are your short-range objectives? Your long-range objectives?

6. What professional in the field do you admire most, and why?

Plus Industry Questions

1. How are profits maximized — improved cost cutting, marketing, strategy, superior product, or service?

2. What is responsible for the positive or innovative trends in the industry? Are they social, political, or individual trends? How has the overall economy affected your industry?

3. What factors are responsible for the growth of the industry?

4. What specific research has the industry found useful in terms of profits or growth?

5. How has the industry developed, and what new strategy is being used to continue or diversify that development?

6. What are the overall earning potentials of your industry?

Plus Company Questions

1. What is the overall philosophy of management here in your organization? How is that specifically implemented? How can you personally measure that philosophy?

2. How accurately are new developments and markets perceived, and what is the management style? Open, vertical, horizontal?

3. What are the long-range goals of the company? The short-range goals?

4. What has been the major achievement of the company in the marketplace?

5. What makes your company better than others in the same field?

6. What combination of aggression and analysis has been used to capture the market share?

Minus Personal Questions

1. If you could do whatever you wished to do professionally, what would that be? What would it mean for your organization? What prevents you from doing it?

2. What feature of your position would you change or eliminate?

3. What development has occurred in your field that you did not envision in your career plans? What did this development mean for your future and the future of others in the field?

4. What does increased government activity mean to your profession?

5. If you had to do it all over, would you join the same field and the same organization? If yes, why? If no, why not?

6. What is the opinion of professionals you respect about the growth potential in your field in the next five years?

Minus Industry Questions

1. Is government regulation — local, state, and federal — in the industry a plus or minus?

2. Are you affected by environmental restraints? Do any interest groups affect your industry?

3. Is your growth fast or slow? Is it typical of the field?

4. What material supply problems are there? Are you able to attract and keep good people?

5. What specific trends affect you? (Markets drying up, hostility toward the industry, cost factors, and so on.)

6. Do you have too much competition, too little? Why is the competition better or worse?

Minus Company Questions

1. How does your firm respond to government regulation? What costs have been incurred as a result?

2. Who is responsible for responding to government regulations? What other political factors are at work in the industry?

3. How are you attracting people to keep up with your growth (if growth is unusually fast)? What markets will you lose if you cannot attract people? What particular skills and abilities do you look for to help you increase your share of profits and earnings?

4. How is quality control maintained? By whom?

5. What influence do inflationary or deflationary trends have on your business?

6.   What are you doing to capture and keep your share of the
      market?

As rapport develops between you, move to the minus questions
about industry, then to personal matters, then to company issues. Move
back and forth, being sensitive to the other person's reactions. Your
skill as a questioner will increase with each interview. The entire
process is designed to develop your self-confidence, knowledge of the
marketplace, and an awareness of your talents. It will lead you to your
passion.

In your journal create an interview grid to help you create your
own questions for each individual interview. Your target is the minus
questions about the company, the problems. Your ultimate purpose
during the interview is to identify the problems, to see these are the
problems you want to solve. Picture your grid as you work through
the interview.

If you make others feel important by focusing on their areas of
expertise, they will enjoy your visit. Remember to rely on your
instincts. They will guide you when you are in doubt. Preparation is
important. Read, practice, think, inform yourself. Then in the face-to-
face meeting, be flexible and receptive: "Play the ball as it comes to you."
Don't stay longer than thirty minutes. Look at your watch when you
think enough time has gone by, then get on your feet, shake hands, and
say, "Thank you very much for your time." Sometimes you will not be
let out the door — one of my clients went to meet with a manager of a
training department and stayed all day. The manager had arranged to
include several employees at the meeting with my client, who was surprised but delighted. Naturally, his agenda changed accordingly. He
had five interviews in one day!

Be flexible. If you are asked to stay longer, stay until your instincts
tell you it is time to leave. Remember that you can always come back for
a second or third meeting. In fact, it may be best to suggest that you
come back rather than talking longer than an hour. You don't want to

exhaust yourself or the other person. He or she may not want to see you again! Always leave any situation when people still want you to stay. Don't wear out your welcome.

WRITING THANK-YOU LETTERS OR EMAILS

After my client left the meeting he sat down and wrote a brief summary of each of the five people he had met with, including details about his or her background and position. Then he took an extremely important step: he wrote each a personal, handwritten thank-you letter. In some cases you can write an email, but nothing matches the elegance of an individualized letter written on fine stationery.

The First Paragraph

Write a thank-you letter to the person you meet no later than a day after your meeting. This letter should be as carefully written as your approach letter or email. It also contains three paragraphs. The first paragraph goes something like this:

> Thank you very much for the time you so generously gave to me in our meeting on [date]. I know how many demands there are on your time, so your courtesy, attention, and advice are especially appreciated. You obviously like what you do, and your enthusiasm is a tribute to that commitment.

Keep it simple and in your own style. Do not be afraid of friendliness or of an unusual way of turning a phrase. If you have the skill to write in an upbeat fashion, as long as you are sincere and respectful, your thank-you letter can be even more powerful. One client wrote:

> You're the most inspirational marketing pro I've ever met. When I left your office my head was full of ideas, and my step

was several degrees lighter! Now I know why your products are so successful in this town. With people like you, your company has the market cornered. Your encouragement of me made my day. No, it made my week! I thank you.

Mailed promptly, your letter will arrive in time for your interviewee to recall your presence in a positive way. It's almost like having a second meeting with you. Think about how you feel when you receive a positive, personal letter. You feel special. The golden rule is golden because it works. Treat everyone as you would like to be treated, and people open doors for you.

Once you are in your new job, send everyone a note telling him or her how your search ended. Also tell each person how he or she helped you in that search. One client told me that piece of advice was worth my entire fee! "Three people called to thank me and invite me to lunch to celebrate, and one of them offered me a great job with him if I became dissatisfied with my new employer," he said.

The Second Paragraph

Now let's work on your second paragraph. Concentrate on the subject matter covered in your interview. Refer to your Research Interview Data Sheet. Make up one of these for each meeting, including those "accidental" advice calls (the talk with someone you met on the bus, the casual encounter — any time you gain more knowledge about your passion). It is like coming to class on Wednesday after your professor's lecture on Monday. He asks, "What did I say on Monday, class?"

You raise your hand and say, "You said the influences that affected the development of the laissez-faire economic system were social, political, and religious." Then you give examples of developments in those three categories. Bingo.

In your interview, you covered — by subject headings — the outline of your "professor's" (contact's) presentation. Do the same in your thank-you letter:

In our recent meeting, you said the communication industry faces many challenges in the future: technological, social, political, and personal. The industry is changing so fast that today's invention is obsolete almost as soon as it is invented. I was fascinated to hear about the high demand for trained personnel in the cable television industry — and that the demand for home entertainment products has led to an unending need for good software. I'll follow up on your suggestions to talk to the people you mentioned. From what you told me, my skills will be needed in the exciting future ahead.

The writer paid the recipient of the letter the highest compliment: she listened and heeded what was said. Nothing makes a teacher feel better than when a student takes action on his or her hard-learned knowledge. The faster the action taken, the brighter the student.

One part of your second paragraph should focus on a time in the meeting when you were both enthused. Think of eyes, body language, voice tone — at one point you were on the same wavelength. Repeat that moment in the letter. Re-create your mutual enthusiasm by mentioning the pace of change in the industry. Be assured that experience was an exciting one for both of you.

The Last Paragraph

The last paragraph of your thank-you letter is a statement of your future intentions:

I appreciate the suggestions you gave me to call Mr./Ms. _____ [or to check with you later if I need more information, or do more research, or any or all of the above]. I will keep you informed of my progress. Thanks again for your warmth and kindness.

By including a statement of your intentions, you keep the relationship alive. After you have had more meetings, you may find it useful to go back to an earlier contact. In many cases, you will meet a particularly nice person who takes an interest in what you are doing — one you will want to meet more than once.

VARIATIONS ON THE INTERVIEWING PROCESS

So far this chapter has covered the steps to take using the interview approach. But there are numerous ways your niche may become apparent to you. As I said in the introduction, the light may go on while you are reading the book or working on your values. You may see an advertised opening that's just right for you. Someone might call you with an opportunity. Feel free to respond! If you are interviewed, however, make sure that you use the plus and minus questions I've outlined in this chapter. Just because you are being interviewed, don't be afraid to ask questions, and don't be passive.

You may create a job right where you are after you do the work in this book, as Philip in chapter 7 did in his forest products company. Or you may hear about a business that is looking for someone like you, as Jenny in chapter 8 did after she interviewed the associate of the financial planner to whom she'd written an approach letter.

In every case, identify the decision maker, then write an approach letter or email to that person, or call if you are more comfortable with direct contact. As you progress in your "campaign" you will develop your own style. Your increase in self-confidence will give you a corresponding increase in spontaneity. Some contacts will be personal enough to telephone without writing or emailing first.

Occasionally, you can get the information you need over the telephone. For example, you may follow up on one of your letters and the recipient wants to handle matters over the phone. "Why don't we just discuss this right now. How can I help you?" First, refer to your letter or email. "As I said in my letter, I'm investigating the work that appeals to me. Before I make a decision, I need to know the answers to several questions. Conversations like this are best done in person, I've found. If your schedule is full this week, how about a day next week?"

Usually, he or she will agree to meet if you sound self-assured and interesting. If the person insists on a phone interview, go ahead — ask your questions. A good one to begin with is: "Tell me how you happened to choose this field and your company?" As he or she expands on the answer, the exchange will become friendlier and the possibility of meeting personally will increase. Thank the person for the help you received. Be gracious — it works.

Some of my clients have such superb telephone skills that letters and emails did not prove necessary. Their tone, self-confidence, and approach were enough to establish rapport. They always wrote thank-you letters, however. You too may have an unusual ability to communicate verbally. Use it when your instincts guide you to do so.

ACCEPTING JOB OFFERS

Using your instincts includes the ability to trust that your enthusiasm is the key to career and life success. Enthusiasm sells ideas and products. You cannot be enthused unless you know what inspires you, what makes your energy level rise. For some it is trucks, for others it is art, for others it is computers or satellites. Whatever it is for you — and only you know the answer — trust your instincts and write a letter to someone who shares your enthusiasm. Learn how you can help that person become even more successful.

Job offers will often come to you in the process of holding interviews. Usually, it takes between fifteen and twenty-five of these meetings to decide what you really want. When you have a clear picture of your objective — and not before — the right job offer will appear. Or it may occur to you to start your own business or practice, which I'll cover in the next chapter. Anxiety can affect your concentration in your early meetings; if so, be sure to write down everything you remember as soon as you leave the meeting.

Once you've done a few interviews you won't be nervous anymore. During your second or third meeting you'll be relaxed because you are more informed. Preparation is the key to comfort, so trust that you will like this process once you know how to do it. However, do not move into a job-hunting mode, such as succumbing to the urge to "sell yourself," at any point. Instead, listen carefully, and when the time is right, move into a more assertive exchange, such as asking who makes the hiring decisions.

When you know what you want, ask for it. Some of my clients have gotten right to the "close" and then they stop, waiting to be asked. A typical closing conversation occurs like this: "Well, John, you've met with several people here in our firm. What do you think about our company?"

The questioner wants to hear your level of interest. Do not play a cat-and-mouse game that drags on endlessly. If you are excited about the job and the company, say that you'd like to work there. In some cases you can write a rough draft of the problems you've identified and take that with you into your third or fourth meeting. This is how consultants get business. They make a "needs assessment," then they propose a solution (which includes their consulting time) to the employer. If the solutions increase sales or cut costs, the company will most likely hire the consultant.

Problems involve people, data, or objects. Brian, our would-be attorney, combined his data skills (analysis of financial reports) with the people skills that gradually emerged. Brian had seven meetings with bank representatives before his first job offer was extended. Both he and the representatives of the bank gave the relationship time (two months) to develop into a good rapport. Be sure to take your time when you are assessing a job; quick closes rarely stick.

Respect the employer's need to determine if you are the solution to his or her problem. Hiring mistakes are costly, both in morale and money. Be patient. You may be told, "We need to think it over and get back to you." If so, say something like this: "That's understandable. When can I expect your call, or would you prefer that I call you?"

Some people are so intuitive that they move quickly. Even then, ask to meet everyone you'll work with before you say yes. This includes support staff, since they are key to a smooth operation. Ask them the same questions that you asked your initial contact. Meanwhile, keep all avenues open until you make your final decision. You may think an offer is certain, but you should still continue with your other meetings. Things change. Disruptions, which have nothing to do with you, may occur. If you are discouraged or simply tired, take a break. Go fishing or backpacking, or do anything that refreshes your spirit.

You'll work harder getting the job or creating a business than you will after you are in the position. There's nothing wrong with you if you find yourself wishing that the process would hurry along. Finding work that matches your values is hard work; the temptation is to compromise your values and take a job that is not the best fit. But think how few people are doing what you are doing. It takes a rare combination of tenacity and commitment to complete such a task. However, the rewards are endless. They just keep coming: money, satisfaction, and the knowledge that you are in charge of your destiny.

NEGOTIATING

In real estate transactions, making counteroffers is an accepted practice. When it comes to job offers, few of us think we can counter the offer. Usually we are so glad to finally get an offer that we accept quickly, and then we think about what else we could have negotiated for when we get home. Talk to any respected recruiter, and he or she will tell you that negotiation is the rule, not the exception. In fact, one of your interviews should be with a person who recruits in your field of interest. Ask about his or her job and about the strategy that works to make good matches.

Do not talk about money unless you've responded to an ad that asks for salary requirements. You should have a figure in mind, give or take $5,000 or $10,000. The figure depends, of course, on your responsibilities; you need to know what you're going to do before a figure can be determined. In sales, for example, if you will be earning an all-commission income, then the commission figure is what you negotiate.

When asked about your expectations, be truthful. But, at the same time, say that the final figure depends on the job itself. In many cases, as you talk with decision makers, you will uncover other areas where your skills could be helpful. Just because you are pleased by the offer, there is no reason to lose sight of your overall objectives. Look on salary.com for the figure that's appropriate for your education and level of skill in your geographic area.

In chapter 8 Elaine showed her employer that she could recruit and, at the same time, lead in-house career development training. She wanted to work part-time from her home so that she could set up her own schedule. The owner had no way of knowing about her energy level and desire until she told him what she could do for him. It was a case of one entrepreneur talking to another!

Three Questions to Ask Yourself

Let us say, for example, that you are offered a base salary of $40,000 with benefits (medical, vacations, profit sharing, and so on) that total $5,000. Do not accept the offer on the spot unless you are absolutely sure. Take twenty-four hours or the weekend to think about it. Ask yourself three questions:

1. Does this salary match my earlier goals? Do not forget the figure you wrote in your affirmation exercise in chapter 3. How flexible do I want to be?

2. Is this position a match for my current abilities? My values?

3. Most important, since finding my passion is a process, will this package prepare me and provide continuing growth for my long-range goals? In other words, is this the next step in the process, and will this job prepare me for the next step?

If your answer is yes to all three questions, accept the offer. If you answer no to any of the questions, design a counteroffer that will give you what is missing. If the money is not sufficient, ask for 15 or 20 percent more. Or you can ask for additional sheltered fringes, such as a car, a parking space, travel, vacation time, or entertainment expenses rather than money. Your tax bracket will make the difference here. Check the tax tables to see what you would actually take home. What matters is your net, not your gross, figure.

Most job offers encompass a range of $3,000 to $6,000 a year, depending on your skills and background. In a very small firm that employs fewer than ten people, for example, be sure to ask about profit sharing. When someone extends an offer, you are in a good position to counter it. Do it. What can you lose? At the very worst, all they can say is no. Then it is up to you to ask in turn for an early salary review or some written commitment that ties your performance to the salary or bonuses you want. Try to structure a compromise in which everyone wins. It is a matter of maturity and realism on both sides. Finding and keeping competent people is hard: ask any employer. Remember that you are the kind of dedicated worker they hope will walk in the door. But they don't know you exist until you put yourself in front of them.

The second question you ask yourself refers to your job function. Ask your employer for the duties you would like. Show him or her why these are important to you. As in all negotiation, this conversation is best conducted face-to-face. Your sincerity and accurate self-knowledge are very persuasive. Do not force issues or try to sell yourself. Present your requests calmly and confidently. It is in this negotiating stage that you will most appreciate all the experience you have gained by using the process that leads to your passion. You already know the alternatives, and you do not limit your thinking, believing that you must settle for less than what you really want.

The answer to the third question, whether this offer will assist you in your total development, comes after you have reviewed all the work you have done (the autobiography, the exercises, and the results of all your meetings). Add up the pluses and minuses. Be realistic. Listen to your instincts. Then write down your assessment of your unmet needs and how the job can be expanded to meet those needs. Perhaps the job can be designed to include those areas after you have proven yourself. Take a copy of your draft with you when you meet with your prospective employer so you can quickly come to an agreement that satisfies you both.

RANKING JOB CHARACTERISTICS

To avoid confusion while you are interviewing with different companies, copy the following Factor Evaluation Work Sheet into your journal and use it to rank each of them on a scale of 1 to 10, according to how fully the job and the company fit the job characteristics you are looking for. This is a good time to review your work on values in chapter 3. What job characteristics were most important to you then? Have your values shifted at all?

For example, often my clients select independence when they do the exercise in chapter 3. Then it turns out that they value security, at least for now. If you find this to be true for you, alter your goal accordingly. If compensation is more important now than creativity, find a job that pays well. Once you are financially stable and you have money saved, creativity may move up on your list of values.

Factor Evaluation Work Sheet

POSITION: _____

Job Characteristics	Company I	Rank 1–10	Company II	Rank 1–10	(etc.)
1. Achievement					
2. Advancement					
3. Aesthetics					
4. Affiliation					
5. Altruism					
6. Authority					
7. Climate					
8. Commute					
9. Compensation (initial)					
10. Compensation (in two years)					
11. Creativity					
12. Equity opp'ty					
13. Ethical harmony					
14. Harmony with Career Objective					
15. Independence					
16. Intellectual Stimulation					
17. Pressure, Stress					
18. Recognition					
19. Security					
20. Status, Title					
21. Variety					

Write your reaction to the job offer, using the above guide to rank the characteristics of the job. The job that meets the most needs is probably the right job. However, sometimes your intuition will override logic. If so, a still, small voice will say, "I know you think you want

268

that job and your chart's great; but I want this other job." Listen to this voice; it's helping you to select the job that will make you grow.

WRITING RÉSUMÉS

A résumé can be an important tool when you are looking for a job in the same field, but it can actually get in the way when you are changing careers, positions, products, or services, and of course a résumé is not necessary when you're starting your own business Then you need to design a brochure or some other marketing material that showcases what you can do for your client or customer, which you will see how to do in the next chapter.

It's best to meet people in person before you write a résumé. That way, you can find out how your skills and background can help them to achieve their goals, then tailor your résumé to fit their needs. Of course, if you are a match the résumé is already fine as it is.

If what you are already doing is transferable — fund-raising is very much like sales, for example, and marketing is the same process regardless of the product or service — then a résumé can reflect that transferability. The important question is, Do you connect emotionally with the product or service? When you make this connection you have identified your passion. There is a wrong and a right time and place to use a résumé. I've summarized those times below.

The Wrong Time and Place to Use a Résumé

1. Mailing it before an informational interview. This sends a mixed message.

2. Handing it to someone as you begin a meeting. The paper just gets in the way if used prematurely.

3. When answering an anonymous or blind want ad. The organization you want is honest and direct — there is no need for any subterfuge.

4. Circulating it in response to every opportunity in hopes that someone will respond (mass marketing yourself does not work).

The Right Time and Place to Use a Résumé

1. After you have defined your objective.

2. When it is targeted to the specific place and person you want to work with.

3. When requested by the individuals you meet with whose values match yours.

4. When you know it is right. (Follow your instincts.)

A good résumé follows logical rules. Your objective is your major premise; your qualifications the minor premise; and your education, training, and experience are the evidence that backs up your initial claim. A clearly written résumé shows the recipient in a step-by-step format that you are the person who can solve specific problems in his or her work setting. By looking at one or two pieces of paper, the recipient can follow your presentation to its logical conclusion.

For examples of how to write chronological and other kinds of résumés I recommend Joyce Lain Kennedy's book *Resumes for Dummies*.[2] Kennedy is a reporter whose "Careers Now" column appears in more than one hundred newspapers. The latest edition of her book (check out the positive customer reviews on amazon.com) helps you to create a résumé that takes advantage of today's technology, such as submitting your résumé online and choosing the format that is right for you. For people who want to move up the corporate ladder, I recommend William Montag's book *CareerJournal.Com Resume Guide for $100,000 Plus Executive Jobs*.[3] Montag is a career consultant with an outplacement firm that serves blue-chip companies such as Xerox.

The right time to send a résumé is usually after the fact — after you know what you want, and when you need to let the other person know that you have the right qualifications. Sometimes a proposal or a summary of your background is the appropriate response following an interview. Following are examples of how to write this kind of proposal.

WRITING PROPOSALS

A proposal defines the problem and presents a solution to it (you) in detail. Describe your background and the situations in which you have solved similar problems. With this approach you display your knowledge, with the language peculiar to the field — buzzwords, if you will.

The following proposal format sample is Eric's (the client who was interested in the trucking industry discussed earlier in this chapter). You will recall that Eric had met several times with individuals in both labor and management and had uncovered the need for pleasant, down-to-earth, communicative problem solvers with an understanding of the industry. Eric's personality, education, and experience as a trucker appealed to top management because they knew the "macho" style of middle management in the trucking industry was fast becoming out-of-date. Notice the logical process in Eric's thinking, the result of a great deal of introspection. The conclusion to his presentation was inevitable: I'm the person for you!

RÉSUMÉ

Objective

My short-term objective is to obtain a supervisory position in the trucking industry. My intermediate goal — within a year — is to be an operations manager. In the long run, I envision myself as the chief operations officer of a company like Delta Industries. This decision has not been taken lightly. I have worked in the trucking business as a truck driver, tester, trainer, and foreman. I am completing my degree in industrial relations at the University of San Francisco. For the past few months, I have met with senior executives in the transportation industry and have become reasonably familiar with current transportation problems: deregulation, labor, recruitment, and competition. On the basis of my experience, education, and discussions, I have decided that I wish to pursue a career in the trucking industry, primarily in operations. In this field I would use my talents to schedule and organize routes and supervise drivers in order to solve traffic-flow problems. The results would be greater profits and more satisfied drivers.

What I Have to Offer

1. *Communication.* I am an honest and friendly person who communicates well with all types of people. I've specialized in industrial relations and I know about workers' problems and can communicate effectively with them. My wide range of experience with different groups of working-class people has taught me to be patient, understanding, and adaptable. Additionally, I am a good listener and learn from each person I meet. Because I know how to listen, I can get close enough to people so that they feel free to open up. Then we're in a better position to exchange ideas. Patience with people is a key to effective communication, and I have patience.

2. *Organization.* Organization of others begins with organization of self. I've taken the time to think through my goals and objectives. I've put my priorities in order and considered my options. The foundation of good management is the ability to critically analyze information: financial and technical data on operations, market research studies, and proposals for new investments. Organizing the affairs of a company, then, begins with personal objectivity and an understanding of how to problem-solve.

3. *Creativity.* Creativity is involved in everything — from deciding on how to decorate an office to reorganizing a work schedule to calming down an angry driver. I organized and led a creative volunteer project at an elementary school in San Francisco when I was a student at

San Francisco State University and learned that creative ideas like the ones I have are always available for future use in yet unforeseen circumstances. Once I drove home a disabled truck by using a coat hanger I found on the side of the road. Creativity is merely a matter of looking at a problem in a different (and sometimes unconventional) way.

4. *Leadership.* Leadership results from early and varied experience with independence. I was raised to be independent. Rather than blindly following someone, I choose colleagues I can learn from. I choose those I follow based on what I want to accomplish. By selecting my mentors wisely, I have strengthened my own leadership qualities.

No wonder this proposal proved irresistible to the man who received it. Because Eric knew himself and his values, he got the job.

When to Use a Proposal

The proposal format is suitable for situations in which the position you are seeking is still to be defined, in which the employer or potential business partner or client is still in the stage of thinking about his or her needs.

It is a myth that company owners, managers, and clients always know what they need to solve their problems — as any management consultant can tell you. Many times they are not even aware they have a problem. An objective outsider (you) can often see a problem and its solution very quickly. You can use this aspect of human nature to your advantage when you find a position, a niche you would like to fill. Take time to summarize the problem, then the solution. Then set up a meeting during which you go over your conclusions. Writing a proposal is a good way to check out your impressions and to show what you can do on your own. This approach is also effective for project and contract work.

HONESTY WORKS

When all is said and done about interviews — and other job-search techniques — doing what one is not supposed to do often proves to be the solution. There are never hard-and-fast rules; use your instincts, as I've said many times by now. Many years ago, when I was interviewing for a government job-training contract, I stopped in the middle of my presentation, since the woman to whom I was making the presentation kept jiggling back and forth in her swivel chair, which I found distracting. So I turned away from my flip chart and said, "What are you doing in this place?"

Janice looked startled; then she sat back in her chair.

"What do you mean, what am I doing here?" she asked, as she drummed her fingers on her desk.

"Well, you're so restless, it makes me think you don't want to be here. You seem to be the entrepreneurial type — I can't imagine that you'd be happy in government work." After she got over her shock, Janice said she had owned a public relations business, but it went belly up during the recession so she'd taken the job as director of the government program to make ends meet.

"Oh," I said. "No wonder you're so restless." Then I went back to my presentation.

Janice told me later that she decided right then that if I had the guts to tell her what I thought of her with so much money at stake, then I was the person she wanted to work with her clients — street-smart, low-income people who knew how to con most social workers.

"Well, you were so obviously bored, I had to say something," I laughed.

The government contract with the city gave me a steady income while I wrote the first draft of *Work with Passion*. Janice later went on to become an executive recruiter. Today she travels all over the world to find the right people for her clients, a great job for a restless extrovert.

In the next chapter, I will discuss the characteristics of people who start their own businesses. I will also provide examples of clients who decided to take the narrow path to freedom.

SUMMARY

Passion Secret *9* *Trust your instincts.*

1. Pay attention to conversations that excite or fascinate you (passion clue!). These may be interviews in disguise.

2. An interview is like a racquetball game: stay flexible and play the ball as it comes to you.

3. The right work for you may not be what you'd choose consciously, but it is the work that will make you grow to your full potential.

4. Passion places money secondary to satisfaction.

5. You are responsible for creating the agenda in an interview. Your three objectives are: (1) to present yourself, your strengths and goals, (2) to gain information, and (3) to ask for referrals.

6. Ask "plus" and "minus" questions in your interview in three areas: personal, company, and industry. Focus especially on the "minus" company questions, because here is where the problems are, and ask yourself if you want to solve these problems.

7. Always write a thank-you letter or email following all your meetings.

8. Learn how to negotiate a job offer.

9. There is a right and a wrong time to use a résumé.

10. Write a proposal when the job position is still in the stages of definition.

11. Summarize what you learned after each meeting using the Research Interview Data Sheet.

12. Use the Factor Evaluation Work Sheet to assess each company you visit. Evaluate the companies and the jobs based on whether both use your top-five strengths and fulfill your top-five values.

13. Do what you are not supposed to do. Honesty can be disarming. If it is motivated by genuine concern, candor is irresistible.

10 STARTING YOUR OWN BUSINESS

During your job search you may have discovered that you are primarily a solo type. If so, you'd probably be happier working for yourself. One way you can tell that it's time to go out on your own is when you have learned all you need to know working for someone else. If you are not aware that you've gone as far as you can in the current job, sometimes there is tension between you and your bosses, supervisors, and co-workers. Your creative self screams for room to spread its wings. If you do not take the initiative you are often fired, demoted, or moved laterally.

Before you start your own business, I recommend that you master the basics of business. Mastering the basics is best achieved by working with or for someone in the same business for three to five years. It also helps if you had entrepreneurial experience when you were young, or if one or both parents were entrepreneurs. Here is where your autobiography comes into play again: When did you learn about business, and from whom? What was your impression of people who work for themselves? Was it positive or negative? Your past business experience will color your view of business today.

For example, you may have a negative view of business because of your parents' attitudes toward it or because of what you experienced while working for incompetent people (these people are like teachers who turn kids off to learning). Competent chief executive officers and owners of well-run businesses leave you with a completely different impression of business because they treat people as their most important assets. They will not tolerate those who mistreat their subordinates or who can't or won't do the jobs for which they are paid.

Always look at the top of any company to assess that company's future, since the leader's philosophy filters down into every aspect of the organization. Notice what kind of people they hire. Remember that first-rate people hire first-rate people, second-rate people pick third-rate people, and third-rate people choose people they can control.

In the decades since *Work with Passion* was first published, I've noticed a trend toward entrepreneurial activity that is still growing by leaps and bounds. This trend is in large part due to technology and unpredictable economic times. While it is distressing to be worrying about the economy's ups and downs, anxiety can be a creative force that increases your ability to think. The more your mind adapts to change, the more flexible it becomes. And the more flexible you are, the more likely it is you'll make a good entrepreneur.

Thus the benefit in the center of technological and economic change is the creation of entrepreneurs, high-energy men and women who bring the economy and the world to new heights. They succeed because they focus on what works: satisfying their customers' needs and adapting as those needs change without sacrificing their own core values.

The fastest growing businesses these days are information businesses, started and run by people who use their intelligence to help others live better lives. Overhead is low when your inventory is between your ears. If intellectual stimulation is one of your top-five values and you have the discipline, maturity, and desire to succeed in your own business, then using what you know will make that dream come true.

Passion Secret *10* *Freedom comes from self-discipline.*

The entrepreneur usually makes three tries before he or she gets it right. The first try at business is usually something like, "You take the East Coast, and I'll take the West Coast." Of course it fails because the goal was unrealistic. The entrepreneur may have to go back to work for someone else for a few years to recoup his or her losses. (Here I'm not implying that you are in partnership or part of a team when you start a business, although you may be. I'm simply describing the overly optimistic thinking that characterizes beginning entrepreneurs.)

The next attempt at starting a business is something like, "Okay, you take the southern part of the state and I'll take the northern part." The second try at a business almost succeeds, but it doesn't flourish because the entrepreneur's values are still unclear. The final try at a business goes like this: "Okay, you take your street and I'll take my street." Then success comes because the entrepreneur now knows his or her values. The "street" he or she takes can be as a sole proprietor, with a partner, or a group of people whose values are a match. By this time the entrepreneur knows exactly what to do, how to do it, and what not to do.

The process of getting your business right does not necessarily mean that you open and close three businesses before one of them works. Nor is it always chronological. You can go through this three-step process in the same business, tweaking it until it works. In other words, as soon as you get your values straight, and you become more realistic, the enterprise succeeds. In that sense, your business is a good therapist, since it makes you face reality.

All along the way you are learning and growing, making mistakes and (I hope) correcting them before they become disasters. When you are willing to make the extra effort that independence requires, entrepreneurship offers rich rewards — emotional, spiritual, and financial. If you have outgrown the need for supervision and structure, then your foundation is secure.

CHARACTERISTICS OF THE ENTREPRENEUR

Following are nine characteristics of successful entrepreneurs. Check the ones that describe you. The ones you leave blank will tell you what you need to work on in order to live life your own way.

1. You are responsible and ethical. You do not play the roles of victim, rescuer, or persecutor.

2. You are organized and efficient.

3. You are intellectually honest. You see people and events as they are, not as you want them to be.

4. You are mature. You make molehills out of molehills.

5. When it comes to money, you pay on time. You don't take on more debt than you can handle. You know exactly where you are financially at all times.

6. You are quick to adapt to change; serving your customers is more important than being right.

7. You are wary of fast growth, so your pace is slow.

8. You achieve balance between your needs and the needs of others.

9. You are independent and do not want to work for anyone else. You prefer to make your own decisions.

You may not match all of the above characteristics all the time, but on the whole you live according to these principles, either by yourself or in tandem with partners. Does the thought terrify you? Good! Terror is another characteristic of entrepreneurs, but it is creative, not the kind of terror that paralyzes them.

My Story

I became familiar with terror when I started my own career counseling practice. I was so scared to go out on my own it took a showdown out of a 1930s gangster movie to blast me out of a plush office I shared with a partner in a skyscraper in San Francisco. But to my surprise I was much happier when I landed around the corner from the skyscraper in which I used to work, in a back-to-basics basement office, where I began to write *Work with Passion*.

Although I was sure I would wind up as a bag lady, pushing a grocery cart down some lonely street, instead I got the government contract I mentioned in the last chapter, and then I changed my entire life: I left an unhealthy marriage, moved, moved again, and eventually began working with clients out of my home, a radical way to work in the early 1980s. Yet it turned out to be the ideal setting for my clients and me, and it is to this day.

I would never have succeeded had I not spent hours, days, months, and years learning the business with partners who had been in the business before. Even though I disagreed with their policies, the experience prepared me to change the business into a reflection of my values when I went out on my own. From them I learned how to get the money in the door, how to advertise, how to service the sale, and to be patient with the rhythm of the business, so I knew not to give up hope during slow cycles.

The problem was that I wasn't sure career counseling was right for me when I got into it. But when my partner lost interest in it, I took over because I could not abandon clients who had already paid an up-front fee (I wasn't charging by the hour then, as I do now). As soon as I did the business my way, however, I discovered that I liked it, which was why I survived. Remember the subtitle of this book is "how to do what you love for a living." You may be in the right business too, but if you're like me you won't fall in love with it until you do it your way.

My emotional strength surprised me as well as those who watched me go through traumas that would have staggered many other people. But I could not imagine getting a job; the freedom to experiment was enough to keep me going every day. It also helped that I had a book to write, something creative to do while slogging through my clients' and my own fears. I also had the support of clients who thought I was great, even when I fell forty floors into my basement office. This "failure" proved to be an opportunity in disguise, since my clients all said they felt more comfortable in the quaint, down-to-earth office.

Perhaps my clients stayed with me because I never treated them as though they were sick and I was well, although there were times when I wondered why they came to me for help when I had so many problems of my own. Yet regardless of my circumstances they knew that I was not afraid to tell it like it is. They also knew that I did not want to sit around listening to problems unless my client was willing to solve them by taking big risks: leaving an abusive person, whether spouse, lover, family member, or so-called friend; getting the necessary counseling; selling the house; quitting the job; starting the business; sending the grown-up kids out on their own; writing the letter or email. Make no mistake, I know how frightening it is to take risks; you must be clearheaded, which is hard to do when your lips are numb and your heart is pounding like a hammer against your rib cage. But I would rather risk the chance that I could be wrong than wait until I am 100 percent sure. I could be dead by then, life gone on without me. A good rule of thumb for me is that if I feel bored and restless I had better take action, or I send out signals that draw change to me, sometimes in unpleasant ways.

The most frustrating times in our lives are when we do not know what to do, the "hell of not knowing," as Jung called that miserable state of mind. When I am uncertain, I concentrate on what I can control, and I turn everything else over to God. Meanwhile, I take care of business details, check more books out of the library, go for longer runs in the morning, or I focus on everyday interactions. Often some unconscious information surfaces that needs to be assimilated, insight I could never have gained in busier or more successful times.

In our highly extroverted society, we are so bombarded with information that our minds need to download periodically, emptied of useless thoughts and ideas. Once my mind is quiet and clear I know what to do or not do. Until then, I wait.

WHEN IT'S TIME TO GO OUT ON YOUR OWN

When you've decided that it's time to take some big risks and go it alone, always begin with a small step. One of my clients, George, had the choice of early retirement or part-time employment. I suggested that he stay on in the part-time position because he would need the income while he developed his business. After two years, George was making enough money to cover his expenses, so he quit his job.

Yet if you have enough income saved and you are experienced at what you want to do, the wisest move may be to leave your job so that you can concentrate on the new work. One of my clients had two years' income saved when he plunged full-time into his new business, writing newsletters and brochures for his customers in technology businesses. Within ten months, Carl was making as much as he had in his old job; in eighteen months, he had surpassed his old income. A decade later, he cut back on his business and his overhead so that he could finish his first adventure novel for young people. Carl's story is another example of how the process of finding your passion works; as he grew in confidence he took on new challenges.

Another client, the top salesperson in his small company, felt as though the owner stifled him, so he thought he should start his own business. I suggested he talk to the boss first about what was bothering him since people often misread their bosses. To his surprise, the boss said he understood Alec's frustration and then he suggested that Alec consider golf lessons to see if that could be a career possibility. The boss had been out on the links with Alec, so he knew Alec was an unusually gifted athlete. "Golf will probably be your passion," I laughed.

Within a few months, Alec was able to keep up with his golf teacher, who told Alec to think about going on tour.

"I know I can do this, Nancy," he said, his tall, athletic frame sprawled on my couch. "But how do I make money while I learn?"

"Why do you have to quit your job?" I asked. "You have the kind of schedule that would allow you to play golf in the early morning and make sales calls the rest of the day, don't you? And your boss is flexible, right?"

"Yes, he is; my time is pretty much my own," Alec said. "In fact, he says he feels proud of me."

"You'll know in a year if competing in golf tournaments is right for you. I'd be surprised if you leave your business expertise behind. In the meantime, you'll have fun, make more sales, and learn about the game."

Alec's pent-up energy and perfectionism were ideal for the game he loved.

"I see all those senior men on the golf tours, and I think, gosh, I could do this the rest of my life."

Alec's natural athletic ability was a theme in his autobiography; he had kinesthetic gifts that he needed to apply in order to not self-destruct. But it took the passage of time for him to see how those gifts could be used. History had to catch up with him: when senior golf tournaments become popular, Alec was inspired to begin the game in his thirties. He needed an activity that he could do on his own, not a business. Of course, this presumed that he had enough talent to develop into a profitable golfing career.

Many of my older clients find new ways to apply what they know later on in their careers, thanks to the changes in societal attitudes toward aging. Retirement is death to creative types, like the personal banker who came to see me toward the end of her career.

"You need more than the work you do in the bank," I said. "Why don't you write a book about how to manage money?"

"How can I write about what I don't do well myself?"

"Writing the book will force you to discipline yourself," I said. "That's what writing did for me. You were an English teacher, you know how powerful the process of writing can be."

Chris lived on her severance pay while she wrote draft after draft. Her book changed over time, as did her behavior.

"Unemployment is a great leveler," she said as she described how she felt about the meetings she attended. "They really liked my presentation on how to survive during unemployment."

"That can be one of the chapters in your book," I suggested.

"As I wrote I realized how childish I'd been with my boss in my last job. She was my mother, and I was rebelling against her. I spent money to cover up for my feelings of inadequacy. But I was not aware of that at the time."

Chris went back to work as a personal banker in a smaller, friendlier bank. She said her wealthy clients were a source of pleasure and information.

"It's no accident you're back in that job," I said. "You can learn from those clients about how to manage wealth."

After a few months in her new job, however, the same old problems cropped up again. Chris felt pressured by the constant demands on her, the interruptions, and the continual push for more customers. We discussed how to relieve her stress, when suddenly she said, "Well, I don't have to get everything done every day, do I?"

We laughed — Chris's impatience was out in the open.

"Maybe it's not your job, but your attitude that needs changing," I suggested, knowing how many times excessive striving caused me to lose my balance. "Isn't patience the key to success with money?"

"Of course. My wealthy clients didn't get there overnight. They worked hard for their money, or if they inherited it, they still manage it well."

Often we are placed in situations we would not choose consciously, but a higher wisdom than ours knows what is best for us — and frustration is our greatest teacher. As human beings, we can be perverse in our belief that a quick-and-easy way to solve our problems exists. Rather than resenting her job, Chris learned to adopt the attitude of her clients.

"I'm getting paid now for my speaking engagements," she said the next time we talked.

Chris stayed with the small bank until retirement; then she started an English tutoring business for high school students. Like Philip and Brian (from chapters 7 and 9) she'd come full circle, back to her love of language and teaching, but with solid financial skills under her belt. Her story demonstrates how following your passion remodels every part of your life. When she was mature emotionally and financially, Chris was ready to start her own business.

"Now I'll never have to retire," she said.

Her situation is an example of what it's like when you have a skill that comes so naturally that you take it for granted. Naturally does not mean easily, however; giving birth is natural, but as every mother will tell you it isn't easy! Chris loves language enough to work hard at it, but she is an extrovert, so she didn't have the patience to work on her book until she got it right, so she let that project go. However, she never loses patience with her students as she did while working for the bank, a sign that she is in the right job now.

Another older client, Jerry, was in a partnership with a man I knew was dishonest, although Jerry did not want to acknowledge this fact because he thought he could not make it on his own. But until he saw his partner as he was, Jerry was doomed to failure. (Remember that intellectual honesty is a hallmark of the successful entrepreneur.)

"I know this scares you, Jerry, but you're not going to succeed until you're on your own — you're not a partner type, you're a solo," I said.

Jerry was afraid to be alone because he'd learned early to give up his need for privacy to be a companion to his single, alcoholic mother. When he married he gave up his need for solitude to please both his first and second wife. This was why he turned a blind eye to his partner's dishonesty, and why he drank so much; that was his way of getting away.

"You must have been miserable all those years," I said. "No wonder you drank all the time."

On the contrary, Jerry said he thought he'd led a "charmed life."

"Oh, you were under a spell all right," I laughed. Jerry's first written want list (see chapter 4) was full of material possessions: boats, houses, cars, and money — goals he set in a seminar he attended before we met.

"What do you want all that stuff for at your age?" I asked. "I'd be worn out just thinking about it."

Jerry said he was so upset by what I said in our meeting he took the wrong turn off the freeway on his way home.

"Well, that's symbolic, isn't it?" I asked, and we both laughed.

As Jerry thought about what he really wanted to do, his new want list began with "time to think and research," a much more introverted and therefore authentic goal. Though he made his living as a certified public accountant, he wanted to use his financial knowledge to be a witness for trial lawyers. "If you want to testify in court, I'd suggest you get your life in shape first," I said. "Make your clients pay you on time. Discipline your staff, and set better boundaries with your wife. When you're in court you'll need to project confidence. As it is now the jury will pick up on your lack of confidence and question your authority."

People like Jerry often fail because they are afraid if they are honest people will get angry with them. As a result of this fear, Jerry was a magnet for people who took advantage of him, like his dishonest partner, his demanding wife, and his lazy staff members. Jerry's inability to set limits with himself and others was rooted in a childhood that was bereft of affection. So he had adapted by deciding to give and give, hoping that he would get love in return. Changing that decision was difficult, but when Jerry decided to love himself enough to say no he became the expert to whom lawyers turned for advice and counsel.

As I've said, success in our careers must be preceded by the willingness to accept responsibility for our choices. When our behavior doesn't work, we must change it without self-recrimination. Then our lives and careers can move forward.

LETTING YOURSELF CHANGE FOR THE BETTER

As I've stated earlier, any change, even for the better, is stressful. We are so used to struggle that it is hard to adjust to a life that works. My client Chris, who got laid off from the bank, wondered how she ever tolerated the life she had led in more chaotic times. Meanwhile, a former co-worker remained fastened to a negative attitude toward the bank. Depressed and burdened by a mortgage, she was forced to take a job she did not like. Chris, on the other hand, sold her house, sent her grown children on their way, and eliminated the clutter from her life. It took a decade of change and personal growth before she started her tutoring business.

"Well, I couldn't expect to correct a lifetime of mismanagement overnight," she said wisely. With her attitude, Chris can't fail. And imagine how her students will benefit from what she's learned. They'll be learning much more than English!

One of my clients found it hard to believe that after a long career in computer systems he could start a photography business. I encouraged Dan to use his considerable talent after I received his Christmas card. On the front of the card was a spectacular color photograph of a mountaintop in Peru. Dan was an avid traveler and mountain climber; the pictures he took on his many trips got rave reviews from many people, he said.

"Work as a systems contractor while your photography business grows," I said. "In five years you'll make all the money you need from your photography. Meanwhile, you'll be learning how to do a business you can do for the rest of your life."

Just to show you how the unconscious mind cooperates when you are on the right track, the night after we spoke Dan had a dream in which he was with a group of people who were preparing for a play. The director in the dream was a woman who said Dan had no part — he was late, so she'd given it to someone else. He walked over to the person who had his script and took it from him. As Dan thumbed through the pages, he thought the others in the cast needed to know the context of the play — the past — otherwise they would never be able to understand it.

"I think the dream means that I lost what was mine because of internal conflict," Dan said. "And that now I'm going to do what I want to do I'll reclaim that part with joy." Several years later, the Society of American Travel Writers selected Dan as the Photographer of the Year. Recently, his stunning photographs appeared in a best-selling coffee table book about the San Francisco Bay.

Sometimes the need for security can draw us back to the familiar when we feel overwhelmed by the unknown. The void is frightening, but our tolerance for not knowing is a direct measure of personal growth. One of my clients kept going back to the past, working for bosses in the insurance business who lied and overextended themselves, then blamed Larry for their failures — a repeat of Larry's interaction with his alcoholic father.

"You'll never be happy until you're on your own," I said.

"But then I'd have no one to blame, would I?" he laughed. "But I've tried so many things, Nancy, I'm not sure I know what I want to do."

"What fascinates you?" I asked.

"Houses and buildings," Larry said. "I subscribe to every home magazine and journal you can imagine. And I watch all the home improvement shows on cable television. I just love to see them take a home or a room and remodel it."

Today Larry works as an independent appraiser of houses and buildings with two older partners. Since he is a partner type, the dynamic of give and take is perfect for him. In his spare time, he finds and fixes up houses for resale. Finding the right appraisal position took a great deal of trial and error. Just when he was ready to give up, Larry would write long emails to me that always ended with, "Well, I'm not going to give up, but I sure am frustrated."

I'd write back to Larry each time, encouraging him to be patient with the process and himself. In time, I knew that he'd find the right niche, but first he'd have to become more self-disciplined, which the process was forcing him to become.

When he went to work with his new partners Larry's email was full of appreciation for the journey. He said he kept hoping to find an easy way out, which had been his father's problem.

"I understand Jim better now. I hate to admit it, but I was in a hurry too," Larry said about his father. "That's made it easier to forgive him."

Larry's father's impatience had left Larry feeling hesitant, unsure, and afraid to make mistakes, which is the case for all children whose parents or teachers are impatient. As he learned, his father was not the problem, but he had provided Larry with a bad example. When Larry took on failure as a challenge rather than something that should not have happened to him, he understood his father better; then he found the right business.

EXPAND ON WHAT YOU KNOW

As you master your craft you invent new techniques, such as the drapery hanger who invents a pleating machine, the computer expert who develops new software and creates a company in the process, the champion ice skater who writes a book about his career and life, or the doctor who creates a new medical device: all these breakthroughs were the result of expanding on what they knew.

Normally, it takes eight to ten years to become good at what you do. At that point, you are ready to innovate. Notice that when you do anything over and over you get better at it, whether it is baking a loaf of bread or running a restaurant. Your experience is valuable; expanding on what you know how to do is so simple it is hard to believe you can get paid for your expertise. As Krishnamurti says in his book *The First and Last Freedom*,[1] quiet observation of any problem reveals its solution.

If you had a paper route or a cottage business of some kind when you were young, such as making or selling a product or service out of your family's home — or even if you were a waiter or waitress — you have entrepreneurial skills, since you made your own decisions. Be proud of that experience, no matter how little money you made. The courage and energy it takes to wait tables, for example, is often underestimated. Some of my clients who were waiters and waitresses changed their minds about restaurant work after we talked.

"Working in a restaurant is demeaning," Joan said to me when we talked about her current job.

"Not if you think of the restaurant as your own business," I said.

"What do you mean, my own business? They own the restaurant."

"I know, but you have access to five or six tables that are cash-flow sources. You are like an independent contractor; the restaurant picks up the overhead, and you and your effort produce income. Your tables and what happens on your shift are your business," I said.

Joan's eyes lit up. "I never thought of it like that — but it's true! My attitude determines my tips. Of course the kitchen has to run smoothly, too. But overall, the cash I generate from my tables depends totally on my performance."

Before our discussion Joan was not aware that her waitressing job or working in her parents' convenience market when she was in high school could be considered entrepreneurial.

"Now you know why you're not happy working for someone else," I said to Joan. "You're like your parents; you're independent."

When Joan was offered a job managing the restaurant where she worked she decided to accept it and, in her off hours, take classes at a culinary school.

"I need to develop my management skills," she said, explaining her reason for accepting the managerial position at the restaurant. "I want to develop a client-based cooking business rather than manage a restaurant, though. That way, I can control my time. I've talked to so many couples lately who have come into the restaurant. They all say they'd love a personal chef and to give them a call when I get started."

Do you see how Joan used interviews right where she worked to find her passion? She did this with customers who already knew and trusted her, high-earning individuals who wanted a personal chef like Joan to make life easier for them.

GET PAID FOR TEACHING WHAT YOU KNOW

If you have a skill you would like to teach others, offer to speak to groups that would be interested in hearing what you have to say. If you are shy about appearing in front of a group, join Toastmasters, or take speech classes to learn how to present yourself. If you are a skilled speaker, consider developing a brochure that markets what is close to your heart. Contact a speakers' bureau and let them know you are available.

Teach courses at the local community college or in a university extension program — an excellent way to develop yourself and your business. You may have a seminar organization in your city. Contact the owner and let him or her know about your topic. Use the interviewing approach discussed in chapter 9; learn about others before you ask for the sale.

One of my clients loved languages and Europe. She was fluent in three languages, largely because she grew up in a multilingual home (you see how your autobiography holds the key to finding your passion?). Francesca wondered how she could make money using her love of languages while living in Europe.

I suggested that Francesca create a business teaching conversational language in social settings, since I knew she'd be bored in a classroom setting. She was very excited about the idea so the next step was to hire a graphic artist to design business cards, stationery, and a brochure with images of a woman working with others in business and social settings, such as conference rooms and museums. He also included a beautiful picture of Francesca. What follows is the text of the brochure she and I put together. Francesca tells me she feels so fortunate to live and work in a beautiful country like Spain, with people who are happy to pay her for what she knows.

Conversational English and Italian in Business and Social Settings

Language Service to Businesses

The success of your business depends on your ability to communicate effectively with your customers. If they speak American English or Italian, I can help you and your employees improve your conversational skill in one or both of these languages in individual and group sessions. I also offer intensive language study before important events, such as formal speeches, meetings and conferences, sales or other presentations, and job negotiations. My extensive training in theater is especially useful when you need to improve the way you present yourself to an audience.

Language Service to Individuals

For individual clients who wish to learn conversational American English or Italian, I offer a relaxed, fun way to master both languages. Together we go for walks to cafés, museums, and stores, weaving in and out of the language you want to know. These interactive sessions last from 1 to 2 hours, depending on your needs. This service is one-on-one, or with a maximum of two people.

Fees

Individual and business rates are by the hour.

Francesca expanded this brochure by discussing her extensive language education, training, and experience. She concluded the text with the following: "Because of my education and travels within the United States and in Europe, I possess the ability to understand both the European and American client. I am adaptable to various work environments and personalities; I communicate with patience, always listening to my clients' needs so that I can help them to become fluent in their target language." Here you have the entrepreneur who embodies the concept of working with passion: Francesca loves what she does and where she does it; she focuses on her customers, and in the process she makes all the money she needs.

Just as Francesca found a way to charge for something she knew well and that came naturally to her, if you find that other people are always asking for your help, consider charging by the hour for your time. You are not going to be a lawyer without training and certification, but many services begin as an extension of what you've mastered: making baskets, home remodeling, gardening, upholstering, or editing. There are a myriad of ways to serve customers' needs.

To get ideas for what you'd like to do on your own, study the many how-to books in bookstores and look at websites that abound with helpful information for viewers. The originators of these e-businesses worked until they figured out how to go online with their expertise. The Internet is a fertile nursery for business ideas and will be for a long time to come. Visit entrepreneurial websites. The best is entrepreneur.com, a site that contains a wealth (no pun intended!) of information on all kinds of start-ups, home business, management, finance, and links to experts in every area of business. You can also go to any bookstore and walk down the how-to aisles — you will be amazed by the ingenuity and the variety of the information offered to readers.

SETTING BOUNDARIES WITH OTHERS

Any successful enterprise requires a great deal of time and energy, much more than you expect when you begin. So to succeed in your business you must use your energy wisely. If you are married or living with someone you need to set good boundaries, especially if you have children. Relationships take time, which means you must not scatter your energy with too much socializing. Even the smartest entrepreneurs founder on the rocks of overextension.

One of my clients who worked out of her home was forced to confront her tendency to get distracted. Alice spent long hours on the phone with her mother, who could not understand why she couldn't talk with her daughter whenever she wanted since she worked out of her home. The mother was from a different generation; she had never worked, so she did not understand that the calls interrupted my client's business.

Finally, Alice asked her mother to call at a certain time twice a week. At first her mother was angry since she was used to getting her way; but when Alice persisted she adapted to the new schedule. This greatly reduced Alice's anger, since she had been stewing over her mother's intrusiveness for years. Not surprisingly, Alice set better boundaries in all areas of her life, with her husband, her children, and her clients.

Owning your own business demands so much of you it is vital that you select a compatible personal relationship. If you share values with your intimate partner, you will have few conflicts, which will free up time that is wasted in arguments and misunderstandings. If your partner is not sympathetic to the demands of your business, he or she may think you are a workaholic when the business and your customers are on your mind.

When you work with passion all sides of you fit well together, like a well-designed garment. This cohesiveness between the private and public life is not the case for most employed people. So be sure you live with or marry an entrepreneur or a person who loves his or her work; otherwise you may conclude that there is something wrong with you because you are so excited about your work.

Many of my clients are surprised and dismayed when the person who is closest to them starts to sabotage their success. Before he or she was supportive, because my client was miserable and, as we all know, misery loves company. But once my client was happy, envy disguised as criticism raised its ugly head. Be prepared for that all-too-human emotion to arise when you love your work with all your heart and soul. Give the problem back to where it belongs, to the person who is envious of your happiness.

Difference in temperament is also the root of many battles at home. Time alone is vital when you are an introverted entrepreneur. If you are an extrovert, you are energized by contact with others. If you are an introvert and you choose an extroverted partner, make sure that both of you allow for the needs of each other. For example, if you said that you were a number 3 on a scale of 1 to 10 in the introvert/extrovert scale on page 174, you need to be alone 70 percent of the time, at work and in relationships.

Conversely, if you said you were a 7 on the same scale, you will need to be alone 30 percent of the time, at work and in relationships. It is not difficult to see what happens when you marry or live with an introverted partner. He or she will be overwhelmed by your need to spend time together, and you will feel lonely when your partner wants to be alone. Go back to your five values; when your partner shares most of these values, your relationship will work like a charm.

We are all a mixture of introversion and extroversion. It's important for you to know what that mixture is for you, and for the person with whom you live. Accurate self-knowledge leads to good boundaries and mutual respect, which are crucial to your mental, emotional, and physical health — and to working with passion.

SUMMARY

Passion Secret *10* *Freedom comes from self-discipline.*

1. You are ready to start your own business when you have mastered the basics of business: responsibility, organization, efficiency, honesty with yourself and others, adapting to change, managing money, balancing your needs and the needs of others, making your own decisions, and trusting in your judgment.

2. Be brave enough to let go of behavior that does not work.

3. When it is time to go out on your own, start with a small step; then set up a plan of action for the long term.

4. Be open to the unknown. Allow time for integrating the past before you proceed to the future.

5. Know that age is on your side when you sell what you know.

6. Consider writing or teaching what you know. You may be surprised by how much you know once you begin to write about it. Consider marketing that knowledge. Who knows? You may create the next search engine or award-winning website!

7. Attend entrepreneurial meetings. Arrange meetings with owners of businesses you find interesting. You may have heard something you were not ready to hear the last time you

met with an entrepreneur. Check out entrepreneur.com. You will be inspired by the wealth of information available.

8. Do not go backward. You will only antagonize people when you associate with people who are not at your level of development.

9. Keep the job you have while you grow in skill.

10. Be careful not to overextend yourself. The symptoms of overextension are irritability, fatigue, and pessimism.

11. Choose your life partner wisely. Make sure your partner loves his or her work before you walk down the aisle! Check to see if you are forcing yourself to be with others more than is comfortable for you. Or, if you need more companionship, do not isolate yourself. Knowing who you are and what you need to be happy and content is your responsibility — no exceptions.

11 CELEBRATING WHEN YOU GET THERE

You have read most of this book, you have done all the exercises, and here you are, at the end of the journey — at least at the end of our journey together. Now you are ready to take the eleventh and final step to finding your passion: celebrating when you get there. How do you know when you have?

In the words of Kahlil Gibran,

And all knowledge is vain save when there is work. And all
    work is empty save when there is love.
And when you work with love, you bind yourself to yourself,
    and to one another, and to God.
And what is it to work with love?
It is to weave the cloth with threads drawn from your heart,
    even as if your beloved were to wear that cloth.
It is to build a house with affection, even as if your beloved
    were to dwell in that house.
It is to sow seeds with tenderness and reap the harvest with
    joy, even as if your beloved were to eat the fruit.[1]

Passion Secret *11* *Celebrate your achievements; then continue to move on and up.*

HOW TO KNOW WHEN YOU'VE MADE IT

In the introduction I said that awakening from emotional numbness begins with a decision. You finally get tired of avoiding reality. You want to experience *life* with all of its trials, tribulations, and joys, rather than play it safe. Before, you may have thought if you were uncomfortable there was something wrong with you. But now you know that discomfort is a sign that you are stretching beyond your limits, and that if you persevere in your efforts you will soon feel as if you are in a new and better world.

Below I have listed twelve ways to know when you've left your old self behind. Remember that when you are fully alive the process of challenge and growth is never ending. You set and then reach a goal, you celebrate your victory, and then you move on and up in your life.

You See Every Part of Your Life as a Success

You know that you have arrived when you see all your experiences as necessary to your growth. As you look at past choices, you understand that you did the best you could at the time, given your level of awareness. You are patient with yourself during this process, forgiving yourself quickly for not seeing what may now seem obvious. You know that awakening from emotional numbness takes time, so you do not rush that dynamic process. As soon as a shift in your thinking occurs, insight comes.

Your World Is Vivid

When you have made it you experience your world as vivid and intense. All hues sharpen and become more defined — as they did for the great English poet John Keats. The editors of the *Norton Anthology of English Literature* write that since Keats combines all his senses in his poems, the reader is able to fully apprehend Keats's experience. Keats experienced an intense delight at the sheer existence of things outside himself, an astonishing poetic power that reminded Keats's friends, as it has so many critics since, of the language of Shakespeare.[2] As the English critic, editor, and journalist John Middleton Murry said about Keats's emotional intensity and short-lived genius, "his uniqueness is such that he can be adequately interpreted only by himself."[3]

Keats embodies the principle of working with passion. He used his skill with language to imbue his poetry with his mind, body, and spirit. His short life (he died at the age of twenty-six) is a remarkable study of love's power, and his poetry reflects that power — intellectual, sensuous, aspiring.

Just as the images of great poetry startle you with their originality, feeling intensely gives you a unique experience of yourself and the world. It is as if you are in a dream and yet fully awake. You see and feel more because your heart is open and receptive, just as it was before you shut it down. Like Sleeping Beauty, you came to life with the kiss of true love: self-acceptance.

If the sun shines, that is fine with you, and if it rains, that is fine too. If a job or a relationship ends you grieve the loss and move on. In time you accept the loss as necessary to your growth and to that of the other person.

You Are Selective

At the same time that you avidly court life's experiences, you become highly selective. (Passion clue: discrimination marks the truly passionate.)

In his autobiography, the Irish poet William Butler Yeats described gathering carefully chosen experiences "as if for a collector's cabinet."[4] You reject experiences that are not good for or helpful to you once you have "gotten there." You turn down experiences that cause you to feel pain, sorrow, or guilt. You do not force yourself to be with people you do not like — including family members — or to do what you hate doing. No one can "trap" you because you do not trap yourself with illusion and self-deception. You examine your motives in the clear light of honesty, the most beautiful word in the English language.

You Are Honest and Forgiving

Our lives sometimes go in directions with traumatic results (unwise marriages, divorce, loss of life, and financial loss). You are quick to admit to and learn from your mistakes, and you set about making things right. You apologize and ask for forgiveness whenever you hurt others. You forgive those who injured you, just as you forgive yourself. You build anew from adversity and do not linger in self-recrimination or blame.

You Find Meaning in Your Experience

Those of us who have experienced the magic of giving birth have an understanding of the driving force behind creative experience. The child decides the moment of birth, not the mother. "Why all the pain, why so much time?" you ask yourself. You finally understand that nature has its own rhythm and cycle. Realizing that, you do not choose to suffer anymore. You accept all your experiences, and that is what makes them significant.

In his book *Man's Search for Meaning*, Viktor Frankl described the attributes of those who made it through the horrors of the concentration camps.[5] Those who went on to productive lives after their release saw meaning in their imprisonment. Jung says that all experience is acceptable to the conscious mind when it is given meaning.

On a lighter note, you give meaning to your experience in much the same way as the characters in the *Peanuts* comic strip do. Lucy, Charlie Brown, Linus, Schroeder, and Snoopy eventually make sense out of the conflicts in their lives, all the while making us laugh at them and ourselves. The same principle can be seen in the structure of music: tension and disharmony are resolved in the final chords, the artist's goal.

You Develop Mastery

Your desire to master a task is another clue that lets you know when you have made it. You are not satisfied with less than your best effort. Mastery is the accomplishment of a task for which you are given recognition. When you are the best, you perform with the precision of a champion. People who do what they do best do not look like they are working; rather, they look like they are playing. Olympic athletes look like they are playing when their event goes well, as do Academy Award–winning actors and actresses.

You are relaxed and confident when you are at the top of your game, whether you rear children, breed show dogs, doctor the sick, start businesses, serve the sick and needy, or take care of your customers. A young woman who works for the automobile dealership where I bought my car calls me after every service visit to see if I am satisfied. She is so sincere I doubt she realizes the effect she has on me. She just does what comes naturally — relating well to her company's customer.

Another woman I know is the director of my favorite charity, a faith-based organization that provides shelter and job assistance to homeless and battered women and their children. Her letters to donors are so full of hope and compassion it is obvious that she loves her work and the women and children she serves.

When you master what you do, you do not overcorrect or overcriticize. A good tennis coach, for example, says, "Turn your wrist half an inch; lean your body forward, into the ball; keep your knees slightly flexed." Like the master coach, you correct as you go since a slight adjustment makes all the difference between success and failure. Navigational devices on aircraft are good analogies for the principle of adjusting as you go. During flight, the computer constantly adjusts course from takeoff to landing. Rarely is the aircraft exactly on course. Ask any pilot, and he or she will tell you that being slightly off course is the norm, but the plane always lands on the right runway. Your personal navigational computer is your heart; you trust its wisdom, and so you always land right where you need to.

You Are Alert

When you have made it you are alert. You pay attention to clues in the environment, since you know there are no accidents. You take careful note of daily life, as well as the people who come into your life. You are like the movie camera that records data for later recollection.

You Are Healthy

When you have made it you are rarely ill. But when you are sick, you examine your illness to see what part of your thinking is off balance. Emotions, particularly suppressed anger, are behind so many of our physical ailments. You do not dam up anger for years, months, or even days. Instead you deal with it constructively. When you have made it you laugh frequently; you exercise vigorously; and you eat and drink moderately. You rest when you need rest. In other words, you use common sense.

You Listen to the Unusual

Prophets are sometimes found in unlikely places, like the woman you converse with at your bus stop, or they are young in years, like your own child. Prophets are always idealists, but they make us think. Nearly every major advance in civilization was once a cockeyed scheme that most people ridiculed. If you are worried that civilization now seems to be headed in a self-destructive direction, realize that the best help you can be to your world is to improve yourself and to follow your passion, since passionate people change the world for the better.

You Use Growth Resources

When you have made it you use resources that help you to assimilate and integrate your experience. You work with a therapist; or you go to group therapy, such as recovery programs that help you to maintain clarity. You attend workshops, seminars, and other courses that help you to learn and grow. Your rule of thumb for any resource is: Does it work? You and only you know the self-awareness tool that works for you. You are self-oriented in the most positive sense.

You Have a Strong Sense of Self

Having a strong sense of self is not the same as being selfish, although self-confidence can appear as selfishness to people who see themselves as victims. Confident people will not sacrifice their mental, physical, and emotional health for anyone. Others may interpret this as arrogance, but love of self precedes all relationships with others.

When you love yourself you examine all your choices, not only to be an example to others but also because you know there are consequences to your choices. Thinking before you act takes self-control, but you know from experience that it is the way to make wise decisions.

Your Spirituality Is Individualized

When you have arrived, your spiritual life is intensely personal. You are aware of a presence that fills your heart and mind. You radiate the joy and confidence that come from knowing you are a beloved child of God, however you conceive of God. As the prophet Jeremiah said about people who feel loved, "their souls shall be as a watered garden; and they shall not sorrow anymore."

FIVE HAPPY ENDINGS

The following five stories are about people who were successful in the eyes of others. Yet even those who appear to have "made it" can hit low periods. All they need is to make a slight correction before they finally arrive.

Robert's Story

Robert had two graduate degrees, an MBA and a law degree. He was not getting along with his supervisor, and he was not performing well in his job as a financial analyst. His work was sloppy, his lunchtimes stretched to two hours, and he was frequently late.

His autobiography showed a consistent pattern of early discontent and rebellion, starting with his relationship with his father (a pattern you are familiar with by now!) and continuing throughout his early school years. It was in high school that Robert finally found a constructive use for his outspoken energy and his need to challenge authority. He joined the debating team and consistently won honors in every competition.

After he graduated from high school and went on to college, Robert's highest achievements came when he made presentations. He was a natural leader whose ability to communicate earned him frequent praise. Robert believed that graduate school, in both law and business, was the road to success, and he continued his education into his late twenties.

"It was one law school professor who told me that a person's writing ability was the key to passing the bar exam. (Remember Brian from chapter 9 who learned this lesson after the sixth try?) He said that even if you knew the law, unless you could write it, you'd never pass. I made up my mind that my focus in law school would be written and verbal analysis. And I passed the bar," Robert said.

Robert's top strength was communication, the skill he had continually developed since his high school years. He loved the excitement of performing before an audience, and had finely honed his skills at a professional level. But his present position did not require the use of his most valuable abilities.

"Why did you get into financial analysis — a position that requires you to sit at a desk and move numbers around?" I asked. (It is easy to get off track when you attempt to fit an image of success that society rewards.)

"I came to the company as a tax lawyer. Because I found I didn't enjoy tax law, my company transferred me to cash management, thinking it would be more exciting for me. It wasn't. I'm bored, and I'm not doing a good job. Until I did the assignments you gave me, I was beginning to think of myself as a failure," he said. (Do you see how even those who from all appearances have "made it" can hit low periods? Robert was not in a position where he could lead, and being in charge was his passion.)

When I met with Robert's supervisor and heard her story, I understood Robert's problem. (This was early in my career, when I accepted corporate clients.) I use his story to show what happens when someone discovers a better way to use natural gifts. "For a whole year I've tried everything. He just can't do the work. I'm behind on my deadlines, and

I must replace him soon," Robert's boss said. Her patience was exhausted. I asked her what she had seen Robert do well in the year he had worked for her.

Her face brightened as she described a course he had taught to all the accountants on financial report analysis.

"He was superb. He worked for days on that course. He wrote a manual, a course outline, and when he was in front of the group, he had total control. I was surprised at his teaching skill. Robert's a natural leader. After the class, many people asked me who he was. They thought he was the best instructor they'd ever heard," she said.

"Yes, and annual reports are not exactly 'up' material," I said. "If such a dry subject can be taught so excitingly, then why not have Robert teach and train people in the company, rather than do the tasks?"

She paused to reflect for a moment.

"Of course!" she said. "He's so good at communicating, no wonder he's bored. He hates his present job because there's no chance to perform, to do what he really loves."

Like bored children, extroverted adults create disruption when they work behind the scenes. They need to be in front of people, not computer screens. The tax department in Robert's company needed to teach salespeople about the tax benefits to customers who bought the firm's expensive computer equipment. This task required someone who knew tax law and who could communicate. Enter Robert!

"It's exciting to think about what I can do with this opportunity, teaching dynamic marketing types about tax benefits. I get along well with salespeople," Robert said.

"You're a born performer, that's why. You just didn't know how to combine business, law, taxes, and cash management with sales," I said.

Robert's renewed self-confidence showed in his face. His body movements had changed in just a few weeks. His chin was forward, his eyes sparkled, and he was leaning on the edge of the couch.

"I feel great. I've learned so much this last year. I was trying to be something I'm not, a financial analyst. I thought that particular position in the company would give me prestige and status. But a position in which I do well is the best one for me," he said. (And because he is so highly regarded, he also has the "prestige and status" he coveted!)

Robert has made it. He will have other challenges, and he will meet them with confidence now, rather than rebelling in passive-aggressive ways like showing up late to work.

You may be in the right company, too, like Robert, but perhaps you'd be better off in another department. Before you change jobs and companies, research inside your organization to see if there are internal problems you can solve naturally and enjoyably. Businesses dislike turnover. It is costly and hard on morale. Because Robert found his niche in his company, both he and the company reaped the benefit of a motivated performer. His natural interest will help them to solve problems, increase sales, and reduce costs.

The key to change of any kind begins with using what you have more creatively. Finding the right fit for you is your responsibility, not your boss's. Remember that you need to think like an entrepreneur in these competitive times, which means you have to figure out the problem. If you have great ideas but cannot convince your supervisor or other decision makers to try them, then look outside your company to find people who will respond to you. Check to see if your personality is a partner, team, or solo type, using the exercise in chapter 6.

Before Robert researched within his company, he considered other job offers, thinking that the solution to his discontent was to move elsewhere. But once he saw how he could make a contribution to his company, he changed his attitude. "The next step in my career will be international sales. The company has asked me to travel and train personnel in all their subsidiaries — a dream job," he said.

Robert spends much of his time thinking about better ways to teach what he knows. He realizes now that setbacks are opportunities, not failures. Now he travels to other countries to help salespeople with their presentation skills, a job that is more like play than work, he says.

Jan's Story

One of my clients was an idealist who was always carrying a banner. Jan had been involved in Zionism, had lived on a kibbutz, and had tried Silva Mind Control and other group workshops: her goal was to change the world. Jan had always focused on fitting into a group. She had a dynamic personality, so she usually wound up leading whatever group she joined. Now, however, she wanted to look within herself for solutions. Individuation, Jung's term for accepting our separateness, was under way, and that process scared Jan. Her break from her causes had left a void. "I know what I don't want. I don't know what I *do* want," she said.

Because Jan always rose to the top of whatever organization she joined, she seemed successful to others. Her present state of mind disturbed her, something she had never experienced. (Passion clue: You choose experiences that scare you just enough to force your growth.)

"What is the benefit of a flat period in your life?" I asked. "Instead of resisting it, take advantage of the time you have to think, analyze, and consider other alternatives."

I asked Jan to keep a daily journal, writing at least a few sentences each day. This technique would assist her in staying alert to clues in her environment.

"It doesn't matter what you write. Nor does it matter what time of day you write. Record whatever is on your mind — comments about what's happening in the world, at home, at work. Just make a note of your reactions," I said.

After a month of journal entries Jan began to understand what she was learning and why she had to take a new path. One journal entry in particular became the key to a long-locked door.

"I started writing in my journal one day after seeing children on their way to school one morning. (See the clue she picked up in the environment?) I remember how terrified I was when I came to this country as a child. I couldn't understand or speak English, and for weeks I didn't say a word. Remembering that time let loose a flood of memories — how important it was for me to find a new family! Could the reason for joining all those groups be based on a need to belong to a new family?" she asked.

"Yes, that's a good insight, Jan. Your desire to blend in, to identify with a movement, could very well have started then. Seven years old is a tender age to be uprooted and placed in a strange country," I replied.

As Jan thought more about herself, she began to see her past as good preparation for work that was more independent. She had come full circle, to the point where she felt she could never work for anyone else again.

"I have to be on my own. And my work as a systems analyst is too oriented to 'things' and 'data.' I like people. I come home after a day of work and have trouble talking to my husband. His work as a sales-person is so people oriented that it's disturbing to adjust to his conver-sation at the end of the day," she said.

We had come a long way in a few months. It appeared that Jan was ready to start a business. We reviewed her passions, skills, and values. Jan's collage (from chapter 4) was extremely revealing. It contained many scenes of food, dinners, picnics, and other gatherings where food and drink brought people together.

"I love food preparation. I always took charge of the food arrange-ments in all the organizations I joined. I've put on dinners for five hun-dred people. Every time we have company for dinner, my guests want my recipes. I just have a good sense with food," she said.

I suggested that she make several advice calls on caterers of various kinds. She called me one day after several meetings to tell me about a young woman she had met.

"We're like twins! She has a similar background, and she worked with computers until she couldn't stand it anymore. She loved to cook, and she took cooking classes and started trying out her new skills on guests. One friend asked her to prepare the food for her wedding, and several wedding guests asked her to cater for them. After six months she had so much business that she quit her job and now caters full-time. She's so busy that she asked me if I'd like to help her with her next big job!" Jan was excited and enthused.

You can guess the story's ending. Jan is now a partner with the other woman, learning the business with no financial risk. She is happy, works hard, and sees limitless opportunities.

"Our next venture will be to teach cooking classes, and we're collaborating on our first cookbook," she said in a recent conversation.

Jan had "made it"; she just had to take time to sift through her thoughts before taking action. Powerful people know what to do when they get stuck. They go back to the past, regroup, and then proceed. They do not stop growing; reflecting passion secret 11, after they celebrate their achievements, they move on and up with their lives. Success is a motivation in and of itself. Successful people want to see what else they can do. They love a fresh challenge.

David's Story

Another example of how a subtle correction can alter a life's course occurred when a very successful salesperson came to me for help with his career. David was trying to break into international trade in the Middle East. His attempts to reach multinational corporations had been fruitless. With every letter and phone call, he ran into the proverbial brick wall. David's skill as a salesperson was apparently ineffective in his new career search.

The number-one salesperson in his company, David continually worked on improving sales skills, so he had many of the qualities necessary for success. But what he needed at this time was to open his mind to a different way of operating.

At first David resisted my suggestions that he follow a definite program to achieve his objectives. He thought that all he needed was to improve his phone technique. He did not want to spend the time writing an autobiography or taking any of the other steps in the process. He wanted a quick answer that would solve his problems.

"You can't beat your way into a company with a résumé and slick phone techniques," I told him. "There's some pattern you're repeating that is holding you back, and we have to find out what it is. Your obstinacy stands between you and the dream position you say you want. Go back and find out when and why that pattern started," I said.

David's autobiography revealed a fascinating story, unusual and rich with variety, showing an early exposure to religious, social, and political conflict. The Middle East, where he grew up, with its turmoil, secrecy, and suspicion, had been the crucible that produced a fighter. With his permission, I have reproduced excerpts from David's story (I changed his name to protect his privacy), which was originally thirty pages long, so that you can see an example of an actual autobiography and notice its revealing patterns. My comments are in brackets to show you what to look for in your own story.

Some of the earliest memories I have go back to my first year in kindergarten at the Armenian School in Jerusalem. All the children there wore red dresses with white lace collars. I remember sitting in class, hands clasped behind my back, reciting excerpts from the Bible. A very uncomfortable position to be in, reciting meaningless — to me — verses in the company of strangers. [David's earliest memory is feeling uncomfortable with his peers and his faith. He felt constricted. Remember that your earliest memory sets the theme of your story.]

Mother had the maid deliver fresh juices to me every day during recess, and I hated juices. All the kids used to gather around me and ask me to share the drink, a request to which I gladly obliged. By local standards, we were well-off, though my mother always complained about money. She came from a traditional upper-middle-class family and married a middle-class man. She never got over that, especially since class distinctions are so important in that traditional culture. [David's mother's frustration with her husband and her class consciousness are a big red flag. It might mean that she made David her surrogate husband, which could explain why David has trouble with women. Our parents' beliefs affect us for years unless we examine them for accuracy, rejecting what does not apply to our lives. In your autobiography it is important to record the beliefs and values of both parents. Since David's father is in an "inferior" position to his mother, will David repeat this dynamic with the women he chooses? Will he always feel — as his father did — that he is not good enough? Will he remain bound to his mother forever?]

Most of the people around us were poor, especially since the Arab-Israeli War of 1948 was only four to five years earlier. Occasionally there were skirmishes on the border and life was not very safe. [Even though he was young, he would absorb the fear around him.] Many people had lost loved ones and property. My family lost their home and business, and my father had to start all over again. We fled Jerusalem in 1948. I was a few months old when we lived with the Bedouins in the desert. I don't remember anything of my experience there. I was about three when we returned to the now-divided city of Jerusalem. The house we lived in was a huge thirteenth- or fourteenth-century house of Arabian architecture with thick walls and big domes.

Rapid Change

After I spent two years at the Armenian School, my parents enrolled me in a German school for one year, and then a French private school for boys. I stayed there until graduation in 1967. This French school was nothing more than a stalag with "Brothers" running the show. Discipline and conformity were of primary importance. [Frequent change and then a repressive religious environment fostered his rebellious attitude.] Classes would start at 7:20 A.M. and end at 4:30 P.M. with two fifteen-minute recesses and one hour for lunch. I hated school until perhaps my sophomore year. My grades until that year were average or below average.

I used to feel very envious of those who excelled. I also considered them "sissies." They were the teacher's favorites. [David likes to be the favorite, to get attention.] I distinctly remember an episode during catechism class where the Brother asked the model student and myself to come forward. Johnny was an A student, blond, blue-eyed, clean clothes and fingernails. I was dark, had disheveled hair, and was meager looking. He asked us both to kneel and proceeded to outline the differences between devils and angels. Johnny was the example of the angel. I was so angry that I hit the Brother, who later punished me by giving me ten lashes and a detention. That was quite a venturesome act on my part, since at that time one did not dare even look in the eyes of a teacher when talking to him. [This is wonderful spirit — I laughed out loud as I read this story. David can be a devil when he wants to.]

Early Self-Image

I was an ornery brat. I spent most of my time climbing trees, and exploring caves and holes. I collected and lynched lizards, despite the pleas and advice of my mother and aunt. I explored old castles or churches with some neighborhood kids.

I used to collect bottles, make some funny perfumes out of spices and liquid color, and sell them to the Bedouins who came to town on Fridays. I also hired neighborhood kids to run tiny concession stands at busy street corners. Later I found that those kids cheated me blind. I started buying squabs and chickens and other domestic animals and raised them for family consumption and for sale. [The early signs of the solo personality, the entrepreneur.] I knew a lot about animals at the age of ten or twelve. I also loved handcrafts. I built things like doghouses, carved model ship hulls out of pine bark, and won prizes at several Boy Scout and craft fairs. Carpentry was my best hobby.

I hated books. I never had time to study or do my homework. That enraged my mother. Since she was well educated by local standards, especially for a woman, she wanted me to stick to my books. I hated school and did not make good grades. Corporal punishment was common. I had a few lickings, but it was hard to pin me down since I fought back. As I grew up, I was so surprised to know that some teachers did like me. I was made prefect to ensure that all the other kids complied with the stupid rules. I "played the game." [He's adapting to the system, making other kids comply with "stupid rules." David looks out for David. He's getting shrewd.] At fourteen or fifteen I spent most of my time in sports.

Exposure to an Audience

Then I became interested in music, and I got in a band — the first such band in the Hashemite Kingdom of Jordan. I was popular. The band gained nationwide popularity. [David is as good looking as he is talented, so it is no wonder that he was so popular.] We performed mostly on stage. We argued and fought a lot among ourselves. I fought the most with the lead singer, who was the best musician of the four of us. I felt he monopolized the group. Today this person is my best friend. It's funny how jealousy has matured into such close friendship.

My Home Life

Our house was the gathering place for all our friends. Women dropped by — very unusual in those days. Mother could not stand the gatherings. She had migraines. Mother has always been ailing. [Mother is probably an introvert, forcing herself to conform and her body is rebelling!] I had my first sexual experience at fifteen with a beautiful married woman of twenty-two or so. Scared the hell out of me!

Dad encouraged our music and was really proud to see me perform as a musician and as an athlete. What an easygoing man. [Too easygoing?] He rarely got angry, and I can't remember his ever hitting me. He was my friend. Mother did the disciplining. [You can see that the mother took over the father's responsibility, which made her the bad guy.] She really worked hard, even with the help of a maid. The house was always in immaculate condition. Dad had many important dignitaries and business associates visit us. I was so proud when the governor of Jerusalem used to visit with military escort.

I was very westernized then. Blue jeans and T-shirts, singing *West Side Story* with my pals. We acted tough and got into many fights. America was an inspiration. When John F. Kennedy was assassinated, we were very sad. It is interesting to see that those who felt that way then are now very anti-American and are PLO supporters. America has got to play a more evenhanded role in the Middle East. I enjoyed the outdoors a lot then, as I do now. I used to backpack in the Judean wilderness and visit Greek monks in remote monasteries. What a simple life it was. [I wonder if he will come back to this at the end of his life?]

College Days

I won a scholarship to Drew University. It was timely, since it came after the Six-Day War in 1967. That was the worst time I spent in Jerusalem. Neighbors were shot, and shops were looted. It was never reported in the American press. Israel certainly did not exercise its democracy with the Arabs. Every time I go there I get interrogated. I feel I am in an alien land. After coming to the United States, I got a deeper appreciation of politics, propaganda, and the American political process. Drew was an ivory tower. I loved it. I enjoyed my teachers and the academic atmosphere. My grades were very good, and I enjoyed books for the first time in my life. I made a lot of friends there.

I got involved in the civil rights movement and the anti–Vietnam War movement. I was also involved in many extracurricular activities. I started and headed the International Club, joined the varsity soccer team, and went to the Nationals in soccer. I became president of my class. I also dated a lot. I enjoyed my education. I finally majored in psychology, met a wonderful girl whom I later married, and moved to Boston to attend school there and work. We were so antiestablishment at that time that I refused to work for a corporation. I took a mechanic's job; then I temporarily worked as a foreman in a factory. Those two years in Boston were a lot of fun.

My wife, Dianne, was the first girl I emotionally got involved with. I had really never had a steady girlfriend. We had the same aspirations and interests. [Not much experience before marriage.]

Kentucky

The back-to-the-land movement was a dominant factor in our move to Kentucky. We wanted to live on a farm, and after two years in Kentucky, we bought one. Little did we realize how difficult it was to live on one, and the investment it would take to start and run it.

Kentucky was the heart of America to me. I became involved in social work. I still did not want to work for profit. What naïveté. I was very proud of the fact that I was working for humanitarian and constructive reasons. Slowly I started realizing how tied up and interrelated the social structure is. I enjoyed work tremendously. The director and two people on the staff and I became very close friends.

Then politics came into the social agency, and our director was axed for trying to reform the system. I got involved in lobbying at the state legislature to pass a new bill, which would create a separate services department and which would ensure that the appropriate federal funds were spent intelligently. Politics and the democratic process definitely was one of the most interesting experiences of my life. I started realizing what power and connections meant. At the same time, I started losing interest in my work, since I was not being rewarded enough materially or even spiritually. I stayed on to fight for what I believed in, for more than one year. We finally won, not only through justice, not only because we had proof, but because we essentially had accumulated political power. My friend and former director was reinstated to his post. It was time for me to leave.

I started looking around for alternative careers. I did not want any more schooling. After taking special classes in work evaluation at a couple of graduate schools, I felt that formal education was not what I wanted to pursue.

Betrayal Number One

In the meantime, I was very much involved with Common Cause, the Sierra Club Issues Committee, and my farm. I was also building a large addition to our house. I got involved with cars, photography, and other hobbies. My wife was not a part of my world. She did not have the same interests, and I was not sensitive enough at that time to notice us drifting apart. To my shock and dismay, she fell out of love with me and in love with a very dear friend.

To this day, it amazes me how well I took it and how accepting of them I was, to the point where I helped them out on several occasions. Up to that point, my relationship with my in-laws had been very good. I respected and admired the character and industry of my father-in-law. My mother-in-law was lethargic, extravagant, disorganized, and very insecure. She was also a very loving person. [Wait a minute. How can she be a "loving person"? She sounds manipulative — David needs to define what he means by the word *loving*], but there was a resentment in me about her unfavorable qualities. [I doubt he ever expressed these feelings.] There are very few women whom I have ever admired, especially among the older generation. Perhaps society never gave them the chance to excel. [Here he is really talking about his mother. I pointed this out to him. I suggested that women in earlier generations used all kinds of covert behavior to get what they wanted. David's generalizations about women reflected his repression of his own feelings — toward his mother, the former wife, his "best friend," and his in-laws.] So after my separation with Dianne, I started feeling coldness from both of my in-laws. Kentucky was not a place to stay anymore. I wanted to move on. The urge to move into a cosmopolitan atmosphere was dominant. I felt I needed to uncover my buried drives and interests.

Off to California

Dianne by then had broken up with her lover. We were still friends. She got a transfer to California and asked me to join her as a pal until I found a way out. We sold our house, bought one in California, and moved. We had a platonic relationship. [David never ended his connection with Dianne. He is getting ready for more hurt. Why?] She quickly found a boyfriend in California and moved in with him. [Dianne is dependent.] I started a company on my own selling bath chairs and related accessories for the handicapped. I enjoyed it but did not make enough money. After about six months, I joined a pharmaceutical company and moved out of the house. Dianne and her boyfriend moved in. We had a verbal agreement on the settlement of the property. I got about 80 percent of the joint ownership in cash. We got an uncontested divorce, with the promise that she would pay me the rest when she had the chance to save the money.

Betrayal Number Two

To my utmost disappointment, she later reneged, claiming that I got more than my fair share. [David would have seen this coming if he had seen Dianne as she was.] That was the worst thing she could have ever done. It really hurt. It sure does surprise me to this day that I still feel a certain loyalty to her and that I'll help her out when I can. [This does not make sense. Where is his anger? David, the fighter, rolls over and plays victim. He has yet to develop intellectual honesty; he'd rather get along than end bad relationships.] My in-laws added more salt to the wound by severing their relationship with me. [Which is what David needed to do with them!] They don't call even when they're in town, although they are very nice when I call. [David does not listen to his feelings; otherwise, he would say how he really feels to these people. He is afraid to terminate contact; he lets them take the responsibility to end what is hurtful to him, once again copying his father's passive behavior.]

I hated my current job at the outset. I took rejection personally. I did not know my customers, the territory, or the products. After about a year things began improving, to the point where I looked forward to starting a new day. Every day is a learning experience, leading me to where I want to go. I enjoy the company of most of my business associates. I don't feel I am selling, but providing a service. It has surprised me to see my sales results. If I am so good now, just imagine how much better I will be with more experience.

Conclusion

Reading what I have just written, I don't think I have changed much on the inside since I was a child. [This paragraph is a key shift in the writing. He is commenting on his life; he is now the editor, analyzing his choices, seeing with a new perspective. He likes who he is, problems and all.] I'm not sure if I regret turning antiestablishment, picking up social work, and shutting off my material needs. The consciousness and experiences of that period of my life were worth it. I have a life ahead of me to build and enjoy. The future sure looks bright. Doing my best is what I firmly believe in. It's the ultimate source of my happiness. I know I'm asking a lot out of life. I'm giving a lot. I will get what I want. There are many people in this world who will benefit from my success. Giving certainly is more fulfilling than only receiving.

The development of character begins early for all of us. In David's case, his cumulative experiences taught him about his judgment. His judgment was correct in many cases, except in regard to his mother, father, former wife, in-laws — and himself. He pays more attention to his feelings now and acts directly when necessary rather than retreat or play the victim, like his father.

"I always did well at whatever I tried. I'm disciplined, and I finish what I start. I was proud of my social work. I am proud of my sales career. I always gave everything my best," he said.

USING EFFECTIVE MARKETING TOOLS

For competitors like David, self-correction is subtle. Remember the earlier tennis analogy? A tennis player may be coached to turn the wrist an eighth of an inch. That slight shift may make the difference between winning and losing. David was trying to "close the sale" before he had defined the problem. His approach was, "Here I am. Where can you use me?" He distributed résumés that usually landed on desks in the personnel department, only to be filed away later.

When David's résumé and letter were circulated, they met with little interest. A general résumé is an ineffective marketing tool because it does not address specifics — the needs of the organization and of the person who has the problems. A job is created as an attempt to solve business problems.

The international arena was David's area of interest, a touchy market for many American businesses. For many businesses, international involvement comes second to domestic emphasis. Especially if domestic markets are providing good return, there is a natural resistance to become involved with the uncertain markets and politics of other countries. Stockholders want return on investment.

The heads of multinational companies know from experience that it takes unusual political, economic, and social savvy to obtain and keep business. American technological and business know-how is improving because of the global marketplace. David's task was to convince an American company that profits would increase if they capitalized on his international knowledge.

David's New Way

David stopped mailing résumés and began to use the interview approach I describe in chapter 9. He selected people in his area who had an interest in international marketing. He contacted the Arab-American Chamber of Commerce, trade representatives, and other businesses, large and small.

The approach letter and email technique worked. David started having extremely productive meetings. He learned that several businesses could use his talents, and he received two offers. Neither was the right niche, but the success of the process raised his self-confidence.

"I see now that I was trying to 'close' people too soon. I wasn't listening; I was trying too hard. People have been so helpful in my meetings, and I think I've located the company I want; it's headquartered right here in the city. I'm sending a letter to the vice president of international marketing. His name was mentioned in one of my meetings with the Arab consulate. I was told his company had considered expanding its Middle East activities but had run into some difficulties. I need to learn more. Their products would have a huge market in the Middle East," David told me.

The meeting went very well. The vice president was open to hearing about David's goals and spent considerable time explaining his company's position.

"Only three percent of our market is in the Persian Gulf area. With so many recent political developments, we're not sure our staff understands all the social, political, and economic problems. We've drawn back from expansion until we can figure out the best approach. We know the market is there, but corporate strategists are more comfortable with domestic markets," he told David.

David listened carefully, and then he asked several questions. The vice president's response encouraged him to ask for a chance to meet with other people in the division. Their perspective would provide him with more pieces of the puzzle, and at the same time he could get a feeling for the personalities involved. Their cooperation and enthusiasm for expanding the market in the Middle East was vital to any proposal David would make.

After many meetings spread out over a number of months, David was ready to make his proposal. During that time not only had he become familiar with his target company, but he had kept himself informed on the latest developments in the Middle East. His proposal included an orientation time that would allow him to become thoroughly conversant with all the products and marketing strategy of the corporation.

David's final letter to the vice president, written after the job offer was verbally extended, summarized what he could do for the company. David went on to the next step in his career. He had "arrived." By making a subtle correction in his attitude, he had achieved his objective.

You may need to shift your thinking in order to allow your self-correcting mechanism to go to work for you as it did for David. He limited himself when he depended on traditional methods to gain entrance into companies. But when he tried a new approach, he found that it worked.

Since David first wrote his autobiography, he has made another move. After two years he accepted a position as regional manager of the Middle East for a large hospital supply firm. This is a major step forward, financially and personally. He is coming full circle. He is going back to his roots. I believe David's story will climax when he combines his social conscience with his marketing skill. Before he left for Athens, he told me of his dream.

"Nancy, it's the nuances in business and political relationships that are important. I want to become a master in liaison between major government figures in the Middle East and American businesses. The culture of the Persian Gulf countries demands a study of nuance. I want to help create mutual understanding and respect," he said.

Naive? Idealistic? I think not. The faith and energy of people like

David are hopeful forces for change and international understanding. He is learning patience, becoming the best he can be. The world changes because of people who do what they love and do it well.

Cynthia's Story

A thoroughly discouraged woman came to see me with so much negativity in her personality I wondered if I could help her at all.

Cynthia was a high school teacher who had had a successful career in education. However, she was seriously disturbed with the continuing lack of interest by her students, fellow teachers, and especially the administrators. She felt her enthusiasm waning, and her normal commitment to her classes and her career was at the lowest point in her life.

"I have to exert great effort to get out of bed in the morning, and I dread the start of each day. The students are apathetic, especially about the subject I teach, social studies. I feel as if no one appreciates me. The other teachers have given up, just putting in their time, and the administrators only do what is required to keep their jobs. Education is a losing battle," she said, her whole face a study in frustration and fear of the future.

"Cynthia, how long have you felt this way?" I asked.

"For years, really. I knew five years ago where public schools were headed, but I couldn't think of an alternative for myself. I've been teaching seventeen years; it's all I know. What else can I do?" she asked, nearly in tears. (Here was the evidence of a big challenge being set up, something that can be painful but will lead to the opportunity for change and fulfillment.)

Cynthia had worked for days on a résumé, then she had sent it to several companies and had met with a few people, all with no results.

"I'm more confused than ever. My friends tell me I'm crazy to want to leave a secure position. I'm a good teacher, but I want to explore other areas, especially the business world," she said.

I explained to Cynthia that any career shift would take months to pursue and asked if she could bear up under the uncertainties that are part of a job search. I was concerned about the years of security that teaching represented and how that part of her life would weigh against an unpredictable future.

"I have to try," she said. "If I don't change now, I know I never will," she assured me, saying that with my help she could do it.

"Cynthia, I'm not a magician. You will do most of the work in this process, and that's as it should be. I won't let you become dependent on me, for then we will be reproducing the past. From what you've told me, I see that you're trying to become independent, to grow in new directions. That is not so easy when you've had a life of relative certainty for seventeen years," I said.

Cynthia's completed exercises revealed that she was group dependent, that she was not sure about her ability to make decisions, and that she preferred a team setting in work. I knew the process of finding a new job would be painful for her, but during that time she would gain enough knowledge to make her own decisions and feel confident about them.

During our discussion of her exercises, I pointed out her strengths as well as the areas where more internal work was needed.

"Your work shows that you are outgoing, assertive, venturesome, and fairly stable. You are intuitive, bright, and forthright. You are also dependent on a group for decision making. To me, this means you don't trust your own judgment — you doubt yourself," I explained, adding that working with her would be a balancing act for me.

"What do you mean — don't you think my chances are good?" she asked, looking worried.

I laughed. "Yes, Cynthia, your chances are excellent. The balancing act I speak of is my ability to encourage you to think for yourself. That means I have to refrain from giving you answers, since responsibility and personal choices go hand in hand. I want you to know I'll enjoy working with you even on those days when I tell you what you don't want to hear."

Cynthia would remember that statement months later when her

resolve was shattered from a week of disasters. Everything had gone wrong. The job she thought she had in the bag did not come through. She was not sleeping well, her health concerned her, her money reserve was low, and all her interviews seemed a total loss. She was even thinking that she should go back to teaching.

"Was the experience with the business world so unpleasant?" I asked.

"No, I loved meeting so many interesting people. Everyone did what he or she could to help, but no one wanted to hire me in sales — that is what I want to do. I know I can sell, but I've been told I don't have enough experience. That's not true. I sell education, so any other product should be a cinch," she said.

Cynthia had interviewed for a good sales position. The sales manager liked her, but his supervisor did not want to risk the training cost on an unknown. She was still feeling the bite of disappointment.

"If you want a sales career, you have to be able to take rejection. I realize you're discouraged and want to conclude this search. Remember, you only focused on sales as an objective just two months ago and you have come very close to a firm offer. Since you're worried about your finances, how about a stop-gap position to give you some money and thinking time?" I asked. I felt that Cynthia needed a respite from the pressure, an alternative.

She listened and then asked, "What kind of position?"

I told her that a friend of mine, Les, had called the day before and asked if I knew someone who could help him manage his office. He supervised the field sales staff in a financial planning services firm.

"I need someone who is mature and bright — able to handle prima donnas," Les had said, laughing. I had replied that I would think about it and call him back.

I knew Cynthia's personality matched Les's. He would be an excellent boss — dynamic, firm, sharp, with a good sense of humor. Cynthia was very much at ease with this type — a man very similar to her father, with whom she had an excellent friendship. (Finally, a client without a father complex, you must be thinking.)

Cynthia called Les and scheduled an appointment with him to interview for the office manager position. Les called me the same day and said he was so impressed with her he wanted to hire her, but not to manage his office.

"If she's what I think she is, I'd like her on my sales staff. The financial planning field needs sharp, hardworking women. She expressed herself well, and she really knows her strengths," he said excitedly.

I was delighted, and Cynthia was amazed. I asked her how she had handled herself in the interview.

"I did what I always do in my meetings. I tried to find out about him and the business. After an hour talking nonstop, we took a break, had coffee, and got back to discussing his business. I was fascinated (passion clue!) with what they do for people. What a great service, helping people manage their finances and investment needs!"

Cynthia was more excited than I had ever seen her. This is a good example of someone experiencing a previously unrecognized passion. Sometimes the career search happens like this. All the research and interviews seem fruitless. You feel like giving up and, suddenly, you find your niche!

As with many companies, even though the boss liked her, it was necessary for Cynthia to meet with other department heads before a final decision was made. After six more interviews she was hired. Les sent me a personal note of thanks, and Cynthia came in two months later to see me. Her eyes were bright, her step was light — she looked great.

"I made my first big sale, Nancy. It was to another teacher, a friend whose inheritance had put her in a precarious tax position," she said.

During the training program with her new company, Cynthia had called on her old friends in teaching. (See the importance of maintaining contacts?) Her friend trusted her enough to allow the company staff to analyze the problem. Their solution finalized the sale. Cynthia will in time be able to analyze the financial problems herself. She is now in training and plans to return to school for a graduate degree in financial planning.

Cynthia's story illustrates that we sometimes lose our perspective and cannot see that we are "making it." I gave Cynthia some suggestions, but her own self-awareness and natural abilities got her the job. In her meeting with Les, she focused on him and his company and forgot her own concerns. She had the same attitude that all high performers have — "the show must go on," no matter what.

Cynthia succeeded because she trusted herself and she communicated openly and honestly. Her years of teaching had served her well. All the times she had gone into the classroom perhaps not feeling great, she still gave her best. The following is what Cynthia wrote about her self-image and her balanced image when we started working together (see chapter 2). You will find her honesty refreshing. Although it took time for her balanced image to become reality, Cynthia's life today matches her words.

How I See Myself

I see myself as a person desirous of getting more from life in the sense of personal achievement and fulfillment. Because I can be very disciplined and determined when I decide on a course of action, I feel that I am capable of facing new challenges and willing to undergo the necessary hard work. Even though I am enthusiastic and hopeful, I do harbor self-doubts and concern about my real abilities, which perhaps have never really been tested. I can be more of a romantic than a realist and recognize that I need to become more pragmatic if I am going to be successful in a role other than that of a teacher.

I have learned to be self-sufficient and independent. I can be happy by myself and don't feel lonely when I am. I learned many years ago that loneliness is a state of mind, not a state of being. However, I hope to have a satisfying relationship with a man someday, for despite the fact that I can function on my own, my life certainly would be enhanced by a caring relationship.

Physically, I feel attractive and sexy. I try to keep in shape by jogging and watching my diet. I am conscious of my appearance and sometimes worry about growing older. But then if I were younger, I might not be as wise! I feel really healthy and energetic.

My Balanced Self

My balanced self would be far more confident and less cautious. Perhaps I could acquire these characteristics if I learned how to channel my energies and focus on some specific goals. With more confidence, I would be more decisive and willing to take risks. I would like to learn how to develop my psychic abilities and use them constructively. Also, I would like to associate with more people who are successful, that is, people who make real contributions to society. With this kind of exposure, I might have fewer negative thoughts — being critical and jealous, for example — and put more energy into constructive projects, things that will lead to a happier me. In summary, I want to learn how to be in full control of my life and destiny.

All of us want to be in control of our lives. Cynthia expressed this need as she began the process. Months later, she achieved it. So can you.

Burt's Story

"Your system sounds wonderful, but it's not working for me, Nancy. My letters are being sent to the personnel departments. One guy even told me not to bother him, that he had no openings," Burt said, looking ready to explode with anger at this treatment.

When we calmly analyzed his ratio of letters sent and subsequent meetings held, he was averaging 50 percent success! Even so, I was not pleased. When this technique is used well, the success average is usually around 80 percent. I discovered that Burt had mailed two-thirds of his letters to the advertising field, a highly visible target. Many people are attracted to the glamour of advertising.

"Why did you send such a high proportion of your letters to advertising agencies? I have a feeling your niche is in a company where your function would be to work with the ad agencies on your company's account. Let's contact more people within companies who do that," I said.

Burt's average rose, and at the same time he realized that the high-pressure atmosphere of an ad agency was not for him. People under pressure usually are not very receptive. Burt was "pushing the river," trying to break into a field that resisted his efforts. Because he was off target, his results were not what he expected. With a change of direction, his ratio improved dramatically. He sent more letters, did further research, and enjoyed good rapport in his meetings.

"I'm amazed at the reception I'm getting. I have so many people to call, so many referrals from my meetings, that I'm not sure I can keep up!" he said, enthused and delighted.

The end result was a job offer inside a company where he acted as liaison between the company and its advertising agencies. Burt made a subtle shift in his approach and found that he could follow his passion — advertising — in a niche that he had not anticipated.

MASTERING YOUR LIFE

Above you have read the stories of people who have learned to master their lives. As you read, you no doubt concluded that this mastery takes a great deal of hard work, faith, belief, and imagination. Faith is the strongest and most productive of all our emotions. Faith is a state of mind; it is emotional muscle that gets stronger with each risk you take. Skepticism, or disbelief, is the opposite of faith, but it is part of our internal warning system. Used properly, skepticism keeps us from making mistakes of judgment. As your faith grows, your negative beliefs are replaced with an optimistic outlook on life. As a result, you are quick to let go of behavior that does not work.

Unless you act you remain a passive receiver, living a vicarious existence through others' excitement. Think of all the money people pay to watch and listen to others work with passion, at concerts, in movies and videos, on television and CDs, and during sports events. It's wonderful to enjoy top performers, they can be inspiring and uplifting, but why not be one yourself? You were not designed to just watch others having fun and making money. That is like owning a Porsche and only driving it to and from the grocery store once a week! Your mind is a rich resource, the creator of your experience of life. You have what no Porsche has: imagination, the source of art, music, science, business, and all ideas.

All your choices are good if you learn from them. You are in control, even when your life appears to be out of control. For example, if you believe, as Cynthia did, that you do not have what it takes to succeed, you make choices that minimize risk. You go for what is safe. Then you feel frustrated and envious of others' success. The lesson is don't hold back from life, since that will force the hand of your creative self who wants to take risks, as Cynthia discovered. Remember that if you hold back your desire to experience life, your emotions will take revenge on you through mood swings, illness, and prolonged depression. But if you jump into life with your whole heart and soul, your future is unlimited.

Cynthia and David show how self-defeating beliefs restrict your experience of life. David believed that he had to be ready to fight for what he wanted, that competitors always lurked around the corner, ready to attack. It was as if he were still living in a war zone. His defensive posture was useful in his early years in helping him to endure a repressive system. But as an adult, in a different environment, he needed to drop his defenses.

Beliefs are subtle. To identify them, look at your life circumstances. Ask yourself what beliefs brought these circumstances into your life? If you want new circumstances, what beliefs would that require? What do you need to do *today* to achieve those goals? In addition, our emotions — both positive and negative — are integral to directing our choices. Take a look at both the positive and the negative emotions listed in Napoleon Hill's book *Think and Grow Rich*.[6] See how they affect your ability to focus and take action.

The Seven Major Positive Emotions

1. Desire

2. Faith

3. Love

4. Sexual desire

5. Enthusiasm

6. Romance

7. Hope

The Seven Major Negative Emotions

1. Fear

2. Jealousy

3. Revenge

4. Greed

5. Suspicion

6. Anger

7. Hatred

Both sets of emotions cannot occupy your mind at the same moment. One state of mind will dominate, depending on how much you practice it. The world is full of people who work very diligently at negativity. Think about how many thoughts it takes to maintain a depressed state of mind. Experts have estimated that we think at least fifty thousand thoughts a day!

How many of your fifty thousand thoughts a day focus on the seven positive emotions? How much of your life is given over to passivity, acceptance of the status quo? How many of your thoughts are trapped in negativity?

Your Story

The people that I have known, met, and served all have similar attributes. They learn to control what they think about and, more important, they take action. (Remember that the definition of power is the ability to take action, to influence.) You have that same ability to take action, to shape the course of your life. Begin to take action with your thoughts, and use your imagination to write your story exactly the way you want it to be. Just fill in the blanks below and see what happens. (See chapter 4, where this affirmation technique is first described.)

I, _____, have an exciting and rewarding career. I make $_____ a year with_____ benefits. I live and work in _____, my ideal geographical location. I provide a service to my company and/or customers/clients that is_____ and _____. I am recognized as a doer and a reliable _____ in the _____ field. I have fine relationships with my co-workers and supervisors. I am seen as likable, warm, strong, and competent. I grow daily in self-awareness, in mastery of my life and chosen work. I truly have combined my livelihood with my passion. My work is fun! My private life is fulfilling and joyous because I am true to myself wherever I am. I have supreme confidence in _____ [statement of faith or spiritual beliefs, if you wish].

I like your story. It is real. Congratulations! Celebrate!

CELEBRATE WHEN YOU GET THERE!

When my clients complete the process outlined in this book, we celebrate the courage that making healthy choices require. The old life (and self), with all its learning and pain, is only a dim memory. We laugh, remembering the struggle together, how we were not sure we would make it. We tell each other the story, savoring every step that got us where we are.

Celebration is a vital part of a passionate life. Savor your triumphs.

Open a bottle of good wine, have a party, ring the gongs, blow the whistles. Let everyone in earshot know about you. Your achievement is music to the ears of the discouraged and to those who love you. Now you know your passion in life and how it connects to others. You are here to do what you love for a living. You are here to give heart to the world, through your passion.

SUMMARY

Passion Secret *// Celebrate your achievements; then continue to move on and up.*

1. All your experiences have meaning — all.

2. You live in the most exciting time in the history of the planet. The future can be summarized in two words: alternatives and newness. Train your mind to be open to all possibilities.

3. You are designed to perform at a very high level.

4. How many of your daily thoughts involve the seven negative emotions? How many involve the seven positive emotions?

5. Write your story exactly the way you want it. Then live it!

6. Always celebrate your achievements. Buy yourself something you have always wanted, go away for the weekend, spend a day with friends and family, putter around your garden, or pamper yourself. After you've celebrated your achievements, move on and up.

7. Remember that you are here to give heart to the world, through your passion.

APPENDIX 1

The following are summaries of the eleven steps to passion and the eleven passion secrets. If you look at these two lists regularly they will become affirmations that prepare your mind for success.

THE ELEVEN STEPS TO PASSION

1. Learn to feel as well as you think, then your mind and heart will work as a team to solve your problems. Remember that feelings are slower than thoughts, so be patient as you become aware of them. Acknowledge the value of all your feelings, even those that make you feel uncomfortable. Become familiar with the six basic fears that block the expression of your feelings: the fear of poverty, the fear of criticism, the fear of losing love, the fear of illness, the fear of old age, and the fear of death. Face these fears head-on and they will lose their power over you.

2. Write your autobiography, beginning with a description of your grandparents' beliefs about money, work, sex, gender, religion, and love. Starting your story with your grandparents will give you more objectivity about your parents, which sets you free to be yourself. You may require professional help in taking this step if you have never done any therapy or other personal-growth work. Allow plenty of time for this project. Understanding the past takes time, so be patient with yourself.

3. Identify your top-five strengths and values: material, intellectual, and spiritual. This step builds on the self-knowledge you gained from writing your autobiography. Remember that what you do, not what you say, reveals your values.

4. Make a list of the goals you'd like to achieve by the end of the next six months. Then narrow these goals down to ten wants. Write a description of these goals as if you have already achieved them. Be realistic; make sure to word these goals in such a way that you and you alone are responsible for what you want. Are your desires in line with your top-five values? Make a collage of images and words that you cut out from magazines. If there is a conflict between your written want list and the images on the collage, write a list that matches the images on the collage, since they reflect your deepest desires.

5. Research your areas of interest where you live using the Yellow Pages or an Internet equivalent. The phone book may seem like a low-tech tool, but it is local, and the information is updated every six months. Some of your categories of interests will be hobbies, not your passion. Your passion allows you to use your top-five strengths serving others and making money. Narrow your categories of interest down to your top-six interests. Rewrite as insight

comes about whether or not this category is personal, what you want to do for others, your company's customers or clients, or your own customers or clients.

6. Discover your personality type by observing what you do when left to your own devices. Do your choices indicate that you are a partner, team, or solo type? It is vital that you be true to your type and temperament, since authenticity attracts the work and relationships that are right for you.

7. Research the marketplace to pick the company or activity that suits your personality type and temperament: Are you at home in a large, medium, or small company? Would you be happy working with a small group of people, working alone, or working for yourself?

8. By email, telephone, or letter, contact people who are doing what you want to do. Ask your friends and family members about the people or companies they know in your areas of interest. Each situation has its own rules, so use your instincts. Practice makes perfect; as you meet people and express your interests, you will grow in self-knowledge. This part of the process is much like shopping for a new wardrobe; it may take several trips to get it right. But once you know yourself you select what is right for you at this stage of your life, rather than repeating the past or following the latest trend.

9. Make advice calls (also called informational interviews or networking) with experts or individuals in the field in which you have an interest. If you are changing positions or careers, you may need to upgrade your skills. You may find that you already know how to do what you want to do but that you need to update your computer skills or your understanding of the terminology in this field; or you need to figure out how to make use of your skills in your own business or client-based service.

10. If you are independent and self-starting, consider entrepreneurship as a partner, as part of a team, or solo. Start your search with people you know: local businesspeople and the chamber of commerce are good places to begin. Use a low-key approach, since it puts people at ease. Attend meetings and seminars in your area of interest to learn about present and future possibilities, as well as problems (problems are where the jobs are!). Now that you know your strengths and values, look around in your company. Is there a way you can make better use of these strengths that will reflect your values? Often the solution to your career dissatisfaction is in your own backyard.

11. Celebrate when you "get there." When you find your passion, teach what you know to others who are coming along behind you. Remember it is the journey, not the goal, that matters, so encourage others as others once encouraged you. When you reach your goal celebrate your victory; your achievement will inspire others to persevere in their efforts.

APPENDIX 2

THE ELEVEN PASSION SECRETS

1. Know what you feel as well as what you think.

2. Understand the past; then let it go.

3. Know your strengths and values.

4. Remember that getting there is all the fun.

5. Network with people whose values match yours.

6. Know your niche; always follow your passion.

7. Enjoy doing research; then act on the information.

8. Speak and write clearly.

9. Trust your instincts.

10. Freedom comes from self-discipline.

11. Celebrate your achievements; then continue to move on and up.

NOTES

CHAPTER ONE. FINDING YOUR PASSION

1. Jane Roberts, *The Nature of Personal Reality* (Novato, Calif.: New World Library, 1994) 292–93.
2. Napoleon Hill, *Think and Grow Rich* (New York: Fawcett Books, 1960), 222–40.

CHAPTER TWO. WRITING YOUR LIFE STORY

1. Robert E. Firestone, *The Fantasy Bond: Effects of Psychological Defenses on Interpersonal Relations* (New York: Human Sciences Press, 1985), 273–75.
2. C. G. Jung, *Modern Man in Search of a Soul* (New York: Harcourt, Brace & World, 1933), 122.
3. David Kiersey and Marilyn Bates, *Please Understand Me: Character and Temperament Types* (Del Mar, Calif.: Prometheus Nemesis, 1998), 16.

CHAPTER THREE. IDENTIFYING YOUR STRENGTHS AND VALUES

1. Jane Roberts, *The Nature of Personal Reality* (Novato, Calif.: New World Library, 1994), 340–41.
2. Alvin Toffler, *The Third Wave* (New York: Bantam Books, 1991).
3. Toffler, *Third Wave*, 44–45.
4. D. G. Zyfowsky, "15 Needs and Values," *Vocational Guidance Quarterly* 18 (1970): 182.

CHAPTER FOUR. SETTING GOALS YOU CAN REACH

1. Srully Blotnick, *Getting Rich Your Own Way* (New York: Doubleday, 1980).
2. Gaylon Greer, "How Did the Rich Get That Way?" *American Association of Individual Investors Journal* (March 1984): 23–24.
3. Shakti Gawain, *Creative Visualization*, 25th anniversary ed. (Novato, Calif.: New World Library, 2003).

CHAPTER FIVE. MEETING PEOPLE WHO SHARE YOUR PASSION

1. Napoleon Hill, *Think and Grow Rich* (New York: Fawcett Books, 1960), 105–6.
2. Konstantin Stanislavsky, *My Life in Art* (Moscow: Foreign Languages Publishing House, 1928).
3. Kenneth Branagh, *Beginning* (New York: Norton, 1990).

CHAPTER SIX. FINDING YOUR NICHE

1. Michael Phillips, *The Seven Laws of Money* (Menlo Park, Calif., and New York: World Wheel and Random House, 1974), 8–9.
2. Richard White, *The Entrepreneur's Manual* (Radnor, Pa.: Chilton, 1977).

CHAPTER EIGHT. WRITING AN APPROACH LETTER OR EMAIL

1. Napoleon Hill, *Think and Grow Rich* (New York: Fawcett Books, 1960), 168–69.
2. Jean Renoir, *My Father* (Boston: Little, Brown, 1958), 144.

CHAPTER NINE. INTERVIEWING, FOLLOWING-UP, AND RECEIVING OFFERS

1. Richard N. Bolles, *What Color Is Your Parachute?* (Berkeley: Ten Speed Press, 2003).
2. Joyce Lain Kennedy, *Resumes for Dummies*, 4th ed. (Hoboken, N.J.: Wiley, 2002).
3. William E. Montag, *CareerJournal.Com Resume Guide for $100,000 Plus Executive Jobs*, 1st ed. (Hoboken, N.J.: Wiley, 2002).

CHAPTER TEN. STARTING YOUR OWN BUSINESS

1. J. Krishnamurti, *The First and Last Freedom* (New York: Harper & Row, 1954), 102–3.

CHAPTER ELEVEN. CELEBRATING WHEN YOU GET THERE

1. Kahlil Gibran, *The Prophet* (New York: Knopf, 1972), 29.
2. M. H. Abrams et al. *The Norton Anthology of English Literature*, vol. 2 (New York: Norton, 1968), 503.
3. John Middleton Murry, *Keats* (New York: Farrar, Straus & Giroux, 1968), 14.
4. William Butler Yeats, *The Autobiography of William Butler Yeats* (New York: Macmillan, 1928), 300.
5. Viktor Frankl, *Man's Search for Meaning* (New York: Simon & Schuster, 1970).
6. Napoleon Hill, *Think and Grow Rich* (New York: Fawcett Books, 1960), 201.

RECOMMENDED RESOURCES

BOOKS AND JOURNALS

Abrams, M. H. et al. *The Norton Anthology of English Literature*, vol. 1. New York: Norton, 1968. A wealth of learning and enjoyment awaits the reader who renews his or her acquaintance with the best of English writing.

Blotnick, Srully. *Getting Rich Your Own Way*. New York: Doubleday, 1980. This study of people who achieved wealth is based on twenty years of observation.

Blum, Ralph. *The Book of Runes*. New York: St. Martin's Press, 1982. When you consult the runes — an ancient Germanic form of divination — you are really consulting yourself.

Bolles, Richard N. *What Color Is Your Parachute?* Berkeley: Ten Speed Press, 2003. Bolles covers all the job-search bases.

Branagh, Kenneth. *Beginning*. New York: Norton, 1990. Young, brash Branagh includes fascinating anecdotes about famous theater and film personalities.

Firestone, Robert E. *The Fantasy Bond: Effects of Psychological Defenses on*

Interpersonal Relations. New York: Human Sciences Press, 1985. Firestone probes deeply into the many reasons that we avoid being fully alive.

Fox, Emmet. *The Sermon on the Mount: The Key to Success in Life.* San Francisco: HarperCollins, 1989. Fox's book is an inspiring interpretation of Jesus' transforming message.

Frankl, Viktor. *Man's Search for Meaning.* New York: Simon & Schuster, 1970. Frankl says that imprisonment in a concentration camp was worthwhile to those who found meaning in the experience.

Gawain, Shakti. *Creative Visualization,* 25th anniversary ed. Novato, Calif., New World Library, 2003. Gawain shows you how to create what you want through the power of your imagination.

Gibran, Kahlil. *The Prophet.* New York: Knopf, 1972. Millions of people know and love Gibran's poetic expression of the deepest impulses of the human mind and heart.

Greer, Gaylon. "How Did the Rich Get That Way?" *American Association of Individual Investors Journal* (March 1984): 23–24. Greer's article makes it clear that the rich get that way by following their hearts, not conventional advice.

Harding, Esther M. *The I and the Not I: A Study in the Development of Consciousness.* Princeton University Press, 1973. Harding is a Jungian psychotherapist whose sophisticated insights into the dawning of self-awareness will enlighten and inform you.

Hill, Napoleon. *Think and Grow Rich.* New York: Fawcett Books, 1960. Hill's principles are as applicable today as they were when he wrote the book during the Great Depression.

Hoff, Benjamin. *The Tao of Pooh.* New York: Dutton, 1982. Hoff's charming book shows that Pooh's way of living is consistent with principles envisioned long ago by the first Taoists.

Jung C. G. *Modern Man in Search of a Soul.* New York: Harcourt Brace & World, 1933. In this compilation of Jung's speeches about his thoughts on life, work, and love, Jung's humor, common sense, and erudition make it clear why he was and remains so influential.

Kennedy, Joyce Lain. *Resumes for Dummies,* 4th ed. Hoboken, N.J.: Wiley, 2002. Whatever job you're looking for, Kennedy has a good résumé guide for you to follow.

Kiersey, David, and Marilyn Bates. *Please Understand Me: Character and Temperament Types.* Del Mar, Calif.: Prometheus Nemesis, 1998. Understanding your temperament is the key to making wise choices. Kiersey and Bates show you how to understand others' temperaments as well as your own.

Krishnamurti, J. *The First and Last Freedom.* New York: Harper & Row, 1954. The freedom this wise man describes comes when we break free from the debilitating, all-consuming concern with the self.

Montag, William E. *CareerJournal.Com Resume Guide for $100,000 Plus Executive Jobs,* 1st ed. Hoboken, N.J.: Wiley, 2002. Montag's book is useful for professionals, executives, and managers who want to move up the corporate ladder.

Murry, John Middleton. *Keats.* New York: Farrar, Straus & Giroux, 1968. Murry's book, a respectful and in-depth treatment of Keats's life and work, has been praised for its uncanny depth of divination.

Phillips, Michael. *The Seven Laws of Money.* Menlo Park, Calif., and New York: World Wheel and Random House, 1974. Phillips's first law of money is "do what you love; the money will follow."

Renoir, Jean. *My Father.* Boston: Little, Brown, 1958. The son of an artistic genius writes a moving book about his practical-minded French father.

Roberts, Jane. *The Nature of Personal Reality.* Novato, Calif.: New World Library, 1994. This provocative book provides useful tools for helping us to change the beliefs that wreak havoc in our lives and the lives of others.

Sarno, John. *Healing Back Pain: The Mind-Body Connection.* New York: Warner Books, 1991. Dr. Sarno's book is about much more than back pain. Sarno states that physiological alteration in certain muscles, nerves, tendons, and ligaments is the way our conditioned minds distract us from emotions we don't want to feel. The pain in our bodies is not our fault, he says; it's what the mind does until we reprogram it.

Stanislavsky, Konstantin. *My Life in Art.* Moscow: Foreign Languages Publishing House, 1928. This delightful book by an original thinker will open your mind to new possibilities.

Toffler, Alvin. *The Third Wave.* New York: Bantam Books, 1991. Moving along with the times is the key to adapting to social and personal change.

White, Richard. *The Entrepreneur's Manual.* Radnor, Pa.: Chilton, 1977. The fountain of creative ideas that pour forth from White's mind will amaze you. Many readers say this is the best business book in their library.

Yeats, William Butler. *The Autobiography of William Butler Yeats.* New York: Macmillan, 1928. The artist's life is never easy, but the result is worth the sacrifice.

Zyfowsky, D. G., "15 Needs and Values," *Vocational Guidance Quarterly* 18 (1970): 182. These values are listed in chapter 3 of *Work with Passion.*

CLASSES

I often recommend acting classes to help my clients learn how to connect with their feelings. These classes also improve their speaking and presentation skills. In an improvisational acting class, for example, you get up in front of the group on the spur of the moment and convince them that you are angry, sad, or threatening, depending on what emotion you want to convey. One of my clients pulled his jeans down low, turned his hat backwards, jumped up on stage, put both of his arms in front of him as though he held a shotgun, all the while shouting at the top of his lungs, "Okay, hands up, everyone, or I'll shoot!" The class was so shocked and scared they put up their hands at once. He got an A-plus for that performance. At the end of the acting course his teacher said he could act professionally if that was what he wanted to do! Obviously, the class had helped my client to break free of his inhibitions. You can find acting classes through your local live theater company, community college, university extension program, or under acting, speech, or drama coaches in the local Yellow Pages.

You can also join Toastmasters, a national group that helps participants from all walks of life to speak clearly and effectively. These meetings are usually held in the evening. They're free, they're fun, and their program is a nonthreatening way to get over the fear of speaking in public. Check your local paper for the location of this organization or visit its website, www.toastmasters.org.

A course in critical thinking or logic is an invaluable aid to good communication. You will discover the pitfalls of reasoning, such as generalizations, rationalizations, obfuscation, and confusing facts with personal prejudices. How you describe a problem is often the problem itself. Your local community college and university extension catalogs usually offer logic or critical thinking classes under the categories of philosophy or humanities.

WEBSITES

You'll find many resources to help with the recovery process on www.hazelden.org. If you want to understand and overcome addiction, or the effects of living and working with people who are "under the influence," you'll find just what you need. This site is also helpful if you are interested in recovery work as a career.

Warren Buffet's letters to the stockholders of Berkshire Hathaway make enlightening reading. You can read the Oracle of Omaha's yearly letters on www.berkeshirehathaway.com.

For an example of an e-business whose founder capitalizes on what she knows, check out www.jacquielawson.com. Lawson's talent and business sense may give you ideas about how to use what you know.

For a demonstration of expanding on what you know, read the biographies of the energetic venture capitalists on www.benchmark.com. If you want to start a business or personal practice of your own, entrepreneur.com will help you figure out how to get started.

Mothersky.com is the website of Jessica Murray, an insightful Jungian astrologer who can help you to identify your life's purpose.

You can log on to receive the thought of the day from www.naphill.org, the Napoleon Hill Foundation's website. A dose of Hill's upbeat thinking is a good way to start or end your day.

You'll find a wide variety of inspiring material on my publisher's website, www.newworldlibrary.com.

ORGANIZATIONS

For support while you're bringing your passion online, join local business, artistic, or entrepreneurial organizations whose members share your values. Associating with people of like mind will keep your spirits up during trying times. Finally, find a spiritual home, a church, a synagogue, a mosque, a meditation center, or any place that nourishes your soul.

ACKNOWLEDGMENTS

The chief idea of my life, I will not say the doctrine I have always taught,
but the doctrine I should always have liked to teach, that is the idea of
taking things with gratitude, and not taking things for granted.

— The Autobiography of G. K. Chesterton

I am very grateful to my clients for their willingness to share their stories; to my family and friends for their love and support; and to everyone at New World Library publishing company for their enthusiasm and commitment. We've all come a long way in the last twenty years. Thanks to Marc Allen, president of New World Library, Editorial Director Georgia Hughes, Assistant Managing Editor Kristen Cashman, Manuscript Editor Mimi Kusch, and the design and marketing team; all gave the book the treatment it deserved.

Finally, as Martin Luther put it, "I have tried to keep things in my hands and lost them all, but what I have given into God's hands I still possess."

INDEX

H

I

N

O

P

R

T

ABOUT THE AUTHOR

Nancy Anderson was a Regents' Scholar at the University of California, Riverside, where she graduated magna cum laude with an interdisciplinary degree in English and political science. Following graduation in 1976, she worked as a partner in two career counseling firms for five years before starting her own practice, at which time she wrote *Work with Passion*, based on her experience with her clients.

She lives and works (with a great deal of passion) in Mill Valley, California.

New World Library is dedicated to
publishing books and audio products
that inspire and challenge us to improve
the quality of our lives and our world.

Our products are available
in bookstores everywhere.
For our catalog, please contact:

New World Library
14 Pamaron Way
Novato, California 94949

Phone: (415) 884-2100 or (800) 972-6657
Catalog requests: Ext. 50
Orders: Ext. 52
Fax: (415) 884-2199

Email: escort@newworldlibrary.com
Website: www.newworldlibrary.com